THE FOUNDING OF ENGLISH METRE

JOHN THOMPSON

The Founding of English Metre

NEW YORK: COLUMBIA UNIVERSITY PRESS
LONDON: ROUTLEDGE AND KEGAN PAUL
1961

Library of Congress
Catalog Card Number: 61–16778

Printed in Great Britain

To
I. S. and Louise Keeler

Contents

vii

Acknowledgements

I wish to thank Professor William Nelson, Professor S. F. Johnson, and Professor Elliott V. K. Dobbie for the guidance they have given me in this work. Needless to say, they are not responsible for any shortcomings in it. To Professor Howard N. Porter I am indebted for reading the chapter on classical measures; he disabused me of certain notions about these metres, but again I must say he is not responsible for failures in what remains there.

The authors to whom I feel most indebted are Mr. John Crowe Ransom for all his writings on metre, Mr. George L. Trager and Mr. Henry Lee Smith, Jr., for their work *An Outline of English Structure*, and George Saintsbury for his *History of English Prosody*.

To many others I feel gratitude for their help in making this study. Among them are Professor F. W. Dupee, Professor Charles E. Everett, Mr. Thomas Flanagan, Mr. Eugenio Villicana, and all my former colleagues in Columbia College. There is a conventional coda for notes like this; only those who have had the occasion to write it and those who have found themselves referred to there will know exactly what it means when I say that I owe most of all to my wife.

Introduction

T HIS is not, I fear, a comfortable study. Its intentions and its methods are extreme. Its general purpose could scarcely be larger: to explain what metre is, why it exists, and how metre has developed in English literature. Its method is as narrow as can be: to examine in detail specimens of the verse of the one short crucial period of English poetry.

The six chapters trace the development of the iambic line in English from Tottel's *Miscellany* to *Astrophel and Stella*. There is a considerable literature on this subject, and the general course of the development seems agreed upon: the iambic line goes from a vigorous and disorderly beginning through a dull stretch to a vigorous and triumphant realization. It is not to revise this broad judgement that I write, nor do I make use of any new materials. Rather I intend to explain the development, that is, to show how and why it took place in each of its major stages in accordance with a developing contemporary body of expressed and unexpressed principles of metre.

The possibility of a new and more exact analysis of these things is suggested by certain discoveries of recent structural linguistics. I am not trained in the discipline of this science; I have only borrowed from it the materials for a theory of metre that allows metrical problems to be seen with reasonable strictness on their three levels, as metrical pattern, as the language of speech, and as the actual line of the poem. And I have adopted some of the linguists' simpler descriptive techniques in the interests of accuracy. An explanation of this metrical theory and of its use makes up the main body of this introduction.

The literary materials of the study are chosen from the works of the poets and the collections of poetry that were regarded in their own day and have been regarded since as the most important of the period for their contribution to literature. These include, of course, writers who were competent or outstanding in their metrical practice but exclude those like Thomas Tusser whose works provide chiefly

1

metrical curiosities. Poetry which was not written within the literary tradition of educated men, folk rhymes, ballads, popular religious verse, I have also excluded, although these things doubtless influenced the literary tradition, and a complete history of sixteenth-century metres would have to include them. Such a history would also have to include a consideration of the influence of music on verse. Most of the poems considered here do not seem to have been intended for song; yet music, like verse in foreign languages, surely had some influence on the development of English verse.[1] I omit these things because I am concerned here with the way the essential nature of English metre developed out of internal necessities in the English language. From the works of the poets and from the poems in the collections, I have sometimes chosen for attention things that may not seem generally the most important or the most typical. On the whole, however, I believe the selection reflects the main course of non-dramatic poetry in the period.

The study begins with Tottel's *Miscellany* of 1567, where the iambic metrical pattern makes its first unequivocal and dominant appearance in print in modern English. Before 1557, the history of this line is obscure. Wyatt seems to have been the first poet to use it in modern English to any extent; his way of using it is hard to define, and no explanation of his practice has ever been generally accepted. He did not invent this line in English, but its place in the metrical tradition he inherited is even more uncertain than his own intention.[2] In the Chaucer Wyatt knew, he could not have understood fully the iambic pentameter line;[3] and Barclay and Hawes, if they had that line in mind, provided only very rough models.[4] The line was certainly used by Dunbar and others in Scotland, along with the

[1] For an excellent study of the relations of music to verse in this period, see Bruce Pattison, *Music and Poetry of the English Renaissance*, London, 1948.

[2] On the general problem of Wyatt's originality, J. M. Berdan commented, 'Of course, with our ignorance of what other writers were doing, it is uncritical to assume that all these novelties [of metrical innovation] were first imported by Wyatt—an assumption that would make him one of the greatest verse-technicians in the history of the language—but they prove that the minds of the men in the circle to which Wyatt belonged were seriously occupied in studying the forms of verse.' *Early Tudor Poetry* (New York, 1931), pp. 485–486.

[3] 'It is because this knowledge [of the older pronunciation and grammatical forms] was lost from the fifteenth century down to the middle of the nineteenth that many of Chaucer's most enthusiastic admirers among English poets and critics have regarded his metre as irregular and rough.' F. N. Robinson, ed., *The Complete Works of Geoffrey Chaucer* (Cambridge, Mass., 1933), p. xxvi.

[4] Some doubt exists that they were even trying to write an iambic line. See C. S. Lewis, 'The 'Fifteenth-Century Heroic Line,' *Essays and Studies by Members of the English Association*, XXIV (1938), pp. 28–41.

alliterative line; I know of no reason why Wyatt and his fellow poets at the court of Henry VIII might not have been inspired by the metres of the Scots as well as by those of the Italian poets. It is also possible that the line was not entirely an imported fashion, but was worked out, or accepted, as a result of experiments that seemed necessary when the old four-beat line lost much of its effectiveness as a metrical pattern.[1]

Apparently Surrey picked up the idea from Wyatt, who 'taught what might be sayd in ryme.'[2] His use of the iambic principle was somewhat different from Wyatt's. Just how much different is uncertain, for his poems may have been edited before their publication in the *Miscellany*, as Wyatt's own manuscripts show that his were. But whatever its origins may have been, in the *Miscellany* the iambic emerged clearly as the guiding metrical pattern, even though the way it was used in forming the language into verse was at best erratic.[3] My study closes with Sidney, for in his poetry the metrical principles that dominated English verse for three centuries were fully and systematically developed.

The metrical experiments that took place in the years between Tottel's *Miscellany* and Sidney's *Astrophel and Stella* were not solely matters of a poet's developing his innate 'ear' for a good line or expanding his technical ability to write consistently the kind of line he wanted. They depended on theories, whether expressed or not, about the way the metrical pattern ought to be used in making a line of verse; and these theories or principles changed during this period in a more or less orderly and accumulative development. Yet the change appears, often, only in very small things; and we must be concerned with matters of a syllable or two, of small degrees of stress which are only relative, of the way words seem to be or not to be a phrase. At the same time we must be concerned with these small, scarcely tangible things not only on one level as we would be if we were studying them as linguists, but on the levels of the abstract metrical pattern, of the language of speech, and of the line of verse that comes from the relation of the first two.[4] All these are to a

---

[1] See below, ch. II, 43 ff.

[2] Henry Howard, Earl of Surrey, 'A Third Tribute to Wyatt,' *Poems*, ed. F. M. Padelford (Seattle, 1928), p. 98.

[3] Lacking further evidence, it seems fair to agree with Puttenham and most historians of literature after him that Wyatt and Surrey 'may justly be sayd the first reformers of our English meetre and stile.' George Puttenham, *The Arts of English Poesie*, ed. Gladys Willcock and Alice Walker (Cambridge, 1936), p. 60.

[4] I say 'the language of speech' to emphasize the fact that although the poetry dealt with here is written, this written language has reference to the sounds we

greater or lesser degree matters of personal judgement; one can only hope to be clear and to be persuasive about them. I begin with a few statements, probably quite familiar ones, of some of the first, specific, mechanical things metre does with language. From these I proceed through an examination of what metre is to an explanation of why poets use metre. For, as I said about the sixteenth-century experiments in metre, any judgement of it or use of it depends on a theory or principle, expressed or not. The poet may be under no obligation to be aware of his principles, or to express them, or to explain them; but the historian is.

Poetry need not be defined here; let the very broadest understanding of the term be assumed. We are concerned with verse, a kind of poetry. The word comes to us from the Latin *versus*, a turning round as of the plough at the end of the furrow, and thus it meant also a furrow, a row, a line of writing. In verse the language turns from time to time and forms a new line. It turns at a point determined by the metre; metre is *metrum*, a measure, and in verse it is a measurement of sounds. But in addition to simply determining when the line is complete and the language must take a turn, metre usually functions in a way that makes it more of a pattern than simply a measure or standard for determining extent or dimensions. The features of sound represented in the metrical pattern form a model or guide for the sounds of the language.

The metrical patterns of most English verse are made of the features of sound called stress. The language of this verse is chosen and arranged so that its stronger and weaker stresses fall more or less according to the design of the metrical pattern. Sometimes these stresses occur in exact alternation, as in Milton's line:[1]

> And swims or sinks, or wades, or creeps, or flyes,
> *Paradise Lost*, II, 950

Or the stresses may be arranged more freely as in Coleridge's

produce when we talk, and to the patterns of these sounds. 'There is no such thing in human society as the supplantation of the speech code [the signals of sound of a language] by its visual replicas, but only a supplementation of this code by parasitic auxiliaries, while the speech code constantly and unalterably remains in effect.' (Roman Jakobson and Morris Halle, *Fundamentals of Language*, 's-Gravenhage, 1956, p. 17.) Whenever I say 'language' I mean the system of sounds we use to communicate with one another. The essential structural elements of sound of the English language include those features of sound called stress, pitch, and juncture. These elements and their relations are described below, pp. 10 ff.

[1] Here, and in the brief discussion in the following pages of a few lines from *Paradise Lost*, I assume that Milton's lines are constructed with a certain reference to the iambic metrical pattern. The lines are susceptible of different analyses. F. T. Prince, for instance, in *The Italian Element in Milton's Verse* (Oxford, 1954),

Christabel, where the poet said the pattern consisted only of four strong stresses to each line. There may be as many as eight weakly-stressed syllables or as in the third line below, none at all:

> 'Tis the middle of the night by the castle clock,
> And the owls have awakened the crowing cock;
> Tu — whit! — Tu — whoo!
> And hark, again! the crowing cock,
>   How drowsily it crew.

Other features of sound have also been used to form patterns for verse. In the following lines the metrical pattern is formed only by the number of the syllables, without regard for their degree of stress. These two lines have the same metrical pattern, because they both have exactly nine syllables:

> Prince Rupert's drop, paper muslin ghost,
>   white torch — 'with power to say unkind
>   Marianne Moore, 'Pedantic Literalist'

Subtler features of sound may be abstracted, too, and formed into metrical patterns. In the following line, the pattern is made of 'short' and 'long' quantities. The poet believed these abstractions corresponded to something he heard in the sounds of vowels. People hear these things differently; this metre is rather hard to follow in English. There is also a complex set of conventions about 'short' and 'long' quantities in this metre, a system borrowed from classical verse. The pattern here is that of one of Vergil's hexameters:

> ‒ u u|‒ ‒| ‒   ‒ |‒ u u |‒   u   u |‒ ‒
> Midway of all this tract, with secular arms an immense elm
>   Robert Bridges, 'Ibant obscuri'

A peculiarity of the measurement of verse is that the units of measure are not discarded and forgotten when the measurement has been made and the line is completed. That is why the measure is more a pattern than a yardstick. As a pattern, as a model or guide

argues most interestingly that along with the other prosodic principles of the Italian Renaissance poets, Milton adopted their syllabic metrics, and that the only requirement of his blank verse line is ten syllables, with a stress on the tenth and on either the fourth or sixth syllable. Possibly; and possibly Milton ignored stress altogether as part of his metrical pattern. But Milton knew what English 'Heroic' verse was, and I think Bridges was right when he said Milton *scanned* his verse one way and *read* it another. The disagreements about Milton's scansions, like most disagreements about metrics, arise from failures to distinguish clearly the three separate sound patterns of metrics, first, the abstract metrical pattern, second, the pattern of normal speech, and third, the pattern of the line of verse.

to the making of something, the metrical pattern is strange, too. For it is used not only by the poet in making his line, but by the audience in hearing or reading the line. Ordinarily the audience knows the pattern, or the poet makes his pattern known to the audience by repeating it clearly in his language as the poem begins; once the metrical pattern is known, it has in turn some influence on the way the language of the lines is heard. For as it is generally recognized today, there is in any line of verse a degree of difference between the pattern of stresses which the words and phrases would have as they might occur in the language of speech, and the pattern of stresses in the metre. Thus, if we can imagine such a statement being made in matter-of-fact speech, the following words might be said something like this:[1] It is an ancient mariner, and he stoppeth one of three. The usual understanding of the words as lines of verse

[1] I employ basically three sets of symbols:
  I. ⌐∧⌐∨ for the four degrees of speech stress.
  II. o   s for the weak and strong metrical stress in basically iambic patterns, varied slightly as ø s for the dip and lift in four-beat verse.
  III. u   — for short and long in quantitative verse.
The speech stresses are, from the strongest to the weakest, primary, ╱; secondary, ∧; tertiary, ╲; and weak, ∨. The terminology is that of George L. Trager and Henry Lee Smith, Jr., in *An Outline of English Structure*, Studies in Linguistics, Occasional Papers, 3 (Norman, Okla., 1951). It has been said that 'there is in the field of English phonological investigation no general agreement on the terminology, concepts, and methodology to be used in the description of the modern English stress system.' (Marshall D. Berger, 'Vowel Distribution and Accentual Prominence in Modern English,' *Word*, XI, No. 3 [December, 1955], 361–376.) But the conclusion of Trager and Smith that there are four distinctive degrees of stress in English speech is supported by the observations of students of metre as well as by other linguists. See J. R. R. Tolkien, 'Prefatory Remarks,' in *Beowulf*, ed. C. L. Wrenn (London, 1950), xxx, n.; and George Stewart, *The Technique of English Verse* (New York, 1930), p. 138, n.
   It is difficult to say exactly what stress is. See Wilbur Schramm, 'Approaches to a Science of English Verse,' University of Iowa Studies, Series on the Aims and Progress of Research, No. 46 (Iowa City, 1935). Trager and Smith simply call it loudness. I take this to mean what we usually hear as loudness, or emphasis, rather than what the physicist would describe as an actual variation in the sound wave. 'In functional linguistic terms . . . a sound may be more prominent than another by timbre (or tamber), length, or articulatory energy without being louder in a physical sense (i.e., with a sound wave of greater amplitude or of greater intensity).' W. F. Twaddell, 'Stetson's Model and the "Supra-Segmental Phonemes",' *Language*, XXIX (1953), 420.
   The marks for the iambic metrical pattern are an adaptation of those used by George Stewart, and recommended by John Crowe Ransom in 'The Strange Music of English Verse,' *Kenyon Review*, XVIII, No. 3 (1956), 460–477. Stewart uses four degrees: stressed, s; unstressed, o; light stressed, l; heavy unstressed, O. Since I use the symbols not to indicate how the line might be spoken but only to

seems to be something like that which George Stewart describes in his study of metre, *The Technique of English Verse*. By 'stress' Mr. Stewart means 'strong stress.'

An accustomed reader of English verse hearing the line:

It is an ancient Mariner,

although it is the first of the poem, would hear four stresses even though the person reading might be enough of a logical grammarian to believe that there were only two. The other two stresses might exist only in the hearer's mind, but they would be for him none the less real. . . .[1]

The adjustment of these two things to one another cannot be determined in any way that would have final authority for all readers; it can only be described with careful reference both to the metrical pattern and to appropriate speech intention, with the hope that a certain broad assent can be gained. This difference between the patterns of the line as speech and as metre is often recognized today as *tension*, and is usually highly prized.[2] It exists in Milton's line:

And swims or sinks, or wades, or creeps, or flyes.

The iambic metrical pattern of alternating weaker and stronger stresses is plainly the same as that of the speech stresses of the language. But even here there is some degree of difference. There is no comma after *swims*;[3] does this mean that the words *And swims or sinks* form a minimal complete utterance differing from the shorter utterances *or wades, or creeps, or flyes*? Let the commas represent terminal junctures, and there could be only one primary stress for the four syllables *And swims or sinks*, whereas there would be a primary stress for each of the other verbs.[4]

And swims or sinks, or wades, or creeps, or flyes.

show the metrical pattern, and since I believe the metrical pattern with rare exceptions employs only two degrees of stress, I use only the lower case set of symbols, o, s.

I vary these slightly for the metrical pattern of the four-beat line because the dip in four-beat verse is not quite the same thing as the weak-stressed syllable in the metrical pattern of iambic verse. A dip may include more than one syllable, and since in the iambic pattern more than one syllable for the weak-stressed position is a departure from the metrical pattern, the difference ought to be indicated in the symbols for the two patterns: iambic, o s; dip and lift, ø s.

[1] Stewart, pp. 6–7.

[2] See the symposium on metre in *The Kenyon Review*, XVIII, No. 3 (Summer, 1956), 411–417.

[3] In the edition of 1667. I simply take the line as it appears there, without assuming anything about Milton's intention, or the printer's.

[4] Trager and Smith, p. 49. 'Between any two successive primary stresses there is always one of the terminal junctures, and every primary stress is followed by

If one decides to read the line in this way, it does not mean that one has decided to ignore the metrical pattern, or to deny it. The abstract pattern exists, but there is a difference between it and the secondary degree of speech stress which takes the place of a metrical strong stress.

It happens that in Milton's next line the metrical pattern must be satisfied with a tertiary speech stress for a strong metrical stress:

⏑ ´   ⏑ ˅⏑´⏑
At length a universal hubbub wilde
II, 951

(I have not marked the complete line. The first syllable of *hubbub* and the word *wilde* have stronger degrees of stress than the second syllable of *hubbub*, but how much stronger?)

A few lines further on in *Paradise Lost*, it seems that if the requirement of the metrical pattern for five strong metrical stresses is to be met, one of them will have to be satisfied with a weak speech stress, on *of*; for in speech the phrases would sound more or less like this:

⏑ ˄⏑⏑ ⏑˄⏑ ⏑ ⏑´
Or spirit of the nethermost Abyss.
II, 956

The metrical pattern may endure even greater divergences:

With head, hands, wings, or feet pursues his way.
II, 949

In speech, *head, hands, wings,* and *feet*, each probably requires a primary stress. *Pursues his way* would probably in the usual matter-
⏑ ˄ ⏑ ´
of-fact speech be said thus, pursues his way. In this line, then, there are six speech stresses of more than weak degree. For most readers it probably seems that it is not the one of these which may be least
⏑ ˄
strong, *pursues*, that represents the weak degree of metrical stress, but one of the primary speech stresses, *hands*; and the line would be *scanned* (but surely not read) in this way:

o   s | o   s   o s | o s | o   s
With head, hands, wings, |or feet pursues his way.

The reading, in whatever voice the reader uses for Milton, would

one terminal juncture at some point subsequent to it.' Juncture means the transition between speech sounds. The terminal junctures are ways of interrupting this transition; we employ them in speech, in connection with stress and pitch, to mark the limits of phrases and clauses, either in going from one part of an utterance to another or in terminating the utterance.

probably show some compromise between the metrical pattern and the phrase pattern the ordinary uses of speech would suggest.

The language of verse is ordered, then, by patterns made of language features, and these patterns exist as abstractions, separate from the language of any particular line. But what is the metrical pattern for? Why should language be subjected to the distortion it must incur when it is placed in relation with this pattern? The answer should be valid for all verse, not only for that which we feel is particularly successful; it should be definitive of verse. It should tell us what makes the particular use of language called verse different from all other uses of language. But it should also include the terms that would allow us to distinguish between one kind of verse and another and between successful and unsuccessful verse; on the basis of the definition of verse we should be able to analyse metrical practices in the sixteenth century and say why they changed as they did.

This is where the description of English offered by structural linguistics is of great service. It makes such a definition possible for the first time. For it allows us to see that the metrical pattern contains in itself the reason for its use in making verse. Metre is not added to language in order to provide the poet with the means of making further refinements in language as expression or communication; I do not know how anyone could prove that the King James Book of Job would profit in any way by being set to metre except that it would thus become verse. What metre adds to language is precisely the element of imitation that makes of the two, when they are joined, the art of verse.

'Imitation' here is used in the simplest physical sense. The metrical pattern is a copy, a mimicry, a counterfeit without intention to deceive, of the basic elements of our language and of their order. When this metrical pattern is placed in conjunction with some words or phrases, a tension exists between them, a strained state of mutual relations; the line from 'The Ancient Mariner' is, as we read it, the result of the pull exerted on the natural sound-pattern of the phrases by the abstract metrical pattern of four relatively strong stresses. The language, when we read it as part of a poem, has been strained into something different, into a resemblance to an imitation. It is thus partly imitation itself, and it is this which makes it an art.

Here it is not necessary to pursue 'imitation' into metaphysics, or to try to define or justify art. It seems to me that the best distinction between art and other activities of human beings is Aristotle's: all art is imitation. But we can rest with the assumption that there is an art called poetry and that verse is one kind of poetry. We are concerned with the way verse is distinguished from other arts which use the same medium of language; it is distinguished from them by its use of metre, and while metre may incidentally be exploited for some purpose of expression or communication according to the usual intentions of language, its essential and defining purpose is simply to make the language with which it is joined take on some part of the quality of the metrical pattern, and thus be transformed into the line of verse, an object which is art. A brief review of the discoveries of linguists about the essential structure of our language should establish that the metrical pattern is constructed in imitation of it, and that the essential function of the metrical pattern can only be to make the language also imitative—imitative of its own structure.

The features of sound of a language that are essential to its internal structure are called phonemes.[1] In English they consist of the segmental phonemes, which are those features of sound we call vowels and consonants, and the phonemes of stress, pitch, and juncture. These phonemes are not entire sounds in themselves, but features of sound, which the speakers of a language have been trained to produce and recognize as signals. There are other factors. The relative length of duration of a sound, that feature which Bridges tried to make the basis of his metrical patterns, may be observed in any speech but it is not in English a distinctive feature. It is not recognized by the users of the language as an essential signal in the system.

Stress is an essential signal in the system. It serves to distinguish not only 'words' as when we say convért or cónvert; it serves to form the larger units of speech—phrases, clauses, and sentences—and to distinguish noun from adjective, subject from verb. The word-groups of English sentences are distinguished by patterns of stress and juncture, and these patterns also form the words and word-groups into sentences. The wŏrd, groúps. As complete utterances, word and groups have each a primary stress and are completed by a terminal juncture of a kind that always follows any primary stress.

The wŏrd-groùps. When this is a complete utterance, the primary

---

[1] This description of the structure of English is based on Trager and Smith, cited above, p. 6, n. They regard as essential elements of English not only the segmental phonemes (vowels and consonants), but the elements of stress, pitch, and juncture, which have often been described as 'suprasegmental' or 'prosodic' features of language, and not essential elements. The simplicity, inclusiveness, and symmetry of their description of our language makes it in effect a revolutionary concept, with profound implications for the study of all literature in English.

stresses which *word* and *groups* would have in isolation are superseded by a stress pattern forming the compound word. *The word-*
groups of English sentences. Here the larger unit is again formed by
the stress and juncture pattern. The primary stress is reserved for the
final word in the utterance, unless another meaning is intended, as
for instance, a contrast between English and French sentences. As a
complete utterance, this word-group would normally end with a
rise and fall of tone, and a pause. Should it become part of a longer
sentence, its terminal juncture would change to a rise and a return
to the normal tone level, a signal that the sentence is not complete;
then the rest of the sentence would follow. Beyond this function of
ordering the elements of sentences, the phonemes of stress, pitch,
and juncture work to provide in our speech what we call tone, the
subtle indications of attitude we make when we speak. The intonation patterns of stress, pitch, and juncture, together with those
features of sound we call vowels and consonants, provide the signals
of sound that are our language. Without all of them the signal is
incomplete, and there can be no complete meaning.

Metre is made by abstracting from speech one of these essential
features and ordering this into a pattern. The pattern is an imitation
of the patterns that the feature makes in speech, a sort of formalizing
of these patterns. Actually the metrical pattern represents not only
the one feature it is based on but all the essential features of the
language. And in organizing these into its abstract patterns, metre
follows the principles of our language with the utmost precision.
Perhaps it has always been apparent that the elements of metre are
drawn from the language. Gascoigne observed this, as we shall see,
and the scholar Paul Verrier, writing on English metre, said that
both poetry and song derive their rhythms and their melody from
the language.[1] Roman Jakobson has pointed out that the elements
of prosody are not just phonetic qualities of the language but
phonemic.[2] However, the full meaning of these facts for the study
of English metre could not have been recognized until we were given

[1] Paul Verrier, *Essai sur les principes de la métrique anglaise*, Paris: Librairie
Universitaire (1909), III, 328: 'La poésie et la chant ont pris dans le langage
ordinaire les formes fondamentales de leur rhythme et de leur mélodie. Ils n'ont
guère fait que régulariser le rhythme et la mélodie de la prose par des simplific-
ations de toute sortes.'
[2] Roman Jakobson, 'Uber den Versbau der Serbokroatischen Volksepen,'
Proceedings of the International Congress of Phonetic Sciences, Amsterdam, 1932,
p. 45. 'Deswegen formulieren wir die Grundfrage der Verslehre folgendermassen:
welche wort- und satzphonologischen Elemente machen einen gegebenen Vers
zum Verse und wie werden sie verwendet? [*contd. next page*]

the description of our language made available by Trager and Smith. For the metrical pattern draws not only its elements but its order from the language; it is a model of the way English works. The iambic metrical pattern has dominated English verse because it provides the best symbolic model of our language.

The iambic foot consists of simulacra of two syllables.[1] The order of the simulacra is fixed; that representing the weaker stress comes first, with certain exceptions or variations such as the initial trochee. The stress system of English is represented in this simplified way. It is a model of the way the words and phrases of English are made: phonemes into syllables, syllables into words or word-groups, word-groups into sentences. The primary stress of a phrase will come as near the end as possible in speech, with exceptions for special occasions.[2] Every primary stress is followed by one terminal juncture at some point subsequent to it. Our understanding of the foot as a unit is our understanding of its representation of a phoneme of terminal juncture; a foot has a beginning and an end. Since terminal juncture is a function of pitch, the foot has thus provided simulacra of the four kinds of phonemes essential to English. The line or measure with its combination of feet and its representation of juncture, the end of the line, is a model of the larger units of language.

This is what the metrical pattern is. It does for language what the forms of any art do for their materials. It abstracts certain elements from the experience of the senses and forms them into patterns, as painting abstracts elements from what the eye perceives, dancing from what the body perceives as it moves, music from what the ear perceives. The elements are ordered in patterns similar to those the senses experience all the time, but art characteristically makes the patterns simpler and clearer and the artist regards them as having a

'Es müssen die Gesetze der Beziehungen zwischen dem Versbau und dem phonologischen System der entsprechenden Sprache erforscht werden. Somit wird die vergleichende Verslehre aufgestellt. Ein besimmtes Bündel der prosodischen Korrelationen einer Sprache begünstigt bestimmte Versbausysteme und schliesst andere aus.' (European linguists employ the term 'phonology' for the study of the distinctive features of languages; the usual term among American linguists is 'phonemics.')

[1] A syllable in speech is a segmental phoneme or cluster of segmental phonemes having as its nucleus a vowel which bears one of four relative degrees of stress. 'A stretch of speech-sounds over which a stress extends' is Harold Whitehall's 'practical definition' in his handbook *Structural Essentials of English* (New York, 1956), p. 26. It is merely practical because while everyone can recognize syllables, no one has devised a way of describing a point where one syllable ends and another begins.

[2] Trager and Smith, p. 73.

kind of independent existence they do not have in everyday experience. The forms are used then to order a presentation of the everyday experience of the senses. In the art of verse, metre does these things; if it does other things as well, these are incidental to the function of imitation. The rhythms of verse, like its other features, are an imitation of speech. When we hear the sounds that are our language, it is the rhythmic pattern of stresses and junctures that gives us our understanding of the grouping and ordering of these sounds.[1] There is even in English a tendency for the rhythm to become regular, for the stresses to occur at 'isochronic' intervals.[2] This tendency of our speech, abstracted and simplified into a pattern, becomes the rhythms of our verse. It is not rhythm itself which distinguishes verse from other kinds of language; it is the fact that the rhythm of verse is the result of the process of art. The elements of rhythm have been abstracted from their source in the language and then ordered into patterns; the patterns imitate in a simplified form the patterns that occur naturally in the language. In altering the natural speech rhythms of the language in verse, these patterns of course alter the meaning of the language, and good poets use this fact to the advantage of their meanings; but this use of the metrical pattern does not define all verse. If there is one meaning which the metrical pattern enforces on all language submitted to its influence, it is this: *Whatever else I may be talking about, I am talking also about language itself.*

The tension, the strained state of mutual relations between metrical pattern and language, can be severe or mild; there are two main ways of reducing it. First, the poet can keep it at a minimum by using a metrical pattern which is loose or free and can easily be

[1] 'Stress and juncture work together in signalling the grammatical structure of statements. What happens when we use them to discriminate grammatical function is that we respond to various contrastive rhythmical patterns based upon various arrangements of the two factors. It is stress-juncture rhythm which gives us our most direct clue to grammatical arrangement and permits us to subdivide statements into their constituent words and word-groups. Rhythm is the first essential of the structural essentials of English—the first and basic device of modern English grammar.' Harold Whitehall, p. 28.

[2] 'The timing of rhythm units produces a rhythmic succession which is an extremely important characteristic of English phonological structure. The units tend to follow one another in such a way that the lapse of time between the beginning of their prominent syllables is somewhat uniform. Notice the more or less equal lapses of time between the stresses in the sentence *The 'teacher is 'interested in 'buying some 'books*; compare the timing of that sentence with the following one, and notice the similarity in that respect despite the different number of syllables: *'Big 'battles are 'fought 'daily.'* Kenneth L. Pike, *The Intonation of American English* (Ann Arbor, University of Michigan Press, 1945), p. 34.

accommodated to the pattern of sounds the speech represents; at an extreme this reduction of tension can cause the metrical pattern to be so closely assimilated to the natural rhythm of the language that the tension is very slight, even scarcely noticeable. Of course, the language itself may have very great virtues, and this kind of poetry may well be extremely valuable. Second, the tension may be reduced by using language that does not itself carry any strong suggestion of a pattern of sound from speech; this kind of language can easily be accommodated to an abstract pattern of sound. Perhaps this kind of poetry will always be of less interest than other kinds, because it sacrifices a great deal in giving up a large part of the resources of speech. Finally, the tension is greatest when the metrical pattern is strict and the language is colloquial, and when the mutual relation is strongly indicated by a readily-recognized convention for all the more important individual sound-relations. It is primarily the shifts from one of these degrees of tension to another that form the history of metre in the years between 1557 and 1580. After that, metre for English poets was largely a question of what they could develop for a personal style out of the possibilities in Sidney and Spenser.

I

Wyatt, Tottel, and Surrey

It seems strange at first that some of the effects deliberately worked out after the long evolution of metre should resemble so much the earliest beginnings. The affinities of Wyatt and Donne have often been noted; their poetry has been admired and disapproved for much the same reasons. The likeness begins with their apparent disregard of the iambic metrical pattern, and a certain effect in their lines as of the speaking voice:

> It was no dreme: I lay brode waking.[1]
> Goe; and if that word have not quite kil'd the.[2]

Yet the tradition of the iambic line as it was worked out in Tudor England seems to lie between the two poets not like a road but like a wall. We first see the barrier rising in Tottel's *Miscellany*, where Wyatt's line is revised to read:

> It was no dreame: for I lay broade awakyng.[3]

The small change produces a line that is regular in metre, and the difference makes it clear that it was partly the irregular patterns of stress that gave the words in the original line their strong effect of speech. The line in Tottel offers the suggestion, as Wyatt's does not, that it may be read according to the metrical pattern of alternating stress relatively weak and strong.

> o   s   o   s   o s o   s   o s o
> It was no dreame: for I lay broad awakyng.

[1] *Collected Poems of Sir Thomas Wyatt*, ed. Kenneth Muir (London, 1949), p. 28.

[2] *The Poems of John Donne*, ed. H. J. C. Grierson (Oxford, 1912, reprinted 1938), I, 68.

[3] Tottel's *Miscellany*, ed. H. E. Rollins (Cambridge, Mass., 1929), II, 39.

15

Of course, we do not know how far any reader would have let this pattern influence his voice, but even if the influence was only slight, the words would sound like nothing anyone ever spontaneously said. In this particular line, it is true, a suggestion of actual speech remains, resisting the metrical pattern; it remains, at least, in the phrase we should ordinarily say, I imagine, as *It was no dream*, or even *It was no dream*.[1] The rest of the line no longer demands a clear speech intonation, as did *I lay brode waking*. It seems that if Wyatt himself had any thought here of an iambic metrical pattern, he was willing to give it up for the effect of the phrases. Whoever made the revision was prepared to give up the effect of the phrases for the sake of the pattern. Donne gave up neither; his phrases demand the living voice, and at the same time the line can be reconciled to the metrical pattern, not in speech, it is true, but in that counterpoint of speech and metrical pattern which today we usually recognize and value. The effects of Wyatt's line and of Donne's, then, are similar, but in structural principles the lines are at opposite poles. The third kind of line, that represented by Tottel's Wyatt, is the key to our understanding of how Donne's kind of line was developed from Wyatt's in the sixteenth century.

The tradition began with Wyatt, but about the details of Wyatt's metrical standard there is not much agreement. He has been said to have had no real principles: 'He was the pioneer who fumbled in the linguistic difficulties that beset him.'[2] He has been said to have followed a system of fantastic intricacy of his own invention, based on a misunderstanding of Chaucer.[3] His metrically irregular lines have been presented as expressively effective, in an almost magical way, capable of creating 'a profound feeling of wonder' with a stress pattern.[4] It has been said that he wrote as he did for the sake of a certain 'pausing' rhythm that is quite unrelated to the iambic principle.[5]

[1] The reader will note here that I proceed as though the sixteenth-century speaker had much the same voice as ours. The sounds of the language have changed, somewhat; but in the absence of evidence to the contrary, I assume that the basic structure of the language, in the formation of phrases by sound-patterns, was the same.

[2] Tottel's *Miscellany*, ed. H. E. Rollins (Cambridge, Mass., 1929), I, 77.

[3] A. K. Foxwell, *A Study of Sir Thomas Wyatt's Poems* (London, 1911).

[4] E. M. W. Tillyard, *The Poetry of Sir Thomas Wyatt*, 2nd ed. (London, 1949), p. 21.

[5] D. W. Harding, 'The Rhythmical Intention in Wyatt's Poetry,' *Scrutiny*, XIV, No. 2 (December, 1946), 90–102.

In the three verse Satires,[1] I think he wrote as he did largely for the sake of catching in his verse the effect of the speaking voice, much as he did in the line from the lyric I quoted above.[2] But he also had in mind a metrical pattern. The relation he maintained between the stress patterns of speech and that metrical pattern is what I shall define here. It is certainly different from the relation that was wanted by Tottel's editor in 1557.[3]

Metrically significant changes were made in forty-three lines of

[1] I use the text of Wyatt printed by Kenneth Muir, *Collected Poems of Sir Thomas Wyatt*. This is based on Wyatt's own manuscript, BM Egerton MS. 2711. The Satires are not in Wyatt's own hand. The first thirty-one lines of Satire I are missing from Egerton, and are supplied largely from Devonshire, BM Add. MS. 17492, and in part from Parker, Corpus Christi College, Cambridge, MS. 168. Mr. Muir expands abbreviations, does not indicate overlining or superscript *a* and *i*, and the punctuation is his own.

Richard Charles Harrier, 'The Poetry of Sir Thomas Wyatt' (unpublished Ph.D. dissertation, Harvard University, 1952), supplies corrections of Muir's readings. Two of these affect the metre of their lines, and for these lines I use Harrier's versions:

It is not for becawse I skorne or moke

I, 7 (Muir)

It is not for to be cawse I skorne or moke

(Harrier)

By se, by land of delicates the moost

II, 25 (Muir)

By se by land of the delicates the moost

(Harrier)

Unfortunately, Harrier's version of the text, while it seems to be the most accurate, cannot be used throughout. It is primarily a criticism of Muir's text and Foxwell's. He prints overlines where they have resulted in different spellings by these editors, and otherwise does not, giving a text that is inconsistent except with reference to the earlier printed versions.

[2] Hallett Smith, in 'The Art of Sir Thomas Wyatt,' *Huntington Library Quarterly*, IX, No. 4 (August, 1946), 323–355, describes Wyatt's usual tone in the Satires: 'Again the conversational and spoken has influenced Wyatt's style, away from the aureate and elaborated, toward the language that is plain, is English, is on the tongues of men.' (p. 341).

[3] The editor of Tottel may have been Nicholas Grimald, Tottel himself, John Harington, or all of them together with the assistance of others. In the manuscripts and commonplace books collected for the anthology, the poems were often marked already with alternate readings; I follow the precedent of Rollins, I, 94: 'The word *editor* will henceforth be used without reference to any particular theory or person.' Rollins summarizes the reasons for the changes thus: 'Confronted with a series of poems in manuscript, he found them too archaic in rhythm and pronunciation to please his ear, and in order to make them acceptable to himself and to prospective readers he revised lines without mercy. His editorial procedure was similar to that followed by Bishop Percy in his eighteenth-century *Reliques of Ancient English Poetry*. Both editors, judged by the standards

Wyatt's Satires before they were printed in Tottel's *Miscellany*. These changes are movements in the direction of regularity. Many other apparently irregular lines were not changed; but when the actual changes have been observed in detail, the acceptance of these other lines can be explained. A final comparison of the two texts shows what the metrical standard of the iambic line was in 1557, and how it differed from Wyatt's conception of the way the metrical pattern and the language ought to join in a line of verse.

Most of the changes made were of two kinds. Twenty-two lines were changed to regularize the pattern of stresses, and twenty lines were changed to regularize the number of syllables. One line (III, 47) was changed in a way that affected the metrical pattern but not, it seems, for that reason.

LINES CHANGED TO REGULARIZE THE PATTERN OF STRESS

I. Lines changed into regular lines

Fifteen of the lines which in Wyatt had irregular patterns of stresses are made perfectly regular in Tottel; one more line is made regular except for its initial trochee.

(a) Lines which were irregular in one foot only.

<pre>
           o   s | o   s | o   s | s   o | o   s
</pre>
1. The powar of them, to whome fortune hath lent[1]   W.

The power of them: whom fortune here hath lent.   T.

I, 8

of their times, were justified in "improving" their texts, and beyond question the improvements thus introduced helped both the *Songs and Sonnets* and the *Reliques* to attain their remarkable popularity.' On the identity of the hands in the manuscript, see Ruth Hughey, 'The Harington Manuscripts at Arundel Castle and Related Documents,' *Library*, XV, 4th series (1935), 384–444.

[1] Some readers, following the method of Foxwell (*op. cit.*), might read *fortúne* here for *fórtune*, as Tillyard (*op. cit.*, p. 178) states that in line 100 of Satire II,

Madde if ye list to continue your sore,

we should read *contínue*. Miss Foxwell assumed that a 'Romance accent' such as *fortúne* for *fórtune* survived as an alternative pronunciation in the sixteenth century. The theory is largely based on the evidence of verse, which seems inconclusive. But for Wyatt of all poets this usage appears unjustified. When there are so many lines which no distortion can make regular, why should we distort here and there to produce regularity? It was precisely the sound-patterns of speech that Wyatt was interested in maintaining in his verse. Of course, I do not imagine I am indicating how every phrase must be said by every speaker on all occasions, when I mark these lines. I try to indicate what seems to me the usual modern matter-of-fact way of speaking. On these matters there can be no complete agreement.

```
   o   o | o s |   o   s | s o  |  o s
```
2. Withowt regarde what dothe inwarde resort.   W.

Without regard, what inward doth resort.   T.

I, 13

(b) Lines which were irregular in more than one foot.

```
  o    s  | o   s |   s  o|  s o |  o  s
```
3. I grawnt sumtime that of glorye the fyar.   W.

I graunt, sometime of glory that the fire.   T.

I, 14

```
    o    s|o    s| o   o s|  o   s  |    s
```
4. That raileth rekles to every mans shame.   W.

That rayleth rechlesse vnto ech mans shame.   T.

I, 72

```
   o   s  |  o    s  | o s | o   o s |  s
```
5. They sang sometyme a song of the feld mowse.   W.

They sing a song made of the feldishe mouse.   T.

II, 2[1]

```
    o    s   | o  s | o   s|o   o  s  |   s
```
6. She thought herself endured to much pain.   W.

She thought, herselfe endured to greuous payne.   T.

II, 5

Two lines had clashing stresses and eleven syllables.

```
   o    s  o    s|  o  s  |  s  o|o   o   s
```
7. In stye|and chaw the tordes molded on the grownd.   W.

In stye, and chaw dung moulded on the ground.   T.

III, 19[2]

```
   o s  |  o   s | o  s  |s o|  o   s    o
```
8. So sackes of durt be filled vp in the cloyster.   W.

So sackes of durt by filde. The neate courtier.   T.

III, 22[3]

---

[1] Of this line it might be said that the line in Tottel has an irregular foot: They sing a song *made of* the feldish mouse. For reasons that will appear later, I believe that the editor regarded these monosyllables as capable of being adjusted to the metrical pattern, despite the greater speech stress on *made* in the phrase: or this may have been excused as a reversal following a caesura.

[2] See note above. I think the editor scanned the line not quite by speech stresses, but like this:
```
   o   s|o    s|  o   s|o    s|  o    s
```
In stye and chaw dung moulded on the ground.

[3] This change may have been made only to avoid the unfavourable comment on cloisters; the *Miscellany* was published in the reign of Mary.

19

One line had clashing stresses and twelve syllables.

    o   ó s|o   s|o   o s | s o | o s
9. With the neryst vertue to cloke alwaye the vise.   W.

    With nearest vertue ay to cloke the vice.   T.

                      I, 61

(c) Line with nine syllables.

Seven lines had only nine syllables, and consequently two strong-stressed syllables were contiguous; the changes avoided the clashing stresses by adding another syllable. One of these lines retains an initial trochee in Tottel.

    o s | s| o s | o s|o   s
10. The cause why that homeward I me drawe.   W.

    The causes why that homeward I me drawe.   T.

                      I, 2

    o s| o   s |o   s | s | o s
11. I cannot speke and loke lyke a saynct.   W.

    I cannot speake and loke like as a saynt.   T.

                      I, 31[1]

    o   s | o s| s o |s | o   s
12. To make the crow singing as the swane.   W.

    To make the crow in singyng, as the swanne.   T.

                      I, 44

    o   s | o   s |'s | o   s| o   s
13. The frendly ffoo with his dowble face   W.

    The frendly foe, with his faire double face.   T.

                      I, 65

    o s | o s | o   s | s | o s |
14. Where if thou list, my Poynz, for to come.   W.

    Where if thou list myne owne Iohn Poyns to come.   T.

                      I, 102

    s o| o s | s | o s|o   s |
15. That if she myght kepe her self in helth.   W.

    That if she might there kepe her self in health.   T.

                      II, 34

    s   o |o   s | s o | s | o   s|
16. Sergeaunt with mace, haubert, sword nor knyf.   W.

    Sergeant with mace, with hawbart, sword, nor knife.   T.

                      II, 78

The scansion I have indicated for Wyatt's nine-syllable lines is

[1] Again, the line in Tottel is not regular by speech stress, but may be regarded as regular if the phrase stress pattern is superseded by the metrical stress pattern.

arbitrary. Except for the last, they present only four speech stresses of marked strength. Only the metrical requirement calls for five stresses and thus for the clashes. But this lack of five relatively strong speech stresses is a situation common in Wyatt's ten-syllable lines also. Here, in the nine-syllable lines, because some of the stresses must be contiguous if there are to be five, the metrical requirement appears more arbitrary. Actually it is not. But whether the editor thought the lines unsatisfactory because they lacked a stress or because the stresses clashed is not important. As the nine-syllable lines he did not change will show, it was the stresses and not the syllabic deficiency that he found unsatisfactory.

II. Lines changed to regularize stress pattern, but remaining irregular

One line with clashing stresses was changed so that one clash was removed but another remains, and the line is left with only nine syllables.

       s   s s   s   s
17. But to the great god and to his high dome.   **W.**

    s   s s   s   s
But, to the great God and to his dome.   **T.**
                        II, 105

Three lines escape the clash of stresses by adding syllables, producing regular feminine-ending lines.

       s   s   s   s   s
18. And doo most hurt where most hellp I offer.   **W.**

And do most hurt: where that most helpe I offer.   **T.**
                       I, 36

19. And hath thereof neither charge nor travaill.[1]   **W.**

And hath therefore no whit of charge nor trauell.   **T.**
                       II, 28

      o s | s| o s | s   o| o   so |
20. To seke grapes vpon brambles or breers.[2]   **W.**

To seke for grapes on brambles, or on bryers.   **T.**
                       II, 86

Two lines add syllables within the line to separate contiguous stresses:

      o s| o   s |o   s| o s | s   o|
21. Tho I seme lene and dry withoute moyster.   **W.**

Though I seme leane and drye, withouten moysture. **T.**
                       III, 24

[1] This line could have been scanned as trochaic, with no clashing stresses. I
                                o s   s o
assume the editor changed it because he read *thereof neither*, changing to *there-*
 s   o   s
fore no whit.
  [2] *Breers* may have been regarded as a monosyllable.

21

```
       o   s|  o     o   s  |  o   s  |  s    |o   s |
```
22. From vnder the stall withoute landes or feise.   W.

From vnder the stall, withouten landes or feese.   T.

III, 48

III. Lines changed to regularize the number of syllables

Eighteen lines were changed from eleven to ten syllables, one from eleven to nine syllables, and one from twelve to ten. Twelve of these changes were accomplished by adopting the newer form of the third person singular indicative inflection of the verb, -(e)s for -eth. These changes were evidently made to improve the metre, not to modernize the form. Only one of them affects the relation to the stronger stresses (II, 32) but all the changes produce greater regularity in syllable count. The syllable -eth is retained where it is metrically convenient:[1]

Grynne when he *laugheth* that *bereth* all the swaye.   W.

Grinne when *laughes*, that *beareth* all the sway.   T.

1, 53

The other changes in eleven-syllable lines are accomplished by dropping a word or a syllable. Some of these lines retain clashing stresses.

13. And call crafft counsell, for proffet styll to paint.   W.

Call craft counsaile, for lucre still to paint.   T.

I, 33

14. This maketh me at home to hounte and to hawke.   W.

This maketh me at home to hunt and hauke.   T.

I, 80

15. By se, by land, of the delicates the moost.   W.

By sea, by land, of delicates the most.   T.

II, 25

16. The towney mowse fled: she knowe whether to goo.   W.

The townemouse fled: she knew whither to go.   T.

II, 59

17. That had forgotten her poure suretie and rest.   W.

That had forgot her power, surety and rest.   T.

II, 68

One line was changed from eleven syllables to nine. The stress

---

[1] This inflectional ending is considered in detail in Appendix B.

pattern in the nine-syllable line is regular, except for a missing first syllable.

18. It is not for to be cawse I skorne or moke.   W.
    It is not, because I skorne or moke.   T.
                              I, 7

One line of eleven syllables and one of twelve presented in Wyatt not only the extra syllables but a clear possibility of six relatively strong stresses if they were read with an iambic metrical pattern in mind. The first may even be twelve syllables, if -*est* is syllabic.

19. 'Peace,' quoth the towny mowse, 'Why spekest thou so lowde?' W.
                              II, 43

20. I cannot crowche nor knelle to do so grete a wrong.   W.
                              I, 25

The editors may have been considering the stresses here rather than the number of syllables, in making the changes:

19. Peace (quod the towne mouse) why speakest thou so loude.   T.
20. I can not crouch nor knele to such a wrong.   T.

Twenty-two lines, then, were changed so that clashing stresses were avoided, and nineteen so that the number of syllables was reduced to ten. Some of the changes are ambiguous, but their general direction is clear. Still, the Satires as they were printed in the *Miscellany* are not smooth and regular if the lines are read to correspond with what seems to be the usual manner of speaking. The changes made appear at first to be an insignificant fraction of the total number of irregular lines. A table in which Wyatt's lines are classified by their relation to a regular metrical pattern will show how this appears.

WYATT		*Changed in Tottel*
Regular lines	146	1
Initial trochee	31	0
Lines varying in one foot	30	4
Irregular lines, varying in more than one foot	51	9
Nine-syllable lines	14	7
Eleven-and-twelve-syllable lines	34	22
	306	43

It must be remembered also that not all the lines changed in Tottel became perfectly regular. However, this does not mean that the Satires in Tottel are only slightly less regular than the Satires in Wyatt's manuscript. They are very much more regular. The actual verbal alterations accomplish some change, but primarily they serve to indicate the intention about the correspondence of metrical pattern to language. Where these two plainly did not correspond, the language could be changed. The lines that were not changed show how the editors must have thought the language could sometimes correspond to the metrical pattern even though that language in its normal use in speech would not correspond. The words are the same as in the lines Wyatt wrote, but the lines in effect become quite different, as different as though they had actually been revised. They are the lines like these—I give them first as they appear in Wyatt, with the stronger speech stresses marked, and then as they appear in Tottel, with what I believe was the scansion of 1557.

And to the dore now is she come by stelth.   W.

o   s| o   s| o   s| o s | o   s
And to the dore now is she come by stealth.   T.

                          II, 36

Ne ye set not a dragg net for an hare   W.

o   s| o   s |o   s | o   s |o   s
Nor ye set not a dragge net for an hare.   T.

                          II, 89

In lines like these, the adjustment is not too far from the common practices of later English verse. I include some lines, however, which violently differ in scansion and speech-stress. There is no way to prove that they were accepted exactly in this way in 1557. A few other lines which cannot be reconciled by any means to a regular pattern are accepted. These lines may be, like those others, an indication that the indulgence of irregular lines, or the slipshod quality of the editing, was greater than I believe it to have been.

That cannot take a mows as the cat can.   W.

o   s   o   s   o   s   o   s o   s
That can not take a mouse, as the cat can.   T.

                          I, 46

I cannot, I. No, no, it will not be.   W.

o   s | o   s| o   s|o   s | o   s
I can not, I no, no, it will not be.   T.

                          I, 76

24

The other lines which were irregular in Wyatt and remain un-changed in Tottel may be excused as standard licenses. Ten of the lines have clashing stresses which could be considered as separated by a caesura following the second foot, as in this example:

```
o   s | o   s  |   s   o |  o s |  o   s
```
Of lordly lokes, wrapped within my cloke.

I, 5

Ten lines may be scanned as partly or substantially trochaic:

```
s    o|    s   o  |  o   s|o   s  |  o    s
```
At the threshold her sely fote did trippe.

II, 64

Three lines are irregular because of the way names are ordered in them, and names have often been allowed as extra-metrical elements in English verse, as they were in Latin.

With Venus, and Bacchus, all theire life long.

I, 23

Ten lines remain which resist any attempt at explanation. Seven of these, if they are to have five relatively strong stresses, can have them only in irregular orders. Three lines will not accept more than four relatively strong stresses. Some of these lines cannot be brought into any relation with an iambic metrical pattern.

1. Rather than to liue thrall vnder the awe.
   I, 4
2. With innocent bloud to fede my selfe fatte.
   I, 35
3. And he that suffreth offence withoutt blame.
   I, 70
4. Rather then to be, outwardly to seme.
   I, 92
5. She chered her, with how sister what chere.
   II, 49
6. To freate inward, for losying such a losse.
   II, 112
7. Seke still thy profite vpon thy bare fete.
   III, 42
1. The letcher a louer, and tyranny.
   I, 74
2. For money, poyson, and treason: of some.
   I, 98[1]
3. Madde if ye list to continue your sore.
   II, 100

[1] In Wyatt's line, the last two words were *at Rome*.

25

Wyatt had thirty-one lines of eleven syllables. Twenty-one of these were changed, and in changing some of Wyatt's other lines, the editors added four to this category. Seven of those not changed were lines with feminine endings; the final extra syllable has always been allowed in English verse. Three of the lines may well have been considered to be ten-syllable lines, if -*eth* need not be syllabic following a vowel.

> 1. *Goeth* guide and all in seking quiet life.
>
> II, 74
>
> 2. There *groweth* no mosse. These prouerbes yet do last.
>
> III, 4
>
> 3. Full neare that winde *goeth* trouth in great misease.
>
> III, 36

Of the four eleven-syllable lines added in Tottel, three regularized the stress pattern and became feminine-ending lines. One has the extra syllable within the line:

> From vnder the stall withoute landes or feise.   W.
>
>   o s |o   o s| o s |o s |o s
> From vnder the stall, withouten landes or feese.   T.
>
> III, 48

Two twelve-syllable lines present no reason why they should not have been changed:

> And driuell on pearles with head styll in the manger.   T.
>
> III, 20
>
> Thy nece, thy cosyn, thy sister, or thy daughter.   T.
>
> III, 68

Of the fourteen lines with nine syllables in Wyatt, seven are changed in Tottel. All these appear to be changed because they presented clashing stresses. One of the lines which was not changed has no clashing stresses:

>   s |o   s|o s |o s| o s |
> 1. Praise syr Topas for a noble tale.   T.
>
> I, 50

Supposing they must have five strong metrical stresses, two of the lines have clashing stresses which may be separated by a caesura:

>   o s| o s || s o| s o| s
> 2. To be the right of a Prynces rayghne.   T.
>
> I, 75
>
>   o   s| o s || s   o| s   o|s
> 3. Had not ysene such a beast before.   T.
>
> II, 56

One line could be scanned, with some violence to the normal speech pattern of stresses, as substantially trochaic:

```
       s    o | s      o | s   o| s      o | s
4. With free tong, what thee mislikes, to blame.          T.
                                        III, 87
```

Two lines can include five strong metrical stresses only if the two final syllables in the line are strong-stressed.

```
      o      s  | o   s|o   s  | o    s   | s
5. And scorne the story that the knight tolde.          T.
                               I, 51
    o    s|  o    s|o   s |o s  | s
6. As Pandar was in such a like dede.          T.
                           III, 75
```

One line appears to have two sets of clashing stresses:

```
      o   o  s      s |  o    s    s  | o    s
7. In a rounde head, with sharpe ears: in Fraunce.          T.
                          II, 54
```

Thus, of the 306 lines in the Satires as printed by Tottel, only thirteen remain with irregular metrical stress patterns which cannot be excused in one way or another. Only two remain with more than ten syllables and no excuse for the extra syllable. The editorial work was neither quite thorough nor quite consistent—why should one of these lines be changed and not the other?

Tho I seme lene and dry withoute moyster.   W.
Though I seme leane and drye, withouten moysture.   T.
                               III, 24

And he that sufferth offence withoute blame.   W.
                               I, 70

But the main change is the change of metrical principle. The Satires as printed by Tottel are not Wyatt's Satires. The metrical principle is quite different from Wyatt's; the true difference cannot be tabulated statistically. No doubt many of the extreme distortions of speech to fit the metrical pattern are due to editorial laziness or desperation. A really thorough redaction of Wyatt would have been a considerable undertaking. Apparently neither Grimald nor anyone else was prepared to do what Pope did in 'versifying' Donne's satires. The revisers did not trouble about the relation of speech junctures, of phrase and clause, to the metrical measure, and surely Wyatt's practice in this could not have been agreeable to them. But the metrical principle and what it allowed readers of Tottel to be interested in may be seen at work in places where the accommodation is slight but where, as well as in the more obvious places, the difference is very real.

Here is a change unnoted in the tabular accounts. It is from the second Satire, the letter to his friend John Poyns on the poet's retirement from Court life.

> But here I ame in Kent and Christendome   W.
>
> I, 100
>
> But I am here in kent and christendome   T.

The lines of course indicate the same fact about the poet's location. But there is a perceptible difference in the presentation of the fact. This line comes at the end of the poem, after a long review of conditions in other more splendid but less virtuous places, the English court, France, Spain, Flanders:

> Nor Fflaunders chiere letteth not my sight to deme
> Of black and white, nor taketh my wit awaye
> With bestlynes, they beeste do so esteme;
> Nor I ame not where Christe is geven in pray
> For mony, poison and traison at Rome,
> A commune practise vsed nyght and daie:
> But here I ame in Kent and Christendome
> Emong the muses where I rede and ryme;
> Where if thou list, my Poynz, for to come,
> Thou shalt be judge how I do spend my tyme.

The tone of the whole poem is summed up in this line as a sort of envoy. Its half-humorous geography of the very local Kent and the huge Christendom allows the spiritual significances of the bigger term to reflect on those of Kent, providing connotations which the county named all by itself or in another relation could not have. The county has previously been established as a place of virtue, the place where the poet can live a healthy and independent life. This reflects again ironically on Christendom. The virtues established for Kent make possible, beyond irony, something like an identification of the two terms: Kent is the only Christendom.[1]

All this is borne much better by Wyatt's location of strong stresses on *here* and *am* than it can be borne by the editor's strong stresses. *But I am here* allows the comparison to be invidious and self-congratulating in a way that is out of keeping.

But here I am allows a number of possibilities. *Fortunately, almost to my surprise, I find that I am here: you can be so lucky too, if you*

[1] The proverb had it as 'Neither in Kent nor Christendom'; see Morris Palmer Tilley, *A Dictionary of the Proverbs in England in the Sixteenth and Seventeenth Centuries* (Ann Arbor, 1950). K 16, 353.

like. . . . At this particular place, here, these things are true: come and see for yourself. . . . Come what may, this is my place, here I stay: come and see why. . . . All of them are consonant with the other effects, and the editor has destroyed them by inverting Wyatt's phrase. 'Certain speech forms,' Leonard Bloomfield said, 'have an animated flavour, akin to the exclamatory, as, for instance, the placing first of certain adverbs: Away ran John; away he ran.'[1]

In Wyatt's line, the phrase is strong enough to demand the stresses which must accompany it in speech. And that, I believe, is nearly a complete description of Wyatt's own metrical requirements, as he must have seen them.

For Wyatt, the metrical pattern of the ten-syllable iambic line had one use. It threw into relief the language of a man speaking, with the abrupt shifts from outburst to meditation that allowed him to include in poetry everything from godly things to the swine that chaw the turds molded on the ground. Ten syllables more or less, five relatively strong stresses, more or less: it was a standard maintained steadily enough to declare itself. In doing that it accomplished what the metrical system of Wyatt's immediate inheritance could not do, it emphasized the quality of living speech that brought with it all the qualities of the man. This is not exactly what the editors were looking for, nor what they were concerned to preserve.

In Surrey's verse the principle of the iambic metrical pattern is perfectly clear. He does not have Wyatt's interest in maintaining speech-patterns of stress in strong contrast to the metrical pattern. At least his verse does not usually have that interest, and never has it to anything like Wyatt's degree. His principles seem to have been very close to those of Tottel's editor. Exactly how close they were cannot be determined; no autograph manuscript of Surrey's poems has been discovered. The versions of some of his poems as printed by Padelford come from a manuscript which apparently preserves readings earlier than those in Tottel, although the manuscript itself is late Elizabethan.[2] Tottel's version sometimes has a greater regularity, but the differences do not constitute a difference in metrical principle, as do the changes that were made in Wyatt's Satires and others of his poems.

Even in these versions, Surrey's verse is not perfectly regular.

---

[1] Leonard Bloomfield, *Language* (New York, 1933), p. 156.
[2] *The Poems of Henry Howard, Earl of Surrey*, ed. F. M. Padelford, rev. ed. (Seattle, 1928). This edition is inaccurate in many details, as Rollins points out in his *Tottel* (I, 62–64), and I use here the versions of Tottel, as printed by Rollins, except for the *Aeneid*.

There are differences in the degrees of regularity in each of the chief kinds of verse Surrey wrote, blank verse, lyrics and sonnets, and poulter's measure.

Metrically, the blank verse of his translation from the *Aeneid* is not unlike that of a later day. There is considerable freedom within the line and in the relations of the junctures of the language and the lines.

> A cloudie showr, mingled with haile, I shall
> Poure down, and then with thonder shake the skies.
> Thassemble scattered, the mist shall cloke.
> Dido a caue, the Troyan prince the same
> Shall enter to, and I will be at hand.
> And if thy will sticke vnto mine, I shall
> In wedlocke sure knit and make her his own:
> Thus shall the maryge be.[1]

It is not thumping iambics nor monotonous end-stopped lines that make Surrey's blank verse lack vigour. The lines above have the metrical variations that have been found to characterize all his blank verse: initial trochee; trochees in other positions (In wedlocke sure *knit and make her* his own); anapaestic feet (A cloudie showr, *mingled with haile*, I shall); pause falling after the first foot, as in the second line above; after the second foot, as in the first, third, fifth, and seventh lines; after the third foot, as in the third line; and after the fourth foot, as in the sixth line. Run-on lines, Padelford calculated, make up about one-fourth of his blank verse lines.[2] It is not strict observation of the metrical pattern, but a lack of energy in the language, an aimless remoteness from speech (*the Troyan prince the same shall enter to*) that gives Surrey's blank verse its effect of monotony. Yet even in the blank verse it seems he was at least moving in the direction of Tottel's editor. He was to a certain extent, like that editor, adpating a text 'too archaic in rhythm and pronunciation to please his ear,'[3] for much of his translation is based on Gavin Douglas's Scottish dialect version. Howard Baker has shown how Surrey sometimes changes Douglas's 'awkward clutter of syllables,' as he calls them, towards 'a line which has a smooth flow of alternate stresses,' so that Douglas's

---

[1] Padelford, p. 150.

[2] *Ibid.*, p. 51, and Edwin Casady, *Henry Howard Earl of Surrey* (New York, 1938), 'Appendix I,' where there is a classification of Surrey's metres.

[3] Rollins's phrase; see above, p. 17, note.

> Clam vp againe in the greit hors maw

becomes Surrey's

> Clambe vp againe vnto the hugie horse,

'and thus a gordian knot in metrics was cut.'[1] It was truly a cutting of the knot, and not an untying. Surrey's smoothing of the line by adopting rare forms of speech, forcing the language to conform strictly to the metrical pattern, doubtless helped give that metrical pattern the authority it needed at that stage of the development. But in the process he does not so much reconcile the vigour of speech with the power of the metrical pattern as he begins to abandon the vigour, which in the case of his translations was partly Douglas's 'impelling diction,' and 'awkward clutter of syllables.'[2] In his own verse a great share of the clutter remains; but he showed those who followed one way of solving the problem. The knot was cut, and the two strands of the metrical pattern and the stubborn English phrase remained for some time without as good a union as the knot had been.

Still, in his lyrics and sonnets Surrey sometimes employed the iambic pattern in ways that would not be fully developed until Sidney took them up. He is more regular than Wyatt, even in Tottel's versions of both poets; their translations from Petrarch are well known, with Wyatt's irregular, inventive line and Surrey's much closer approximation to the perfectly regular metrical pattern.

> Wherwith loue to the hartes forest he fleeth,
> Leauyng his enterprise with paine and crye.
> > *Wyatt*[3]

> And cowarde Loue then to the hart apace
> Taketh his flight, whereas he lurkes, and plaines
> > *Surrey*[4]

Yet some of the lyrics printed as Surrey's have a success which depends on a delicate handling of metre and a sensitivity to the patterns of phrase used with it. 'O happy dames' has a stanza of various line lengths:

> O Happy dames, that may embrace
> The frute of your delight,
> Help to bewaile the wofull case,
> And eke the heauy plight
> Of me, that wonted to reioyce
> The fortune of my pleasant choyce:
> Good Ladies, help to fill my moorning voyce.[5]

---

[1] Baker, pp. 63 ff.   [2] *Ibid.*   [3] *Tottel*, I, 32.   [4] *Ibid.*, I, 8.
[5] *Tottel*, II, 15. This poem may be Harington's. See Hughey, p. 418: 'It will be

This is Tottel's version, but the precise syllabic accuracy may well be the poet's own: the structure of the stanza demands that the line lengths be recognized in the number of feet, 4, 3, 4, 3, 4, 4, 5. In the third stanza this metrical structure is retained exactly in the number of syllables, but the phrases given to the lady cut across the pattern of feet, and gain in the movement a reinforcement of their effect of dramatically appropriate speech.

> When other louers, in armes acrosse,
> Reioyce their chiefe delight:
> Drowned in teares to mourne my losse,
> I stand the bitter night,
> In my window, where I may see,
> Before the windes how the cloudes flee.
> Lo, what a mariner loue hath made me.[1]

In the last line the demand of the metrical pattern for five relatively strong stresses could be satisfied theoretically by distorting the language to read,

> o   s|o   s|o s | o   s | o   s|
> Lo what a mariner loue hath made me.

But the most likely way of saying the words is something like this, where only four stresses are noticeably stronger than the others,

> Ló what a mariner lóve hath made me.

If the reader attempts to preserve as much of the metrical pattern as he can, and still stay reasonably close to a possible way of speaking the words, there is this possibility,

> s   s o s o o s   o   s   o
> Lo what a mariner loue hath made me.

This is appropriate; the stresses on *what a mariner* correspond to a modern intonation implying *What a foolish kind of imitation mariner I am; how preposterous that I should be scanning the skies like an anxious mariner, for the mariner really has some necessity for his vigil, but I have only my bad nerves as an excuse; and I am helpless anyway to aid my love, the real mariner, no matter what the weather.*

recalled that the poem "O Happie dames," ordinarily ascribed to Surrey, is printed in the *Nugae* (ed. 1769, pp. 187–8) with the heading "By John Harington, 1543, for a Ladie moch in Love".' Miss Hughey's studies of the Harington MS. led her to ascribe considerable authority to the *Nugae*; Rollins believed its value to be slight (I, 91, 92). Whoever wrote it, the poem has metrical virtues unusual for the period before 1557.

[1] *Tottel*, II, 15.

The lady's wistfully ironic reflection on her own feelings is expressed most fully with the metrical requirement reinforcing and altering the normal way of saying the words. There is also the more indefinable pleasure, throughout the poem, of participating in the play of phrase and measure:

> And eke the heauy plight
> Of me, that wonted to reioyce
> The fortune of my pleasant choyce.
> Good ladies, help to fill my moorning voyce.

The lines of four feet and the lines of three feet, followed by the two lines of four feet and the final line of five feet, all form a pattern recognizable and pleasant in itself, and furthermore the pattern can sometimes become useful in helping to create the appropriate tone for the speech, as it does for this poem in those longer final lines,

> Toward me, the swete port of his avail.
> Now he comes, will he come? alas, no no.

It might seem that poulter's measure could have the same success, with its metrical structure of units of three feet, three feet, four feet, three feet, in a regular order. But it is almost universally regarded as a failure. The form itself seems to be a mistake. The metrical units are apprehended in an entirely different way from our apprehension of the same units in a lyric like 'O happy dames.'

> Layd in my quiet bed, in study as I were,
> I saw within my troubled head, a heape of thoughtes appere:
> And euery thought did shew so liuely in myne eyes,
> That now I sighed, & thē I smilde, as cause of thought
>   doth ryse.
> I saw the lytle boy in thought, how oft that he
> Did wish of god, to scape the rod, a tall yongman to be.
> The yongman eke that feles, his bones with paines opprest,
> How he would be a rich olde man, to lyue, and lye at rest.[1]

This fatal sing-song, not blank verse or the sonnet, was the form that Surrey's immediate successors took up most enthusiastically. It is in this form that Surrey's verse is most regular metrically, and the regularity is of the peculiar kind that dominated English poetry for twenty years after 1557.

The form itself provides the explanation for this. It explains, at least, why poets were obliged to write as they did once they had adopted the form. To some extent it explains why the form was adopted.

[1] *Tottel*, I, 29.

Poulter's measure is a kind of couplet, one line of six feet, the other of seven. Within the lines the measure has another feature as essential as the measure of the entire lines themselves. This is the pause after the third foot of the first line and after the fourth foot of the second line. This pause is sometimes called a 'caesura,' and properly so. It is not the same as the pause that may occur within the iambic pentameter line. This is also sometimes called caesura; but as C. S. Lewis has noted, 'it is a rhetorical and syntactical fact, not a metrical fact.'[1] The pauses in poulter's measure are like the pauses in the ancient hexameter and in the English four-beat line: metrical facts. They are essential features of the metrical pattern. They occur within the line of poetry as it is usually written. No mark was ever agreed upon to indicate this feature of the pattern; there is nothing to correspond to our conventional way of indicating the line-end in writing, although commas and colons were sometimes used for this purpose. The pattern of the language has to serve as the only dependable indicator of a metrical feature. This simple fact is the trouble with poulter's measure.

To retain the sense of the metrical pattern in poulter's measure, the distinction between the units of three feet and three feet in one line, and four feet and three feet in the other, it is necessary to read the lines with an unusual emphasis on the metrical pattern. This was at once the charm of the line for the early Elizabethan poets and its danger. Their attention was fixed on the new principle of poetry that iambic metres allowed. In a line like

> Thassemble scattered, the mist shall cloke,

every syllable has its place in an order which can be instantly apprehended as a pattern. This pattern seems to be a kind we can apprehend clearly even when it appears in a distorted form.

> And if thy will sticke vnto mine, I shall
> In wedlocke sure . . .

Here both the order of stresses and the pause that marks the end of the pattern are distorted by the requirements of the language. In speech, to mark only the relatively strong stresses and junctures, the pattern might be

> And if thy wíll stícke vnto míne, Î shall in wedlock súre . . .

In iambic pentameter a line can depart widely from the pattern without that pattern losing its force. But in poulter's this is not so.

[1] C. S. Lewis, 'The Fifteenth-Century Heroic Line,' *Essays and Studies*, XXIV (1938), p. 29.

Apparently we do not apprehend directly the distinction between six feet and seven feet; we need the internal division of three and three and four and three. If a line should be read so that these distinctions are lost, the pattern is destroyed. The poet has no way to escape this dilemma. If he allows a close correspondence of metrical pattern and the pattern of speech stress, the pattern of speech stress is easily absorbed into the metrical pattern.

> Layd in my quiet bed, in study as I were

becomes

> s   o | o   s|o s || o   s| o s |o ||
> Layd in my quiet bed, in study as I were.

The equal degrees of stress of the metrical pattern, even though they correspond to the varying degrees of stress of speech, cause the language to become a kind of nonsense.[1] The reader is scarcely able to attend to the stress patterns which make the language meaningful. If the pattern of language does not correspond to the metrical pattern, the situation is no better, in poulter's measure.

> The yong man eke/that feles his bones with paines opprest.

Here the punctuation of Tottel shows how the line must be read if the pattern is not to be lost:

> The yong man eke that feles, his bones with paines opprest.

It is possible, of course, that the early Elizabethans did not have the modern reader's difficulty in maintaining a sense of the pattern of poulter's measure without making the metrical pattern so obvious that it completely overmasters the necessary pattern of language. They may have read the line above with its natural pattern of two, two, and two without falling into a confusion between this line of the couplet and the longer line with its initial unit of four. The probability, though, is that they did read poulter's with great

---

[1] It would be more precise to say that the intonation pattern demanded by the pattern of stresses has a meaning of its own which is so strong that it nearly obliterates the meaning of the language. Kenneth L. Pike, in *The Intonation of American English*, has this to say about sing-song:

The monotonous repetition of special sequences of balanced contours in evenly spaced rhythm units—especially if it causes normal grammatical units to be broken up—produces SINGSONG. One such sequence is °3-2 °3-4. [This refers to the intonation pattern usually used in a Mother Goose rhyme like *Mary had a little lamb*.]; it may be said to have a meaning of RECITAL . . . (p. 72).

The meaning of the intonation pattern of poulter's is not exactly clear to me, but it is obviously something very like this, as poulter's is very like the metrical pattern of nursery rhymes.

35

emphasis on the metrical pattern, and did not object to the result; and the evidence of the styles of versification that develop between Surrey and Gascoigne is that they read all measures that way. It remains uncertain whether popular verse like Sternhold's and Hopkins's Psalms was an influence on this more literary verse or whether it was another symptom.[1] We might suppose that the common measure of four feet and three feet would be clear enough without the over-emphasis demanded by poulter's or the fourteener; but here for a clear view we need deeper studies of the English phrase, of the perception of rhythm, and of popular verse of every kind. Without these, I can only say that for nearly all English readers after the 1570's the difficulty of poulters and to some extent of hexameters and fourteeners, is overwhelming.[2]

The quality of much of the verse written in those measures seems to indicate that the poets who wrote in them were encouraged by the form to feel that it was not a bad thing to write verse whose sense mattered very little. It would be wrong to say that the art of writing near-nonsense was Surrey's legacy to English poets, but that is certainly the use they made, for a while, of his sudden success in the new metrical patterns.

[1] On the possible influence of Sternhold and Hopkins, see Hallett Smith, 'English Metrical Psalms,' *Huntington Library Quarterly*, IX, No. 3 (1946), 249–271. 'Their Psalms, commanding an audience roughly equivalent to the whole of the English-speaking race, constituted a body of verse that was plain, bare, regular in beat, iambic, strictly measured. It came at a time when English prosody was in confusion, and it offered some kind of order.' (p. 265).

[2] Ezra Pound (*ABC of Reading*, New York, n.d.), finds Golding's fourteeners in his translation of Ovid's *Metamorphoses* 'susceptible to bad reading,' but successful if read 'as natural spoken language.' The usual feeling about it seems to be that described by Robert Lowell (*Kenyon Review*, XVII, 1955, p. 315): 'Even if one is careful not to tub-thump, and reads Golding's huge, looping "fourteeners" for "sense and syntax," as Pound advises, even then one trips; often the form seems like some arbitrary and wayward hurdle, rather than the very backbone of what is being said.'

II

The Mirror for Magistrates

At about the time when Tottel's *Songs and Sonnets* was being assembled, the editors of *The Mirror for Magistrates* were gathering the twenty-seven lugubrious tragedies that did as much as the lyrics in Tottel to form Elizabethan style and taste.[1] The *Mirror*, unlike the *Miscellany*, is nearly all the work of contemporary hands. But it is by no means all in a contemporary style. Some of the writers were still working their way out of the metrical traditions of the past into the new, working hard at it; and in the early editions the editorial improvements do not obscure this, as the alterations in Tottel obscured the experiments of some of his poets. As a result, these tragedies form an extraordinary museum of metre. The oldest kind of verse in the *Mirror* looks back to Middle English, while the newest kind allows a look forward to the practices in metre for centuries to come. The oldest and newest kinds of verse are easy to recognize; they have names and standard descriptions. But in the *Mirror* there is also a kind of verse that has no name. It has features of two systems of metre, that based on the four-beat line and that based on the line of iambic feet. It belongs to neither; it may be a link between them that shows how and why the old gave way to the new.

One *Mirror* poem not the work of a contemporary is 'Edward IV.' It is attributed to Skelton, and was written perhaps at the time of that king's death in 1483. Even then its metre was not quite in line with the current tradition, although it was more in line than it might seem to have been. 'Edward IV' is in stanzas of twelve lines, rhymed ABAB BCBC CDCD; the last line, in Latin, is a refrain.

---

[1] *The Mirror for Magistrates*, ed. Lily S. Campbell (Cambridge, 1938). The first published edition is that of 1559, but there exists a fragment of a suppressed ~ion dating from about five years earlier.

37

Of the 84 lines in the poem, a few have only eight syllables, a few have as many as thirteen, but more than seventy have ten or eleven syllables. Considering these things, it is not unreasonable to say, as Sainstsbury did, that the metrical basis of the poem is 'decasyllabic.'[1]

Yet the basic structure of 'Edward IV' is not that of the deca-syllabic line but that of the four-beat line. Despite the fact that its alliteration is not systematic enough to identify the form, it resembles in several ways some types of alliterative verse. The fourteenth-century poem *Pearl*, for instance, like 'Edward IV' an elegy, has rhyme also, and its twelve-line stanza, a common one for elegy in Middle English verse, is very like that of 'Edward IV.' The use of a repeated last line (Latin or English) is a common feature of these two poems and of the similar poems which employ this stanza.[2] The lines of both poems have a certain consistency in length between their extremes of thirteen and seven or eight syllables.

About three out of four lines of *Pearl* have some alliteration; in 'Edward IV' it is infrequent after the first few lines. But alliteration, length of line, rhyme, or stanza do not determine the basic structure of verse. The structure of *Pearl* is identified as four-beat by the pattern of junctures and the pattern of the stresses. In these essential features it closely resembles 'Edward IV,' and in these features both poems resemble the more usual Middle English and Old English alliterative poems.

The essential feature of the pattern of junctures is that the line is formed of two half-lines, indicated by the phrasing of the language.

> I halde þat iueler   lyttel to prayse
> þat leuȝ wel   þat he seȝ wyth yȝe.
> *Pearl*, 301–2[3]

> Where was in my life   such an one as I,
> While Lady Fortune   with me had continuaunce?
> 'Edward IV,' 25–6[4]

The essential metrical elements within the half-line are 'lifts' and 'dips,' the lift being the metrical equivalent of a relatively strong-stressed syllable, the dip the metrical equivalent of a relatively weak-stressed syllable. The half-line has two lifts, like the normal Old English half-line; there may be one, two, or three dips; each dip may contain from one to three syllables (or very rarely, four).

---

[1] George Saintsbury, *History of English Prosody* (London, 1906), I, 245.
[2] On the use of this stanza in Middle English, see E. V. Gordon (ed.), *Pearl* (Oxford, 1953), p. 87.
[3] Gordon, *op. cit.*
[4] This and all quotations from the *Mirror* are from Lily Campbell, *op. cit.*

My symbol for the dip, ø, remains the same regardless of the number of syllables that represent the dip in the language. As much as they differ syllabically, all these half-lines satisfy the metrical requirements.

s ⸱ ø ⸱ s Quen þat frech	*Pearl*, 195a.
Where is now	'Edward IV,' 49a.
s ⸱ ø ⸱⸱ s Knelande to grounde	*Pearl*, 434a.
Mercy I aske	'Edward IV,' 9a.
s ⸱ ø ⸱⸱ s ⸱ ø Schadowed þis worteӡ	*Pearl*, 42a.
Absolon profered	'Edward IV,' 69a.
ø ⸱ s ø ⸱ s of ryal prys	*Pearl*, 193b.
your hartes enbrace	'Edward IV,' 81b.
ø ⸱⸱ s ø ⸱ s And Chartye grete	*Pearl*, 470a.
I slepe now in molde	'Edward IV,' 13a.
ø ⸱ s ⸱ ø s in Jerusalem	*Pearl*, 804b.[1]
and to contribute Fraunce	'Edward IV,' 28a.
ø ⸱⸱ s ø ⸱ s ø For neuer lesyng	*Pearl*, 897a.
While Lady Fortune	'Edward IV,' 26a.
ø ⸱⸱ s ⸱ ø ⸱⸱ s ⸱ ø Wythouten mote o þer mascle	*Pearl*, 726a.
nor amend your complaynyng	'Edward IV,' 11b.
ø ⸱ s ⸱ ø ⸱⸱ s ⸱ ø þou telleӡ me of Jerusalem	*Pearl*, 919a.
that was late in prosperity	'Edward IV,' 20b.

'Clashing' patterns in which there is no dip between the two lifts, øss, ssø, øssø, seem to occur within the half-line in *Pearl*. The uncertain adding and dropping of final *e* often makes the intention doubtful—as it makes uncertain the exact number of syllables in a line (Where rych rokke, 68a; Ryche blod, 646a). In 'Edward IV' clashes may occur, but here too they are uncertain. There may be other if less likely possibilities for the strong stresses (or els $\overset{ø\ \ \ s}{of}$ strong

---

[1] Jérusalem in Middle English.

Sampson; or els of strong Sampson, 66b) or the pronunciation might
allow an intervening syllable (vnto wormes meat, 64b). In both
poems there are clearly cases where one half-line ends and the next
begins with a strong stress:

>   As glemande glas burnist broun   *Pearl*, 990
>   And moreover to encroch ready was I bent
>   'Edward IV,' 39

Half-lines, then, with a metrical pattern of two lifts and one to
three dips are the metrical elements which order both the following
stanzas.

> Perleʒ pyʒte . of ryal prys
>
> þere moʒt mon . by grace haf sene,
>
> Quen þat frech . as flor-de-lys
>
> Doun þe bonke . con boʒe bydene.
>
> Al blysnande whyt . watʒ hir beau biys,
>
> Vpon at sydeʒ . and bounden bene,
>
> Wyth þe myryeste margarys . at my deuyse
>
> þat euer I se . ʒet with myn ene;
>
> Wyth lappeʒ large . I wot and I wene,
>
> Dubbed with double . perle and dyʒte;
>
> Her cortel of self . sute schene,
>
> Wyth precios perleʒ al vmbepyʒte.
>   193–204.
>
> Where is now . my conquest and victory?
>
> Where is my ritches . and royall array?
>
> Where be my coursers . and my horses hye?
>
> Where is my mirth, . my solas, and playe?
>
> As vanity to nought . all is wyddred away:
>
> O Lady Bes, . long for me may you call,

$$\overset{s}{\text{For}} \overset{s}{\text{I am departed}} \ . \ \overset{s}{\text{vntill doomes}} \overset{s}{\text{day}}:$$

$$\overset{s}{\text{But love}} \overset{s}{\text{you that lord}} \ . \ \overset{s}{\text{that is soveraine}} \overset{s}{\text{of all}}.$$

$$\overset{s}{\text{Where be}} \overset{s}{\text{my castels}} \ . \ \overset{s}{\text{and buyldinges}} \overset{s}{\text{royall}}?$$

$$\overset{s}{\text{But Windsore}} \overset{s}{\text{alone}} \ . \ \overset{s}{\text{now have}} \overset{s}{\text{I no moe}}$$

$$\overset{s}{\text{And}} \overset{s}{\text{of Eton}} \ . \ \overset{s}{\text{the prayers}} \overset{s}{\text{perpetuall}},$$

$$\overset{s}{\text{Et}} \overset{s}{\text{ecce nunc}} \ . \ \overset{s}{\text{in pulvere}} \overset{s}{\text{dormio}}.$$

Et ecce nunc . in pulvere dormio.
                        49–60.

This reading of 'Edward IV' is, of course, the result of applying a metrical pattern to the language of the poem. The superior marks show where the lifts occur, not necessarily where all the strongest stresses of speech would be heard if the words were uttered. The point and the line-end show where the half-lines end, not necessarily where the pauses of speech would be longest in every case. The pattern is that of *Pearl*. In that poem the expectation of four lifts to the line is announced by the alliteration. This auxiliary of metre works both immediately as it calls special attention to its syllables in any particular line, and less directly but perhaps more essentially as it calls attention to the tradition. The pattern suggests itself for 'Edward IV' because *Pearl* and 'Edward IV' have in common certain secondary metrical characteristics, chiefly the stanza form.

When the pattern is applied to the language of 'Edward IV' it seems to fit. It seems to fit better than a pattern of iambic feet does, although that would fit some lines perfectly. Still there are places where half-line and phrase, lift and strong stress, do not readily coincide. In this poem they may be accommodated, and the kind of accommodation they require is worth noting, for it differs from the accommodations other poems in the *Mirror* will need between the patterns of sound in the language and the patterns of sound the metre requires.

First, it is obvious that the pattern of lifts does not everywhere easily correspond to the stress patterns of the language. In the first five lines of the stanza given above, they do correspond. It is easy to speak the lines with two relatively strong stresses to each half-line; most of them would be spoken in this way without any thought of a metrical pattern. This does not seem true of the second part of this line.

O Lady Bes, long for me may you call.

41

There is some degree of difficulty both in the metrical pattern itself and in the language, if they are expected to correspond. The alliteration of *Lady* and *long* suggests (but in this poem cannot determine) that *long* represents a lift. The language suggests this also, for the adverb in this position can receive a primary stress, as in *Long may it wave*. The possibilities for the other stresses in speech seem to be these:

Long for me may you call: *Others may be able to come at your call, but not me.*

Long for me may you call: *My melancholy reflection is so old and familiar as to be ritualistic, almost a meaningless chant.* An extreme interpretation of this sort could separate the words from one another and give each of them a primary stress.

Long for me may you call: In this case the stress pattern is formalized to indicate a particular tone, a tone of acceptance or resignation, but a kind of emphatic resignation usually employed to convince the other person that he too should be resigned. The pitch of the last word is raised: *Be it as it may be* can be said significantly with this intonation. This pattern is appropriate to the occasion of the language, and allows a correspondence of the stress-pattern of speech to the metrical requirements of two lifts to the half-line. The dip is represented by four syllables. This is an unusual case here and in *Pearl*, although not in four-beat poems of longer lines like *Gawain*

(So bisied him his ȝonge blod . and his brayn wylde. 89) or *Piers Plowman* (For with charite hath be chapman . and chief to shryve lordes. *B-text*, Pro. 64). The real problem these long dips present will be considered later.

This is a long way round to a reconciliation that may not be necessary unless we expect this correspondence. The perfect correspondence of speech stress and metrical pattern plainly does not exist consistently in most poems whatever their metrical system. *Pearl* certainly does not seem to have it. At least in modern speech, the first of these lines requires that the weak or tertiary stress of *schal* must represent a lift, and the second line requires that one of the five stronger stresses be part of a dip (unless the line is said to have five lifts).

þer alle our causeȝ . *schal* be tryed,
702.

A *hondred* and *forty fowre* þouwsande *flot.*
786.

In the same way, the metrical pattern, as I see it, influences the speech stresses of lines in 'Edward IV,' in some cases suppressing a strong stress where it would be expected in speech, and in other cases suggesting a stronger stress than the phrase would require in speech.

       s   s   s   ø   s
O Lady Bes, long for me may you call.

     s
And of Eton the prayers perpetuall.

As it happens, the suggestions of the metrical pattern here make phrases which are appropriate in speech. There is no actual conflict.

'Thomas of Woodstock, Duke of Gloucester,' by George Ferrers, has the same basic metrical pattern as 'Edward IV.' Ferrers was of Surrey's generation. He served Henry VIII, Edward VI, Mary, and Elizabeth with some distinction.[1] As one of Baldwin's chief collaborators, he would of course have been aware of the metrical system based on the iambic line used by Baldwin and most of the other contributors. But his 'Thomas of Woodstock' and his 'Tresilian' in the first edition of the *Mirror* are adaptations of the older metrical pattern. His three other contributions were held up for some reason until later editions; they surely underwent some revision in the interim, as the printed poems did, and may have undergone a great deal. Since it is impossible to determine what the changes were, these poems are not of any great historical interest metrically except as they show what was acceptable to the editors. They resemble metrically the text of Wyatt's *Satires* produced by Tottel's revision, haphazard approximations of iambic pentameter.

The lines of 'Thomas of Woodstock' are formed into half-lines by their phrasing. The half-lines have every pattern of lift and dip, and with few exceptions they possess two stresses stronger than the others in what I take to be a normal, modern, matter-of-fact way of speaking.

    s ø   s   s   ø   s
Articles nyne; lyst for to frowne,
    186a   6b

    s   ø   s   ø   s   ø   s ø
Maye in a moment; hourded a treasure
    7a   149b

   ø   s   ø s ø   s   ø   s
In proofe whereof; tourne vypsyde downe
    8a   7b

[1] Lily Campbell, 'Introduction,' pp. 25–31.

ø   s   ø   s ø   ø   s   ø s   ø
Let none trust Fortune; of suche presumption
          34a   134b

ø   s   s   ø   s   s
Had fyrst nede; of the Cats clawes
      87a   102b

s   s   ø
Sum executed; (none in second half-line).[1]
  128a

With these phrases, Ferrers meets his metrical requirements. It is rarely necessary in 'Thomas of Woodstock' to include one of the stronger stresses in a dip, as in this line:

For princes lyke Lyons haue *long* and *large pawes.*
                                  102

And it is as rarely that we must allow what would usually be a weakly stressed syllable to represent a lift, as *of* or *my*, or perhaps *-ate*, must here:

Towardes the atchiuyng of my attemptate.
                                  107

More frequent are the cases in which the correspondence of speech and metrical pattern depends upon the coherence of the phrase, as in this half-line,

Ouerturning townes,
     51a

Here the relative subordination of both syllables of *ouer* to the stronger stress of *turning* depends upon their being part of a pattern of compound word-stress. If *ouer* is perceived as a unit in itself, its first syllable qualifies as a lift, and the line would have five lifts:

s   s   s   s   s
Ouerturning townes, high castels and towers.

On the whole Ferrers is able to prevent this disintegration of the half-line. To prevent it, he must be careful not to raise the expectation that stresses less than the strongest can function as lifts. He does use half-lines like that cited above.

                                     s   s
Towardes the atchiuyng . of my attemptate,
or

                               s   s
The king enflamed . with *indignacion,*
                                 136

              ø   s ø   s ø
[1] This half-line could be *sum executed*; but as I see it, Ferrers avoids here using the tertiary as a lift.

where a stress clearly less strong than the other strong stress in the same half-line has to represent a lift. But if he used these intermediate stresses as lifts often enough to create an expectation, the whole system would fail. Both his control of juncture and of stress would be lost. A line like the following would then not meet his metrical requirements.

No brasen pyller maye be fyxte more fast,
4

In the half-line *no brasen pyller* the relative degrees of stress are established by the word-stress of *brasen* and *pyller*; and in the half-line *maye be fyxte more fast* the stronger stresses on *fyxte* and *fast* are clear when the half-line is regarded as an utterance in itself. But if the two words *maye be* are isolated as an utterance there will appear a distinction of stress between them, either *máye be* or *maye bé*. In this case, the coherence of the half-line in phrasing keeps the words from breaking off into a unit by themselves where the contrast in stress would allow one of the words to be a lift. Whatever relative strength one of these two syllables possesses, it is overshadowed by the stronger stresses of the complete half-line. For this control Ferrers relies on the patterns of speech which his phrasing indicates, and not on the expectation created by the metrical pattern. The half-line for him is more than a trick of style. It is a necessity, and it must be clearly indicated with all but complete consistency in every line, by the patterns chosen from those of ordinary speech. He does not depend on alliteration or position for the location of lifts; the pattern of speech must locate them, as it must locate the junctures. In this poem the metrical pattern exists as a set of requirements for the language. It consists of two degrees of stress in random patterns and a representation of juncture. The requirement is met by the language only with the degree of stress the syllable normally would have in the particular phrase it occurs in. The metrical pattern is never called upon to assert itself, as it were; there is almost never any noticeable difference between the ideal metrical pattern and the pattern formed by the corresponding elements of sound in the language.

This cannot be true of Ferrers' other poem, 'Tresilian,' unless we suppose that the metrical pattern of that poem is extremely free, so free that it must be really a series of patterns, since at least three different kinds of lines appear there:

s   s   s   s
Possessed the palays, and pillage the countrye
97

$$\overset{s}{\text{Engraue}} \text{ it in } \overset{s}{\text{marble}} \text{ that } \overset{s(?)}{\text{may}} \overset{s}{\text{be}} \overset{s}{\text{razed neuer}}$$
10

$$\overset{s}{\text{And}} \overset{s}{\text{set}} \text{ his } \overset{s}{\text{lustes}} \text{ for } \overset{s}{\text{lawe, and}} \overset{s}{\text{will}} \text{ had } \overset{s}{\text{reasons place}}$$
90

No metrical pattern, whether it be of four, five, or six strong metrical stresses or lifts, can fit all these lines without presenting difficulties of adjustment between that pattern and the corresponding elements of sound in the language. Perhaps the only certain conclusion about 'Tresilian' is just this, that its structure is as free as the 'irregular nursery rhyme movement of *Beryn*,' to which C. S. Lewis compares it.[1]

Yet there is another possibility, and while it can be no more than a speculation, it is an interesting one; it suggests how the iambic pattern may have appeared in English not entirely by imitation of foreign models or through the study of Chaucer, but out of developments from the kind of metre adopted by Ferrers for 'Thomas of Woodstock,' his other poem in the 1559 edition of the *Mirror*.

'Tresilian' begins with a burst of alliteration (even though it sometimes falls on weak-stressed syllables) and phrasing that makes it appear to have the same metrical plan as 'Thomas of Woodstock.'

> In the rufull Register   of mischief and mishap,
> Baldwin we beseche thee   with our name to begin
> Whom vnfrendly Fortune   did trayne vnto a trap,
> When we thought our state   most stable to have bin.[2]

Yet these lines have twelve or thirteen syllables each; sixty per cent of the lines in this poem have twelve syllables, more than twenty per cent have thirteen, ten per cent have eleven. Lines of ten, fourteen, or fifteen syllables are too rare to be significant. This is markedly different from 'Thomas of Woodstock.' This poem, with its system of phrasing, obviously could not indulge in the very long half-line, such as that Dunbar could use in 'The Tua Maritt Wemen and the Wedo':

$$\text{Thair } \overset{s}{\text{mantillis}} \text{ grein war as the } \overset{s}{\text{gress}} . \text{ that } \overset{s}{\text{grew}} \text{ in May } \overset{s}{\text{sessoun.}}[3]$$

And its line length seems more than the incidental result of other

[1] C. S. Lewis, *English Literature of the Sixteenth Century* (Oxford, 1954), pp. 243–244.

[2] The break in the lines is my own addition.

[3] *The Poems of William Dunbar*, ed. W. M. Mackenzie (Edinburgh, 1932), p. 24.

metrical requirements. The half-lines vary in length from three to seven syllables without causing much difficulty in the phrasing; however, no complete line has less than nine or more than twelve or thirteen syllables. Few of them are at these extremes. Half the lines have exactly ten and a quarter of them have eleven syllables. So the line-length of 'Tresilian' suggests both that the poem has a plan, and that this plan is different from that of 'Thomas of Woodstock.' It remains uncertain whether Ferrers could have been thinking of both syllables and stress, or whether one or the other, as part of the plan, determined both. At any rate, both soon become part of a pattern that represents itself clearly in the poem, whether it was Ferrers' conscious intention or not.

> So wurkyng lawe lyke waxe, the subiecte was not sure
> Of lyfe, lande, nor goods, but at the princes wyll:
> Which caused his kingdome the shorter tyme to dure,
> For clayming power absolute both to saue and spyll,
> The prince therby presumed his people for to pyll:
> And set his lustes for lawe, and will had reasons place,
> No more but hang and drawe, there was no better grace.
> 85–92

If Ferrers was indeed thinking of one fairly consistent metrical pattern for all the lines of his poem, there are three possibilities. The first, and least likely in view of the number of lines like those above, is that he intended to write another version of four-beat metre, with long dips of three syllables. The second and third possibilities are much alike: he may have had in mind the pattern usually called dipodic, or he may have been trying to write a line with six strong metrical stresses, a kind of hexameter. The dipodic line is described by George Stewart as basic to the ballad and the nursery rhyme.[1] A strong stress, an intermediate stress, a strong stress, a pause, with a distribution of weakly-stressed syllables, make up the half-line of such verse. The pause is said to make up for a missing intermediate stress.

> Sing a song of sixpence
> A pocket full of rye.
> Four and twenty blackbirds,
> Baked in a pie.
> When the pie was opened,
> The birds began to sing.
> Wasn't that a dainty dish
> To set before the king?

[1] Stewart, pp. 77–91.

47

In such a verse, 'the alternating arrangement, if not perfect, is at least frequent enough throughout the whole poem to establish in the reader's mind the pattern, and so to enable him to feel through the variations the simple fundamental rhythm.'[1] There is, then, in this verse, a pattern which is established strongly enough to make it unnecessary for every phrase to be formed exactly after the pattern; as when today we learn this rhyme we do not say *When the pie was opened*; we chant:

When the pie was opened.

If this pattern were the one adopted by Ferrers, and it is suggested by his interest in the other old oral tradition of the four-beat line, it would not in the end be very different from the other alternative, a kind of hexameter. For the intermediate metrical stress in the dipodic line often enough falls where the phrase presents a strong stress as speech:

Offices, fermes, and fees,
49

and the strong metrical speech where the phrase has some lesser degree:

Vnder the seconde Richarde.
34

The tendency is clearly for them to level out, leaving a metrical pattern of six strong stresses to the line, with a variety of possibilities in adjusting to the phrases of any actual line. The result, as in the last stanza of 'Tresilian,' is iambic, with the usual faults of iambic in the middle of the sixteenth century.

If sum in latter dayes, had called vnto mynde
The fatall fall of vs for wrestyng of the right,
The statutes of this lande they should not have defynde
So wylfully and wyttingly agaynst the sentence quyte:
But though they skaped paine, the falte was nothing lyght:
Let them that cum hereafter both that and this compare,
And waying well the ende, they wyll I trust beware.
141–147

For while the metrical pattern exists here as an independent entity, providing tension between itself and the speech-pattern of the phrases, in 'Tresilian' this is only a disadvantage, and the system of 'Thomas of Woodstock' would seem to be far better in comparison.

1 *Ibid.*

The metrical pattern here seems to serve only to provide emphasis where none is wanted and to set up a rhythmical beat that is monotonous and close to nonsense. This is chiefly because Ferrers has allowed the half-line, so necessary to 'Thomas of Woodstock,' to dominate the structure of metrical junctures; he did not realize that since the measure is established clearly in metrical terms by the succession of weak and strong metrical stresses, the metrical juncture need no longer coincide with the juncture of speech, but could have the same independence, and establish the same tension, as did the metrical pattern of stresses. The two poems are perhaps something more than 'the beginning of one more unfinished causeway across the swamp,' as C. S. Lewis calls them;[1] they may, in showing the route taken by one man, indicate what had once been a main road.[2]

Not every poem of the *Mirror* that is obscure in structure is a part of the movement from the old metrical system to the new. Some of the tragedies appear to have as a metrical principle little more than a refusal to recognize the idea of a consistent metrical structure. Even the editors find 'Richard, Duke of Gloucester,' by one Frances Segars, to be without 'eyther good Meter or order.' 'The Blacksmith,' perhaps by a 'Master Cavyl,' was said to lack 'any exacte kynde of meter'; but of this poem the editors also said that 'a little fyling would make it formall.' 'Richard' appears to be a version of four-beat metre, if it has any consistent metre at all. 'The Blacksmith' has an iambic basis, apparently. Both poems have wide variations in line length. If their disorder has a precedent, 'Richard' may be considered a reproduction of the free stress pattern and varied line-length of *Beryn* or *Gamelyn*; 'The Blacksmith' may be an adaptation of that form in which the lines retain their freedom in length but the stress pattern is somewhat regularized. Finally, however, they are inscrutable.

'Richard, Duke of Gloucester' begins with lines reminiscent of 'Thomas of Woodstock,' with their alliteration and phrasing by half-line:

> What hart so hard, but doth abhorre to heare
> the rufal raygne of me the thyrd Rychard?
> King vnkindely cald though I the crowne dyd weare.

But these could also be read as rough iambic lines; and clusters of

---

[1] Lewis, *English Literature in the Sixteenth Century*, p. 242.
[2] See Frances B. Gummere, 'The Translation of Beowulf, and the Relations of Ancient and Modern English Verse,' *American Journal of Philology*, VII (1886), 46–78. Gummere believed that the pentameter line had evolved out of the four-beat line when the pause between the half-lines, 'giving up its importance caused, by compensation, a new (fifth) stress' (56, n.).

lines occur which in the company of so many iambic poems may much more easily be read as iambic pentameters:

> The Lordes and Commons all with one assent,
> Protectour made me both of land and Kyng,
> But I therewith alas was not content:
> for mindyng mischiefe I ment another thyng.
>   15–18

Or a sort of hexameter:

> To cruel cursed Cayn compare my carefull case
> Whych did vniustly slaye his brother iust Abel,
> And did not I in rage make runne that rufull race.
> My brother duke of Clarens, whose death I shame to tell
> for that so straunge it was, as it was horrible?
>   50–54

Or the three sorts of lines occur together:

> Nor to passe forth out of the same
> As they tendered our favour, and voyd would our blame,
> Doyng therein their pains and industrye.
>   214–216

'The Blacksmith' established a basic iambic pattern in the first hundred lines of regular verse. But later there are lines which will be read as hexameters if that pattern is remembered. Occasionally there is a pair of lines which form poulter's measure.

> With slashers, slaves, and snuffers so falshod is in price
> That simple fayth is deadly sinne, & vertue counted vice.
>   215–216

Whatever the intention of the authors may have been, neither random line-length nor random stress pattern is an acceptable form by 1563. The editors have an amusing excuse for the disorder on grounds of decorum: 'Seyng than that kyng Rychard never kept measure in any of his doings. . . .'

The great bulk of the verse of the 1559 *Mirror* is regular iambic pentameter. Its characteristics may be seen in those poems written by its chief editor, William Baldwin. (He may have written all the tragedies not specifically assigned to others; the consistency of the versifying supports this speculation.) The stories are recited, the morals pointed, always in plain general terms, in sentences readily padded, contracted, or inverted, to reproduce the metrical pattern. An extra syllable is allowed from time to time, even when it would seem no great trouble to remove it, like *my* in the fifth line of this stanza:

> Wherefore while Henry of that name the fifte,
> Prepared his army to go conquer Fraunce
> Lord Skrope and I thought to attempt a drifte
> To put him downe my brother to avaunce:
> But were it gods wil, my luck, or his good chaunce,
> The king wist wholy wherabout we went,
> The night before the king to shipward bent.
> *Richard, Earl of Cambridge*, 36–42

Nearly always the line-end and the end of phrase or clause coincide. But occasionally there is an overflow; a complex verb is divided, subject and verb are separated, or verb and object:

> We sayd for hier of the French kinges coyne, we did
> Behight to kil the king. . . .
> *Richard, Earl of Cambridge*, 47–48

> My father hyght Syr Richard Wudvale: he
> Espoused the duches of Bedford, and by her
> Has issue males my brother Iohn and me
> Called Anthony.
> *Anthony, Lord Rivers*, 162–165

The mechanical elements of later verse are all there. The line is understood. The relation of the stresses of language to the metrical pattern is clear: there need be no exact reproduction of metrical pattern by the language. The metre takes care of too many or too few speech stresses by raising some and lowering others, as the last syllable of *generally* is raised and the word *flesh* is lowered in this line,

> And generally no fish, flesh, fowle, or plant
> *Owen Glendour*, 20

What the bulk of this verse lacks is not metrical accomplishment but an intention in the language large enough to give the metres anything to do. There is very little there to be intensified or controlled. One thing Baldwin does make of the metre is that he sometimes gets from the structure of line and stanza a framework on which to display his structure of language in logic and rhetoric. Rarely, but now and then, the measure provides emphasis when the statements themselves have enough order to bear emphasis. In the following stanza the fact that this historical summary is divided into three parts is little enough, but it is something; it is more than summaries like this usually provide in the *Mirror*, although they make up the bulk of it.

> The spiteful duke, his silly king and quene,
> With armed hostes I thrise met in the field,
> The first vnfought through treaty made betwene,
> the second ioynde, wherein the king did yeeld,
> The duke was slayne, the quene enforst to shylde
> Her selfe by flight. The third the quene did fight,
> Where I was slaine being overmacht by might.
> *Richard, Duke of York*, 92–97

Here, the first, second, third serve some purpose. The long sentence about the first two battles, ending only in the sixth line, has something of the suspense of a periodic sentence lent to it by the run-on of the fifth line and its end in the middle of a line, even though the rhyme word *shield* is not really good enough to bear the lingering attention it gets—a flight is not at all like a shield. The internal rhyme in the sixth line, with the resumption of a stop at line-end, reinforces the rapidity of conclusion: *the third time was different*. Of course, it is all spoiled in the next stanza with a clumsy anti-climactic flashback:

> Before this last were other battayles three,
> The first, etc. . . . .

More rarely Baldwin (perhaps Baldwin—it may be that one of the others wrote this) manages a rapid movement of phrases which not only convey ordered thought but actually achieve a definite and lively tone with the aid of measure and stress.

> We worldly folke account hym very wyse
> That hath the wyt moste wealthily to wed.
> By all meanes therfor alwayes we devyse
> To see our issue ryche in spousals sped.
> We buy and sell rych orphans: babes skant bred
> Must marry ere they know what maryage meanes,
> Boyes mary old trots, old fooles wed yong queanes.
> *Anthony, Lord Rivers*, 127–133

Here the break of the measure after *babes skant bred* and the emphatic stressing lend some effect of wit to the predicate which follows so smoothly in the sixth line. And after all this smooth iambic procession, the brief phrases of the seventh line acquire a certain emphasis from the fact that their stresses in speech—Bóyes mary old tróts—are counter to those we have been expecting. Some additional force is required to read the line however we choose to do it, whether as extra-metrical phrases or according to that metrical pattern as nearly as possible. The emphasis that must result from the additional force is appropriate; these phrases are the most succinct and the most extravagantly indignant in the stanza. They intend to provide a summary of what began as rather abstract comment. The metre is really being used here, but such uses are not consistent, not sustained, not even necessary for all that Baldwin means to do.

Churchyard's 'Shores Wife'[1] won the praise of the editors for 'both metre and matter' by using the same mechanically correct line to string together a repertory of proverbs. This was perhaps the most influential of the *Mirror* poems on the generation that immediately followed its publication; the weakest part of Googe and Turberville already plods limply through stanzas like these:

> The fond desire that we in glory set,
> Doth thirle our hartes to hope in slipper happe,
> A blast of pompe is all the fruyt we get,
> And vnder that lyes hidde a sodayne clappe:
> In seeking rest vnwares we fall in trappe.
> In groping flowers wyth Nettels stong we are,
> In labouring long, we reape the crop of care.
>
> 15–21

Here almost no attention is being given to what is said. The familiar sound of the syllables moving along in order is enough; pomp may begin rather impressively as a blast of sound, but if it becomes a fruit under which lies hidden a clap, it makes no difference. The incoherence has some reference to melancholy fortune, and to listen closely is almost impossible anyway, in that dull continual chant where all things are equal. That regularity of sound was all that mattered.

What the metre could really do had to be shown by poets with more than a chronicler's ambition. The two longest poems in the 1563 *Mirror* demonstrate the possibilities opened to poetry by this new technique. One kind of thing Sackville accomplishes. He knew how to exploit the abstracted prosodical elements of speech in a relation to sonorous basic sounds producing the effect which, for those who regarded this use of language as the highest achievement of poetry, made Sackville's verse clearly the best thing in the *Mirror*, the only real poetry. The 'Induction' and 'Henry, Duke of Buckingham' by this view are the best poems in English between Chaucer and

---

[1] 'Shores Wife' was first printed in the edition of 1563, but may have been written before 1559. See L. Campbell, 'Introduction,' p. 13.

Spenser.[1] John Dolman's 'Lord Hastings' is called by the editor of the only modern edition 'probably the worst poetry in the *Mirror*.'[2] To me it seems the best. But whatever the judgment may be, it is certainly the farthest from Sackville's lines, with their 'words of special colour, weight, and resonance,' which Saintsbury, for instance, says demonstrate 'the extraordinary skill with which the metre is arranged, and with which the diction is selected and adapted to the metre.'[3] If 'arrangement' of metre means, as it seems to, the achievement of a regular procession of stresses to match the iambic pattern with occasional departures from the strict correspondence, and in the relation of line and phrase the same general correspondence with occasional run-on lines and pauses within the line, then Sackville is no different from Baldwin. He has more initial trochaic feet, a few more clashing stresses, but that is all. And it may be doubted whether Sackville's departures from a strict correspondence of language and metrical pattern are truly departures or simply failures to reach a goal. Sackville's manuscript[4] shows frequent corrections; lines that present clashing strong stresses,

> But *false fayth* of commontie alone,

have a syllable supplied:

> But *fickle fayth* of commontie alone.

And these attempts by Sackville to straighten out his lines in the manuscript were carried further in the printed text of the *Mirror*.

> The large kingdomes and the dredfull raigne

becomes

> The large great kyngdomes, and the dreadful raygne.
> *Induction*, 506

It is possible, as Dr. J. Swart says in his work on Sackville, that the poet would have had his verse absolutely regular if he could have managed.[5] At any rate, the verse as it is printed is as regular as the bulk of verse in the *Mirror*. It shows the same use of the principles

[1] Saintsbury's phrase, often quoted with approval, as in *A Literary History of England*, ed. Albert C. Baugh (New York, 1948), p. 399.

[2] Lily Campbell, p. 45.

[3] Saintsbury, I, 333.

[4] *The Complaint of Henry Duke of Buckingham, Including the Induction, or, Thomas Sackville's Contribution to the Mirror for Magistrates. Edited, from the Author's Manuscript, with Introduction, Notes, and Collation, with the printed edition*, by Marguerite Hearsey (New Haven, 1936).

[5] J. Swart, *Thomas Sackville* (Groningen, 1949).

of metre. There is this line, one of those Dr. Swart finds deficient since it 'has only four beats, although the number of syllables is correct':

> And howe she nowe byd me come and beholde
>> *Induction*, 67

But the metrical pattern here can be satisfied with these unemphatic monosyllables, just as in this more impressive line it can, in theory, find the pattern of its five strong stresses reflected:

> That cities, towres, wealth, world, and al shall quayle
>> *Induction*, 445

In each case a regular metrical pattern is obtained, although in each case there is some tension between the metrical pattern and what we might speak at first thought. This is actually a rather intelligent 'weighting' of a more important line, 'lightening' of a less important one. But Sackville rarely had occasion for metres like this. What is hailed as beautiful in his work is the achievement of a line full of adjectives bearing equal emphasis, equally vague and poetical, and typically marked with a Spenserian talent for anticlimactic generalization. These generalizations have the effect of reducing any specific force the earlier adjectives in the string may have had. The line and stanza thus produced tend to allow an equal emphasis at every point, and in so far as the arrangement of the stresses in relation to the metre allows a similar equal emphasis, there may be said to be a metrical reinforcement of the intention of the stanza. In fact, it is the power of the iambic line to impart this same steady emphasis that Sackville exploits, removing the phrases from their patterns which give them meaning in speech. The words have 'special colour, weight, and resonance': sound for its own sake.

Sackville's variations in phrasing and pauses lend a purely sonorous variety to his lines. They have no relation to the structure of his thought. In a stanza of description, which for Sackville means adding one thing after another all more or less equal, in no particular order, these variations within the measure can be pleasant, as they were doubtless intended to be:

> Mydnight was cum, and every vitall thyng
> With swete sound slepe theyr weary lyms dyd rest,
> The beastes were still, the lytle byrdes that syng,
> Nowe sweetely slept besides theyr mothers brest:
> The olde and all were shrowded in theyr nest.
> The waters calme, the cruel seas did ceas,
> The wuds, the fyeldes, & all thinges held theyr peace.
>> *Buckingham*, 547–553

The same descriptive method is applied to scenes of calm and scenes of horror. The addition of adjective to adjective, the anti-climactic 'and all,' these are fitted into the same metrical device of musical phrasing within an observed measure. There is the same lack of intellectual structure.

> Thence cum we to the horrour and the hel,
> The large great kyngdomes, and the dreadful raygne
> Of Pluto in his trone where he dyd dwell,
> The wyde waste places, and the hugye playne:[1]
> The waylinges, shrykes, and sundry sortes of payne,
> The syghes, the sobbes, the diepe and deadly groane,
> Earth, ayer, and all resounding playnt and moane.
>
> *Induction*, 505–511

The iambic line absorbs everything into the same sonority.

Dolman's 'Hastings' is quite another thing. He varies the relation of his metrical pattern to his language according to his dramatic intention, a possibility of the iambic line which no other poet of the *Mirror* realized to anything like the degree he did. His minor departures from the strict iambic form are not of much significance; they can occur anywhere. Like Baldwin and Sackville he allows initial trochee, trisyllabic feet, even clashing stresses. Occasionally, however, he makes an extreme departure, and for good purpose. But the chief novelty of his metrics is his manipulation of phrase and measure. He handles this in a way which powerfully reinforces the dramatic intention of his lines. He alone manages to vary the tone of his speech in significant ways, sometimes by very rapid shifts in which the metre is of central importance.

In his expository and reflective passages his metrical practice is that of the other *Mirror* poets, basically a matter of varying a number of lines with pauses after two or three feet, and then running in a line which has no noticeable pause. His language is not the same as theirs. His rhetoric is the rhetoric of wit. He connects ideas, he plays on words, sometimes in meaningless echoes, sometimes with an effect of verbal analysis.

> Hastynges, I am, whose hastned death whose knewe,
> My lyfe with prayse, my death with plaint pursue.
> With others, fearyng least my headlesse name
> Be wrongd, by partiall bruite of flatteryng fame:
> Cleaving my tombe the waye my fame forewent. . . .
>
> 1–5

---

[1] On the word 'hugye' as a sign of Sackville's and other poets' kind of solution to the problem of clashing stresses following Surrey, see Baker, pp. 63–75.

For dramatic effect he can chop up the line, even making the last foot a separate element of speech, with an exclamatory effect, as in the second line below:

> The restless tyde, to bare the empty baye,
> With waltryng waves roames wamblyng forth. Away
> The mery maryner hayles. The bragging boye,
> To masts hye top vp hyes. In signe of ioye
> The wauering flagge is vaunsd.
>
> 129–133

And there are passages which in isolation appear to have subtler metrical virtues. In the following lines Hastings' friend has come at night to warn him that his life is in danger:

> While thus he spake, I held within myne arme
> Shores wyfe, the tender peece, to kepe me warme.
> Fye on adultery, fye on lecherous lust.
> Marke in me ye nobles all, Gods iudgmentes iust.
> A Pandare, murtherer, and Adulterer thus,
> Onely such death I dye, as I ne blushe.
> Now, least my Dame mought feare appall my hart:
> With eger moode vp in my bed I steart.
>
> 393–400

Here Dolman is realizing a dramatic possibility of the *Mirror* formula which occurred to no one else. The first two lines are part of a long narrative which has continued through some stanzas without interruption. At this moment of vivid recollection the ghost suddenly speaks out against his sin. It is most typical of the *Mirror* that a story should be well laced with moral reflections directed to the audience, but in no other poem do they come with this dramatic plausibility as the ghost suddenly remembers that this is the sin for which he is damned. The moral, as well as the scene it interrupts, is dramatically appropriate. If Dolman seemed always to have a precise control over the details of his metre we could credit the initial trochee of *Fye on adultery* as a metrical reinforcement of the sudden shift, the second *fye* after the two weak-stressed syllables of *adultery* as similarly reinforced. But his general practice is too loose for claims like these.

It is in his long, fully detailed scenes with brilliant description and quick action that his handling of the measure, his peculiar choppy phrasing, and his ear for dialogue are most impressive. Here his lines truly are successful, unlike anything to appear in England for a generation at least, and quite unlike what had come before, with one exception. Dolman's 'Hastings' is not unlike Surrey's 'Aeneid,' or even Baldwin's chronicles, in the mechanics of the iambic line;

57

but it resembles only Wyatt's *Satires* in the energy of the language. Both poets achieve a great tension in their verse between the abstract metrical pattern on the one hand and the actual language on the other. The line-end usually marks also a juncture of phrases, and often the larger units formed by the rhymes, Wyatt's tercets and Dolman's couplets, are measures of sentences in the language; but in both poets there is considerable variety in these uses. Run-on lines are not uncommon, nor does every couplet or tercet round off a sentence. The metrical form does not require, for them, an exact agreement of the language to its measure; but the true strength they share is the tension built up in their lines. Here, as in the larger units, the metrical pattern is strained and nearly broken from time to time by the language. The phrases have a quality akin to that of the words themselves, in both poets so often vivid, inelegant, even brutal, and in their phrase often reinforced by alliteration—the alliteration of proverbs and catch-words, it usually seems, a trick of speech rather than of literature.[1]

> A ryveld skyn, a stynking breth, what then?
> Fede thy self fat and hepe vp pownd by pownd.

So it is with Dolman's 'chopped,' 'nypped,' 'gogle eye,' and lines like this:

> Thus gan at last to grunt the grymest syre.

With Dolman as with Wyatt, snatches of dialogue often push hard against the metrical pattern. The phrases of speech carry with them a demand that they be spoken with their own intonations; a smooth progression of alternate stresses is nearly impossible. Here Dolman is less extreme than Wyatt. He has no nine-syllable lines, and few clashing strong stresses. The metrical pattern is never quite abandoned; it is never really in doubt, as it may be in Wyatt. Perfectly regular lines appear often enough. But what is truly remarkable about the relations Dolman maintains between the abstract metrical pattern and his phrases is the way these relations shift, and the way the shifts are exploited for the dramatic purpose of his narrative. To show this, a long quotation is needed. The scene is the climax of Hastings's tragedy. Richard III is about to turn on his own councillor:

> To Councell chamber come, awhyle we stayd
> For hym, without whom nought was done or sayd.
> At last he came, and courteously excused,
> For he so long our patience had abused.
> And pleasantly began to paynt his cheare,

---

[1] See Tilley, p. vi, for the typical forms of sixteenth-century proverbs; 'Such beef such broth' is an example.

And sayd. My Lord of Elye, would we had here
Some of the strawberyes, wherof you haue stoare.
The last delyghted me as nothyng more.

Would, what so ye wyshe, I mought as well commaund,
My lord (quoth he) as those. And out of hand.
His servant sendth to Elye place for them.
Out goeth from vs the restless devyll agayne.
Belyke (I thynk) scarce yet perswaded full,
To worke the mischiefe that thus maddeth his scull.
At last determynd, of his bloudy thought
And force ordaynd, to worke the wyle he sought:

Frownyng he enters, with so chaunged cheare.
As for myld May had chopped fowle Januere.
And lowryng on me with the goggle eye,
The whetted tuske, and furrowed forhead hye,
His Crooked shoulder bristellyke set vp,
With frothy Iawes, whose foame he chawed and suppd,
With angry lookes that flamed as the fyer:
Thus gan at last to grunt the grymest syre.

What earned they, whoe me, the kingdomes staye,
Contryved have councell, trayterously to slaye?
Abashed all sate. I thought I mought be bolld,
For conscyence clearenesse, and acquayntaunce olld.
Theyr hyre is playne quoth I. Be death the least,
To whoe so seekth your grace so to molest.
Withouten staye: The Queene, and the whore shores wyfe,
By witchcraft (quoth he) seeke to wast my lyfe.

Loe here the wythered and bewitched arme,
That thus is spent by those. ii. Sorceresse charme.
And bared his arme and shewed his swynyshe skynne.
Such cloakes they vse, that seek to clowd theyr synne.
But out alas, hit serueth not for the rayne.
To all the howse the coloure was to playne.
Nature had gyven hym many a maymed marke,
And hit amonges, to note her monstrous worke.

My doubtfull hart distracted this replye.
For thone I cared not. Thother nypped so nye
That whyst I could not. But forthwith brake forth.
Yf so hit be, of death they are doutlesse worth.
Yf, traytour quod he? playest thou with yfs and ands?
Ile on thy body avowe it with these hands,
And therewithall he myghtely bounced the bord.
In rushed hys byll men. one hym selfe bestyrrd.

Layeing at Lord Stanley. whose braine he had suerly cleft.
537–585

59

The cross-play of dramatic events, the effect of the speaking voices, the sudden change of tone, the whole drive of the narrative, these reach the reader through the energy of language in the tight frame of the metrical pattern. In the first stanza, there is interest in the movement and pause of the phrases in relation to the individual lines, to the couplets, and to the entire stanza. (Dolman's punctuation with its excess of points is unique in the *Mirror*, and must be his own.) The first two couplets have a variety of internal pause, and as sentences are self-contained within their rhymes. The third spills over into the fourth, into a sentence that ends with the first line of this last couplet; then comes the smooth, complete, final line that marks the end of the stanza, and as speech brings into the ominous self-possession of his intent the sound of Richard's trivial remark about the strawberries. It is smooth as silk. When Richard erupts, his voice breaks through the iambic pattern:

> Yf, traytour quod he? playest thou with yfs and ands?

Shakespeare's verse of thirty years later is not really comparable to this; it is not narrative, he has not Dolman's opportunity to load the scene with Hastings's sick disgust and fear, or anything like Dolman's brilliant odd use of *distracted*:

> My doubtfull hart distracted this reply.

Shakespeare's Richard breaks out like this:

> If? thou Protector of this damned Strumpet,
> Talk'st thou to me of Ifs: Thou art a Traytor,
> Off with his head; now by Saint *Paul* I sweare,
> I will not dine, vntill I see the same.

Richard III is Shakespeare's first character to have a voice of his own, and it is very like the voice of Dolman's Richard, but at this point it is a less shocking voice, because less concentrated, and not so violently different from the same voice a moment earlier.[1]

> Yf, traytour quod he? playest thou with yfs and ands?

There should be five stresses stronger than the others, stronger at least than the syllables immediately around them. This must mean

[1] In More's 'History of King Richard the Third' (facsimile of Rastell's edition of 1557), the speech is given thus:
  What quod the protectour thou seruest me I wene with iffes and andes, I tell the thei have so done, and that I will make good on thy body traitour. And therewith as in a great anger, he clapped his fist upon the borde a great rappe. *The English Works of Sir Thomas More*, ed. W. E. Campbell (London, 1931), p. 54.

that *Yf* is an outburst great enough to make both syllables of *traitor* weak in relation to it. The madness of the King's justification is all done by Dolman in these two words, when they are said as they must be said here. In this tyranny the slightest doubt is proof of disloyalty. Shakespeare has to spell it out; the point becomes not exactly the same, and Richard, in becoming less absurd, loses some of his peculiar horror. For Dolman, he is always comic as well as frightening. The danger is real, but it is not the danger Richard says it is:

> Ile on thy body avowe it with these hands,
> And therewithall he myghtely bounced the bord.
> In rushed hys byll men. . . .

With *Richard III*, Shakespeare's verse begins to move in the direction that Dolman had been able to take, although he never uses in the plays a metrical form as strict as Dolman's couplet. Perhaps it is not needed in drama. There are enough artifices constantly there on the stage to remind us that something is being done with the speech that gives it the reality of art, not life. Dolman combines his form and his language under nearly maximum pressure to give us this reality.

III

Googe, Turberville, Gascoigne

BARNABE GOOGE, George Turberville, and George Gascoigne were
youths when Tottel's *Miscellany* and the *Mirror* were published.
Googe and Turberville wrote in the metres of Tottel, and neither of
them made any important change in the way Surrey had used the
iambic measure. Their place in a history of metrics is not large. Their
verse has some personal qualities that are worth noting, but on the
whole they were content with the medium as they inherited it.
Gascoigne was not. He saw the principles of that medium and their
implications, and pushed the implications to the logical conclusion.
He wrote a treatise on metrical regularity and practised this regularity strictly in his verse. His conception of the metrical pattern was
something new; it superseded Surrey's adaptation of Wyatt's principles, it cast a new light on the metres of the *Mirror*, and it prepared
the way for the new poetry of 1580.[1]

The measures of Googe and Turberville are those of Tottel's
Miscellany. Googe's favourite is the fourteener, printed in lines of
eight and six syllables; Turberville's is poulter's, with the lines broken
in the printing. Both poets also use very often the ten-syllable line
broken in four syllables and six.[2]

Their verse is generally characterized as familiar themes set to a
monotonous jog-trot rhythm. For most of the verse, this is a fair
description.

> No vayner thing ther can be found
> amyd this vale of stryfe,

---

[1] Barnabe Googe (1540–1594), *Eglogs, Epytaphes, & Sonettes*, 1563. George
Gascoigne (1542–1577), *Flowers*, 1573; *Posies, Certaine Notes*, 1575; *Steel Glass*,
1576. George Turberville (1544–1597), *Epitaphes, Epigrams, Songs and Sonets*,
1567.
[2] See Appendix A, Stanza forms.

eport haue made
Then truste vncertayne lyfe.[1]

Let other then that feelen ioy
Extoll the merrie Month of May,
And I that tasted haue annoy
In prayse thereof will nothing say.[2]

They maintain the metrical pattern with something less than absolute rigidity. Initial trochees are frequent in their verse; occasionally there are lines with extra syllables:

As in Quaiting, Leaping, Singing or
to sound a Bagpype ryght[3]

The fault is neyth*er in hir* nor mee[4]

They also have lines deficient by a syllable, but some of these might well be printers' errors.

With this the sounde begyns to mount
and *noyse* hye to ryse.[5]

That sayde: *pray* you all agree.[6]

By hap a man that could not heare
but borne *deafe* by kinde.[7]

There is scarcely one such small departure in a hundred lines of their verse. They do commit one larger offence against regularity in the realm of pure metrical pattern. They both fail on occasion to keep to an established measure. Googe several times introduces a couplet of poulter's into poems of fourteeners, and one poem he begins with poulter's and finishes with fourteeners.[8] Turberville, in the 'Epitaphes and Sonets' appended to his *Tragical Tales* (1577), twice does something similar, switching from poulter's to fourteeners, and from

[1] Barnabe Googe, *Eglogs, Epytaphes, & Sonettes*, ed. Arber (London, 1871), p. 98.
[2] George Turberville, *Epitaphes, Epigrams, Songs and Sonets* (London, 1567), folio 110, verso.
[3] Googe, p. 58.
[4] Turberville, folio 17, verso.
[5] Googe, p. 124. It is conceivable that Googe intended the diphthong of *noyse* to represent two syllables.
[6] Turberville, folio 2, recto.
[7] *Ibid.*, folio 75, verso.
[8] 'Eglogue 6,' 'Eglogue 7,' 'Sonnet 31,' 'goyng towardes Spayne.'

63

poulter's to an hexameter couplet.[1] With these few exceptions, both poets could subscribe to Turberville's modest claim:

> Yet one thing will I vaunt
> and after make an ende
> That Momus can not for his lyfe
> devise one fote to mende.[2]

The regularity of the metrical pattern alone is not enough to account for the effect of thumping monotony that much of their verse produces. Rather, in the relation this pattern has to their language appears the reason for what seem to modern readers to be their worst failures; and their occasional successes are due to a change in this relation. It is not mere awkwardness that produces these steady thuds of stress and the general effect of near-nonsense. This seems to be exactly the effect the poets usually wanted. Seen in this light, their odd inversion of language from its normal English order and the series of clichés in their phrases both serve the same purpose. This is to maintain the two degrees of stress of the metrical pattern at a level as nearly as possible consistent throughout the line.[3] It can be seen in the passage from Googe,

> No vayner thing ther can be found
> amyd this vale of stryfe,
> As Auncient men reporte haue made
> then truste vncertayne lyfe.

In the line *amyd this vale of stryfe*, the near-equality of the stronger stresses is assured by the phrase itself: Amid this vale of strife. Even the tertiary stress of *amid* cannot be so subordinated that it could be mistaken for a weak-stressed syllable. The next line, however, in a more natural order would present the danger of appearing to require only three strong stresses: As ancient men have made report. The inverted order Googe presents breaks up the phrase pattern of stresses so that the words must be said something like this if they are to be said at all: As ancient men report have made—but there could be no occasion in actual speech to say the words in that way. The poet is thus assured that the metrical pattern will be consulted for guidance, and the result will be what he wanted, a nearly equal degree of stress on each of the strong-stressed syllables, corresponding to the metrical strong stress. Since in this line there is no

---

[1] *Tragical Tales and Other Poems*, reprinted from the edition of 1587 (Edinburgh, 1837), p. 389, and p. 332, noted by J. E. Hankins, *Life and Works of George Turberville* (Lawrence, Kansas, 1940), p. 71.
[2] Turberville, folio 6, verso.
[3] See Chapter I, p. 35.

requirement of rhyme to meet, this consideration must have been decisive unless we suppose Googe simply had a taste for inversion. It was this desire for exactly the metrical effect they secured that determined the style of this period. As has often been noted, the verse of the time is full of adages and old saws, but these familiar sayings are oddly twisted, as no one had ever said them:

> Count not the birds that undisclosed be.[1]

Such verse is so remote from speech that a sort of translation must be made to understand it, and then what is understood is so small a thing that it all seems a miserable joke. Sometimes early Elizabethan poetry can make the modern reader wonder if a kind of idiocy had not descended upon poet and audience alike in that time. Not only 'literary' verse was in this mode; through Sternhold and Hopkins it was heard everywhere:

> O Lorde howe many doe encrease,
> and trouble me full sore.
> Howe many saye unto my soule,
> God will him saue no more.[2]

Yet both Googe and Turberville have another vein of poetry, so close to this jog-trot in its elements that the difference is hard to describe even though it is immediately recognizable. This poetry still has great interest, quite apart from its historical status. Like the bulk of their verse, it is conventional in sentiment and thought, plain even rude in diction, given to echoes of adages, and in metrical pattern all but perfectly regular.[3] Yvor Winters, the champion of these poems, says this of them:

> The wisdom of poetry of this kind lies not in the acceptance of a truism, for anyone can accept a truism, at least formally, but in the realization of the truth of the truism: the realization resides in the feeling, the style. Only a master of style can deal successfully in a plain manner with obvious matter: we are concerned with the type of poetry which is perhaps the hardest to compose and the last to be recognized, a poetry not striking or original as to subject, but merely true and universal, that

---

[1] *Howell's Devises* (1581), cited by Walter Raleigh in his introduction to the reprint (Oxford, 1906), p. xiv. 'If Howell deserves to be remembered as a poet, it is because there were hundreds like him. . . .' Our saying must have been current; Tilley, 96, C–292, gives 'You count your chickens before they be hatched' as recorded in 1616.

[2] *Psalms of David in Metre* (London, 1551), Psalm III. See Chapter I, p. 36.

[3] Lewis calls it 'Drab Age Verse.' *English Literature in the Sixteenth Century*, pp. 222ff

is, in a sense commonplace, not striking or original in rhetorical procedure, but direct and economical, a poetry which permits itself originality, that is the breath of life, only in the most restrained and refined of subtleties in diction and in cadence, but which by virtue of those subtleties inspires its universals with their full value as experience. . . .[1]

I take it that Mr. Winters is claiming for the verse of Googe, Gascoigne, and Turberville, of which he speaks here, a control of language through metre which causes the language to appear with the effect of a real voice; the realization of experience through style means giving to the words all the complexities of intonation that a speaker uses to express his feelings. Of course, this does not mean that the bad poems considered earlier lack intonation and thus have no feeling. Rather, they have an intonation that seems inappropriate: 'The tone is wrong,' we say of such writing, or of such a speaker.

I have said that it was a peculiarity of the measure, its inability to present adequately both the junctures of the metrical pattern and the junctures of the intonation patterns of speech, that caused poulter's measure and the fourteener to destroy the possibility of significant tone in poems written in those forms.[2] This fault usually operates for early Elizabethan writers even when the lines are broken to resemble ballad or 'common' measure, where the conventions of the printed line ought to allow the junctures to work effectively. Sometimes they do allow it, and it is largely this effective use of juncture to control intonation that gives their successes to Googe and Turberville. In a stanza from the little poem 'To an Olde Gentlewoman that Painted hir Face,' Turberville for once achieves a combination of directness and simplicity in diction with an underlying dramatic situation, so that the effect of metrical reinforcement at exactly the right point is enough to make the stanza a realization of truth. There is the sound of a man speaking, a man who knows what he is talking about and has a sense of the person he is speaking to:

> Let Beautie go with youth,
>   renounce the glosing Glasse,
> Take Booke in hand: that seemely Rose
>   is waxen withred Grasse.

It is poulter's measure. But here that deadly caesura is what makes it all successful. If the lines were altered to pentameter,

> That seemly rose is waxen withered grass,

the word *rose* loses its emphasis, the pause which the metre requires

[1] Yvor Winters, 'The 16th Century Lyric in England,' *Poetry*, LIII (1939), 263.
[2] Chapter I, p. 33 ff.

in poulter's is only a matter of choice, and the suggestion that the pause demands is gone; there is no longer the sense that the lady's former beauty is remembered by the speaker with some regret, as well as with a gesture of tact to the old gentlewoman. Without the pause there is in effect only the harsh withered face. With the pause, there are both faces. The experience is real, the tone is one we must admire; both are due to the metre according with speech juncture.

The junctures of his metrical patterns are a curious puzzle in some of Googe's poems. The long lines of poulter's, the fourteener, and the hexameter were frequently printed as two lines each in Tudor books. But even Googe's pentameter lines are printed as two lines, usually but not always as four syllables and six; words are sometimes split between the lines. It is reasonable to suppose that this was done by the printer for his convenience,[1] but the effect is so extraordinary that even if the poet did not intend it, the effect must have been noted after the poems were printed. I would like to think that it was appreciated, and even if accidental it added to the understanding of junctures in poetry and in speech. Here, in a few lines from 'An Epytaphe of the Death of Nicolas Grimaold,' Googe's plain diction and simplicity of phrase manage a sound of mastery like that of George Herbert's short lines:

> For if that wytt,
> or worthy Eloquens,
> Or learnyng deape,
> coulde moue hym to forbeare,
> O *Grimaold* then,
> thou hadste not yet gon hence
> But heare hadest sene,
> full many an aged yeare.
> Ne had the Mu-
> ses loste so fyne a Floure,
> Nor had *Miner-*
> *ua* wept to leaue the so,
> If wysdome myght
> haue fled the fatall howre,
> Thou hadste not yet
> ben suffred for to go,
> A thousande doltysh
> Geese we myght haue sparde,
> A thousand wytles
> heads, death might haue found

[1] See Arber, p. 17; H. H. Hudson, 'Sonnets by Barnabe Googe,' *PMLA*, XLVIII (1933), 293–294. Both men believed the breaking of the lines was only a printer's device.

And taken them,
for whom no man had carde,
And layde them lowe,
in deepe oblivious grounde,
But Fortune fa[v]-
ours Fooles as old men saye
And lets them lyue,
and take the wyse awaye.

Printed as pentameters, the lines of course retain the hard, almost cruel sense of exact estimation of loss, with the wry resignation of the ending; and the stanza form is appropriate to the alternatives Googe lingers over before reaching the final conclusion in the couplet.

A thousand doltish geese we might have spared,
A thousand witless heads death might have found,
And taken them for whom no man had cared,
And laid them low in deep oblivious ground;
But Fortune favors fools, as old men say,
And lets them live, and takes the wise away.

Here again it is a question of 'the most restrained and refined subtleties of diction and cadence.' *A thousand witless heads death might have found* is certainly the primary suggestion of a word-group, followed by the next word-group, *and taken them for whom no man had cared*. But the broken lines suggest the other possibility: *A thousand witless heads—death might have found and taken them, for whom no man had cared, and laid them low....* This substitutes for the ordered but inverted syntax of the pentameter version a sequence of phrases with a suggestion of reflective thought; a subject is expressed, and a series of statements follows, not quite connected grammatically. In the broken lines there is also more suggestion of a speech stress counter to the order of metrical stresses:

A thousand witless ||
heads|| death| might have found. . . .

If the line-end following *witless* is considered a metrical juncture, which in turn suggests a pause, the pause requires that a primary stress be placed on *witless*, the pause after *heads* requires one for *heads*, and since the phrasing read in this way suggests a slow reflective speech, the speech pattern of *death might have found* is suggested rather more strongly than it is in the context of the pentameter line where it might appear as *death might have found*. This emphasis on *might* is not bad, and itself suggests a plausible intonation of speech.

68

But the cluster of strong stresses and the slow movement created by the broken line suggests the reflective and sad as well as the merely invidious tone of *A thousand witless heads death might have found.* Such are the possibilities of the iambic measures; for Googe and Turberville, as for Surrey, their fulfilment is rare, perhaps even accidental.

2

The usual view of Gascoigne's *Certayne Notes of Instruction concerning the making of verse or ryme in English*[1] is that the little treatise may contain the observations of an honest craftsman but that the observations are 'wholly superficial.'[2] In fact, Gascoigne not only attacks the chief fault of the verse of his time and offers a remedy for it, but shows a deep understanding of metre and language. This essay and Gascoigne's own practice in poetry mark one of the major stages in the development of poetic techniques in modern English.

Wyatt's introduction of the five-stress iambic line was followed by Surrey's use of the metrical pattern of that line without Wyatt's interest in maintaining the intonation patterns of language. In most of the poetry of Tottel's *Miscellany* and the *Mirror* and in most of the work of Gascoigne's contemporaries the principle of metre was that there should be as nearly as possible five relatively strong stresses in a line, arranged in alternation with weaker stresses. To achieve this the poets broke up the patterns of English intonation by breaking the word-order of English, as we have seen in the poems of Googe and Turberville, or at best, as in Surrey's and Sackville's verse, they employed a diction so unlike that of speech that the longer intonation patterns of normal speech could not be invoked in reading their lines. They got what they wanted, a steady progression of alternate stresses which tends always to cause the stress-patterns of speech and the patterns of metre to become one. But when the patterns become one, the words lack a real intonation and so lack the best part of that indication of feeling which is tone. Gascoigne changes this. He does not say that there *should* be alternate weak and strong stresses in a pentameter line, presented by the words; he says there *are* alternate weak and strong stresses in a line, whether the speech fits or not. It was a profound change, even if it was largely

[1] *Works*, ed. John W. Cunliffe (Cambridge, 1907), I, pp. 465–473.
[2] Tucker Brooke, *A Literary History of England*, ed. A. C. Baugh (New York, 1948), p. 436. In *English Literature in the Sixteenth Century* (270–271), Lewis says, 'His unpretentious *Certain Notes* . . . are of great importance because they tell us what he really wanted and what difficulties he found. . . .'

only the conscious recognition of a principle that sometimes oper-
ated in verse whether the poets liked it or not. Gascoigne did not
quite realize what could be done with it, and in his verse as a rule it
takes him only as far as this:

> When I recorde within my musing mynde.[1]

Another change in the understanding of the line had to take place,
allowing both the metrical pattern and the pattern of speech to
function, before lines like this were standard practice:

> When to the sessions of sweet silent thought.

In my exposition I must place first Gascoigne's observation on
English word-order. It appears to be only negative, denying poets
the indulgence of breaking phrases after the common manner of the
times. But the demand is a necessary part of the metrical principles
Gascoigne develops.

> You shall do very well to use your verse after the Englishe phrase, and
> not after the maner of other languages: The Latinists do commonly set
> the adjective after the Substantive: As for example *Femina pulchra, sedes
> altae*, &c. but if we should say in English a woman fayre, a house high,
> &c. it would have but small grace: for we say a good man, and not a
> man good, &c. And yet I will not altogether forbidde it you, for in some
> places, it may be borne, but not so hardly as some use it which wryte
> thus:
>
>> Now let us go to Temple ours,
>> I will go visit mother myne, &c.
>
> Surely I smile at the simplicitie of such devisers which might aswell
> have sayde it in playne Englishe phrase, and yet have better pleased all
> eares, than they satisfie their owne fancies by such *superfinesse*. There-
> fore even as I have advised you to place all wordes in their naturall or
> most common and usuall pronunciation, so would I wishe you to frame
> all sentences in their mother phrase and proper *Idioma*, and yet some-
> times (as I have sayd before) the contrarie may be borne, but that is
> rather where rime enforceth, or *per licentiam Poeticam*, than it is other-
> wise lawfull or commendable.[2]

The next passage to be considered in Gascoigne's essay (it precedes
the passage on phrasing) begins with another observation about the
placing of words, but this time it concerns both the words and the
metrical pattern. Every sentence in this passage invites comment.
Three points demand it: how the basic unit of the metrical pattern

[1] Gascoigne, p. 94.
[2] *Ibid.*, p. 470. I have expanded contractions in this and following passages.

is derived from language: how those units are ordered to create the structure of metre; and how, according to Gascoigne's principles, that structure of metre controls the language that fills it out to make a poem.

And in your verses remembre to place every worde in his natural *Emphasis* or sound, that is to say in such wise, and with such length or shortnesse, elevation or depression of sillables, as it is commonly pronounced or used: to expresse the same we have three maner of accents, *gravis*, *le[v]is*, & *circumflexa*, the whiche I would english thus, the long accent, the short accent, & that whiche is indifferent: the grave accent is marked by this caracte, ⌐ the light accent is noted thus, ⌐ & the circumflexe or indifferent is thus signified ⌐: the grave accent is drawen out or elevate, and maketh that sillable long whereupon it is placed: the light accent is depressed or snatched up, and maketh that sillable short upon which it lighteth: the circumflexe accent is indifferent, sometimes short, sometimes long, sometimes depressed & sometimes elevate. For example of th' emphasis or natural sounds of words, this word *Treasure*, hath the grave accent upon the first sillable, whereas if it shoulde be written in this sorte, *Treasúre*, nowe were the second sillable long, & that were cleane contrarie to the common use wherwith it is pronounced. For furder explanation hereof, note you that commonly now a dayes in english rimes (for I dare not cal them English verses) we use none other but a foote of two sillables, whereof the first is depressed or made short, & the second is elevate or made long: and that sound or scanning continueth throughout the verse. We have used in times past other kindes of Meeters: as for example this following:

> No wight in this world, that wealth can attayne,
> Unless he beleve, that all is but vayne.

Also our father *Chaucer* hath used the same libertie in feete and measures that the Latinists do use: and who so ever do peruse and well consider his workes, he shall finde that although his lines are not always of one selfe same number of Syllables, yet beyng redde by one that hath understanding, the longest verse and that which hath most Syllables in it, will fall (to the eare) correspondent unto that whiche hath fewest sillables in it: and like wise that whiche hath in it fewest syllables, shalbe founde yet to consist of woordes that have suche naturall sounde, as may seeme equall in length to a verse which hath many moe sillables of lighter accentes. And surely I can lament that wee are fallen into such a playne and simple manner of wryting, that there is none other foote used but one: wherby our Poems may justly be called Rithmes, and cannot be any right challenge the name of a Verse. But since it is so, let us take the forde as we finde it, and lette me set downe unto you suche

[1] This graph indicates the scansion for the entire couplet.

rules or precepts that even in this playne foote of two syllables you wreste no woorde from his natural and usuall sounde, I do not meane hereby that you may use none other wordes but of twoo sillables, for therein you may use discretion according to occasion of matter: but my meaning is, that all the wordes in your verse be so placed as the first sillable may sound short or be depressed, the second long or elevate, the third shorte, the fourth long, the fifth shorte, &c. For example of my meaning in this point marke these two verses:

I understand your meanyng by your eye.

Your meaning I understand by your eye.

In these two verses there seemeth no difference at all, since the one hath the very selfe same woordes that the other hath, and yet the latter verse is neyther true nor pleasant, & the first verse may passe the musters. The fault of the latter verse is that this worde *understand* is therein so placed as the grave accent falleth upon *der*, and therby maketh *der*, in this worde understand to be elevated: which is contrarie to the naturall or usuall pronunciation: for we say *understand*, and not *understand*.

First Gascoigne observes the phenomena of stress in English. He recognizes strong stress (the long accent), weak stress (the short accent), and what he calls *circumflexe* or indifferent—'sometimes short, sometimes long, sometimes depressed, sometimes elevate.' This 'length or shortnesse, elevation or depression of sillables' is a property of a word 'as it is commonly pronounced or used.' 'For example of the emphases or natural sound of words, this word *Treasure*, hath the grave accent upon the first sillable. . . .' The indifferent degree of stress may be his recognition of the degrees of stress between the strongest and the weakest, or it may be his recognition of how the stress pattern that forms a phrase or a compound word can determine the degree of stress on a syllable, as in *a light house* or *a lighthouse*. He speaks again of the indifferent stress when he considers the adjustment of language to the metrical pattern.[1] But so far as the basic elements of metre are concerned, their source is the distinction in speech of two main degrees of stress, the strongest and the weakest.

Of the representations of these two kinds of syllables the metrical

---

[1] Monosyllables, he notes, 'will more easily fall to be shorte or long as occasion requireth, or wilbe adapted to become circumflexe or of an indifferent sounde,' in a line of poetry. See below, p. 77 ff.

pattern is formed. He next tells how these elements are ordered. 'We use none other order but a foote of two sillables, wherof the first is depressed or made short, & the second is elevate or made long: and that sound or scanning continueth throughout the verse.' His reference to other kinds of feet is interesting, but in other connections. The iambic foot is the only one that counts for him. The metrical pattern is absolute and admits of no variation whatsoever.

He has now presented two requirements for a line of verse. The words must be in the natural order of the language, pronounced according to the common use. And the metrical pattern is simple and rigid: it consists of two degrees of stress in alternation, and nothing in it can be changed. The most important point in the essay is the next: When the language and the metrical pattern come together in the line of verse, it is the metrical pattern that rules. If language and metrical pattern do not coincide exactly, the metrical pattern takes precedence, and what we have is a distortion of language and not a variation in metre. As it applies to Gascoigne's verse, this point is not of supreme importance. His way of making it emphasizes the harshness of his demand for coincidence of language and metrical pattern, but that is all, so far as the verse of his immediate contemporaries is concerned. They must have the coincidence, for if they do not their line will sound like this, it will be no language:

Your meaning I understand by your eye.

'The fault of the latter verse is that this word *understand* is therein so placed as the grave accent falleth upon *der*, and thereby maketh *der*, in this worde *understand* to be elevated, which is contrarie to the naturall or usuall pronunciation: for we say *understand*, and not *understand*.'

A fault, of course; but what must be noted here is that the fault is not that of introducing a trochaic foot into the line. The scansion remains absolutely the same, pure iambic. Furthermore, the scansion determines the sound—'sound or scanning,' as he said. The two must be the same, and it is the metrical stress, 'the grave accent' that 'falleth upon *der*,' that determines both scanning and sound.[1] To

[1] George Hemphill has also noted Gascoigne's insistence on the metrical pattern, in an interesting essay on sixteenth-century metres. He quotes this example of Gascoigne's scanning and reading.

And that said thus: Nemesis, Nemesis
(*Works*, II, 53)

'There is no reason to doubt that the diacritical marks are Gascoigne's. Since stress shift after pause supported by the accent of a polysyllable did not appear to

later verse this means everything. The metrical pattern has been recognized as a ruling principle independent of the stresses of the language in a line. In later verse the metrical pattern may not retain the absolute power over language that Gascoigne gives it, but it does retain its status as an independent element in the line. It is never again only a principle of selection. When the patterns of stress in the language gain a similar status, we have the line in which both patterns can function, and instead of

> When I recorde within my musing mynde

a poet can write

> When to the sessions of sweet silent thought.

As a matter of fact, Gascoigne was demanding such lines although he did not know it, and he was sometimes writing them although he had no way of approving them. His two requirements, a strict metrical pattern and the observation of natural word order, make this practice inevitable. Words in their natural order will of course suggest their own patterns of stress. But to Gascoigne this can only have been an embarrassment, or perhaps sometimes the source of an inexplicable success.[1]

Two other limitations of the theory of regularity must be noted. One is only a corollary of the relation of identity required for metrical stress and word-stress. 'Finish the sentence and meaning at the end of every staffe where you wright staves, & at the end of every two lines where you write by cooples or poulters measure. . . .' The uses of opposing metrical junctures and language junctures are not recognized by him, although they appear in his own verse now and then. The effects gained by Googe (or his printer) in this way would be lost on Gascoigne.

The other limitation is theoretical and more severe. Insisting that there can be no variation at all from the iambic foot, Gascoigne loses something more than mere variety. The metrical pattern without it is a less complete model of the language. With the right to change a foot here and there the metre incorporates a representation of a basic device of our language, the shift-morpheme, as it is called. This is the means by which we indicate by shifting the stresses in a phrase that we mean something a little out of the ordinary: $I\ don't\ know$ or

him to be an acceptable variation, he seems to have inserted the circumflex over the first *e* of the *Nemesis* to ease the shock of the variation; and the acute over the first *e* of the second *Nemesis* enforces a return to normal metre.' 'Accent, Stress, and Emphasis,' *College English*, XVII, No. 6 (1956), 339.

[1] See below, p. 85 ff.

I don't know, for instance, instead of *I don't know*. Typically it involves the primary stress in an utterance moving forward from its normal position on the last element, just as the most common variation in the iambic line exchanges these positions in the foot.[1]

The principles of regularity, then, as Gascoigne states them, continue the direction of Surrey's kind of verse. Metrical pattern and speech pattern there had a tendency to be identical. Here an absolute identity is claimed for them, with the speech pattern completely absorbed into the metrical pattern. The result ought to be nonsense, or near it. But Gascoigne has re-introduced a saving grace, the 'mother phrase.' In practice his principles serve Gascoigne very well.

3

In one sense Gascoigne's *Certayne Notes* contained nothing new at all. He only described what everyone was doing or trying to do. It was all implicit in the use of iambic metres from the beginning. But advances in thought are often little more than summaries of what is already known, making the implicit into the explicit, disclosing principles which can be used in slightly new ways once they are recognized. So it was with Gascoigne's theory of metre, and so it was with his own practice in verse. Most of his verse is not very different metrically from that of other writers of his time. The differences appear only sometimes, and then in those very small matters of a syllable, a degree of stress, the turn of a phrase.

In verse forms Gascoigne follows the writers of Tottel.[2] He sometimes uses the forms with a new degree of strictness, but not always. Gascoigne was prolific, he improvised, he claimed even to have composed hundreds of lines at a time in his head: 'he devised all these admounting to the number of CCLVIII verses, riding by the way, writing none of them untill he came at the end of his

[1] Trager and Smith, pp. 72–73.

[2] See Appendix, Stanza forms; and C. T. Prouty, *George Gascoigne* (New York, 1942), pp. 131–136.

Gascoigne has approximately 3,500 lines of rhyme royal, most of it in a few long poems, 'Dan Bartholomew,' 'Dulce Bellum,' and *The Grief of Joy*. He uses the measure of Surrey's translation of two books of Aeneid for *The Steele Glass*, 'the first original English poem in blank verse.' (Prouty, p. 132.) This and his share of the translation of *Jocasta* he made with his friend Francis Kinwelmarshe make a total of approximately 3,000 lines of blank verse. In poulter's measure he wrote some 2,500 lines, in thirty poems. He wrote thirty-two sonnets. He used the six-line ballad rhymed ABABCC sixteen times in ten-syllable lines, six times in eight-syllable lines, once in twelve-syllable lines. Nine poems are in ten-syllable quatrains. All these and his other forms are in Tottel, except a few which appear to be unique. The stanza of his 'De Profundis,' which he repeats in 'Dame Cinthia her selfe that shines so bright' and varies slightly in 'His libell of

Journey. . . .'[1] He admits imperfect lines and knows it. 'This is but a rough meeter, and reason, for it was devised in great disquiet of mynd, and written in rage, yet have I seene much worse passe the musters, yea and where both the Lieutenant and Provost Marshall were men of rype judgement. . . .'[2] Again, he says, 'The Meetres are but rough in many places, and yet are they true (cum licentia poetica). . . .'[3]

Gascoigne does actually write entire long poems which by his system of metre are 'true'; sometimes they do not even have rough places. By the distinction between 'rough' and 'true' he means that according to his system the metre is true if the syllable count is just and no *word* is placed so that its stresses fall out of relation with the metrical pattern of stresses. When Gascoigne says verse is 'rough' I believe he means that the stress patterns of *phrases* in that verse fall out of this relation, as in this line:

My swelling heart breakes with delay of paine.[4]

Here the intonation pattern of speech would require the stress on *breakes* to be stronger than that on *with*, while the metrical pattern requires just the opposite. Yet the case here is not that of the line in *Certayne Notes* which is 'neyther true nor pleasant,' and cannot pass the musters:

Your meaning I understand by your eye.

Understand will not do, but *breakes with* will. Gascoigne attempts to explain this by saying that 'woordes of one syllable will now easily fall to be shorte or long as occasion requireth, or wilbe adapted to become circumflexe or of an indifferent sounde.' Again he is thinking of the metrical pattern as something very like the intonation pattern of a phrase. These patterns form phrases out of combinations of

request exhibited to Care,' has eleven lines, nine of them ten-syllable, one pair four-syllable, A10 B10 B10 A10 C10 C10 D10 E4 E4 D10. Somewhat similar stanzas appear in Tottel, and frequently in *The Paradise of Dainty Devices*, which was assembled sometime before 1576, although it was not published until 1576. See *The Paradise of Dainty Devices*, ed. H. E. Rollins (Cambridge, Mass., 1927). He has a few variations on the quatrain form, adding to it sometimes two couplets, sometimes one more rhymed line to which at the end of the poem he adds a second, concluding with a couplet (*Works*, I, 44, 338, 424; II, 327, 354). Once he uses a stanza which, like these other variations on the quatrain, is related to rhyme royal, ABABBCCDD (*Works*, I, 47). He is not an innovator in forms.

[1] *Works*, I, 480.
[2] George Gascoigne. *A Hundreth Sundrie Floures*, ed. C. T. Prouty (Columbia, Mo., 1942), p. 65. This is a reprint of Q1, 1573. For the verse I use Cunliffe's edition, which is based on Gascoigne's revised edition of 1575.
[3] *Ibid.*, 159.
[4] *Works*, I, 115.

76

words. Words of more than one syllable may sometimes have their order of stresses changed by the phrase intonation, '*Are you almost ready?*' '*Almost.*' But usually in English the included words of more than one syllable retain the order of stresses they have as complete utterances. Monosyllabic words receive the stress required by their use in the phrase. '*I'm in school.*' '*I'm coming in.*' Or, of course, the situation may require a shift, '*I'm in school, not out,*' or, '*I'm in school,*' or, '*I'm in school.*' Thus, these patterns of sound that form phrases, and carry meanings, are in a way independent of the individual words they are attached to, even though they are conditioned by the stresses of words of more than one syllable.

Thinking of the metrical pattern of stresses as a thing independent of the sounds of the words in the line, and taking precedence over the sounds of these words, Gascoigne sees how it can determine the degree of stress falling on any monosyllable. For him almost any line of monosyllabic words is necessarily 'true.' But if the metrical pattern, in imposing itself upon the words, distorts the phrase-pattern of sound, then the verse is 'rough.' Gascoigne cannot see the possibility of an interplay between the phrase-pattern of the language and the metrical pattern, producing a new pattern of sound for the line, and consequently a new meaning. He can only regret that the difference between language and metre must occur. To later poets, this difference, with the distinction between the distortion of stresses on monosyllables in a phrase and the distortion of stresses within words of more than one syllable, becomes an essential principle to be exploited to the fullest extent in metrical composition.

This definition of the metrically true line, then, allows for the first time a clear recognition of the devices by which such a line can be attained. The first of these adjustments of language is the shift of stress which allows a rough line to pass as true. Others are those tricks of 'poetic licence' which can be classified now that the true line is defined: they are alterations of language and not variations in the metrical pattern. Gascoigne lists some of them in *Certayne Notes.*

> This poeticall licence is a shrewde fellow, and covereth many faults in a verse, it maketh wordes longer, shorter, of mo sillables, of fewer, newer, older, truer, falser, and to conclude it turkeneth all things at pleasure, for example, *ydone* for *done*, *adowne* for *downe*, *orecome* for *overcome*, *tane* for *taken*, *power* for *powre*, *heaven* for *heavn*, *thewes* for good partes or good qualities, and a numbre of other whiche were but tedious and needelesse to rehearse, since your owne judgement and readyng will soone make you espie such advauntages.[1]

1 *Works*, I, 470.

These practices, like the adjustments of stress on monosyllables, occur in relation to the metrical pattern. Like those adjustments of stress, they correspond to what happens in speech under the influence of the patterns that form phrases, as the words *I* and *am* become *I'm*, and so on.[1] In verse these alterations may or may not be based on actual particular speech practices present or past, as *o'er* for *over* is based on speech, but the use of *heaven* as one syllable is purely conventional since the phoneme *n* is syllabic. The principle itself is based on a practice of speech. The recognition of traditional uses here is an important step in the development of the idea of the metrical pattern and its relation to language. What Gascoigne's uses are can be seen in one of his poems which is entirely 'true' throughout.

'Dan Bartholomews Dolorous discourses'[2] is a poem of 371 iambic pentameter lines, rhymed in quatrains. There is one odd failure. In *Certayne Notes* Gascoigne said 'every yong scholler can conceive that he ought to continue in the same measure wherwith he beginneth.' Googe and Turberville did not always 'hold the just measure,' but Gascoigne usually does, and certainly expected it of himself. It is 'either forgetfulness or carelessness,' as he said of this fault, when in this poem following the eighty-first quatrain, ABAB, there are three lines rhyming CBC, whereupon the structure by quatrains picks up again. The fault persists through two editions which appear to have been carefully edited, and in the context of the verse there is no reason for the departure. Again, Gascoigne's practice, strict as it is in comparison to that of others in his time, is still too casual to allow the kind of significant departures from regularity that his precepts ought to have made possible, and which they do make possible for later poets. There are also in this poem six lines of eleven syllables. These are all feminine lines, in pairs, without the slightest displacement of stress.

> With Ippocrace thou banquetedst full ofte,
> With Ippocrace thou madst thy selfe full *merrye*,
> Such cheere had set thy new love so alofte,
> That olde love nowe was scarcely worth a *cherry*.
> 301–304

It is doubtful that Gascoigne regretted the extra final syllable, even though he made no provision for it in *Certayne Notes*.

[1] 'With certain phrase-superfixes some words appear in phonemic shapes involving loss or replacement of the segmental phonemes (the so-called weak forms of auxiliaries, personal pronouns, prepositions, and others . . .). The special contractions or portmanteau forms that arise at times (|donow| for |downt| from |duw nat| and |now|) are instances of the same process.' Trager and Smith, p. 59.
[2] *Works*, I, 106.

With these exceptions the 371 lines are true to the iambic metrical pattern. The adjustments of poetical licence are there. Gascoigne employs here and in other poems whenever it is convenient the *eth* ending for the present indicative third person singular verb inflection. In my observation he always uses it as a syllable; it always fits an exact regular metrical pattern.

> Beholde the man, which *taketh* grief for game
> 199

> My swelling heart, *breakes* with delay of paine
> 345

In the same way, he treats -*ed* endings with perfect freedom as syllabic or non-syllabic according to the requirements of the metrical pattern, indicating the choice by his spelling.

> The freedome *fainde*, which brought me but to thrall
> 32

> And with false love, did cloke a *fained* luste
> 108

> Till I perforce, *constraynd* thee for to seeke
> 167

> When Titan is *constrained* to forsake
> 189

He makes free use of syncopation and elision:

> The *mutuall* love, the confidence, the trust
> 86

> Of *many a* wound received by disdaine
> 42

> In happy *haven*, which saufer was than Dover
> 150

In other poems the device may be handled with a rather cavalier inconsistency:

> o s| o   s| o s|os|
> Promot*ion* not devot*ion* is cause why cleargie quailes.
> *Memories* V, I, 22[1]

By these devices, and with the exception of the eleven-syllable feminine lines, Gascoigne maintains in this poem an exact relation between the ten syllables of the metrical pattern and the syllables of the language.

[1] *Works*, 69.

In the pattern of stresses, he does not place any word of more than one syllable contrary to its usual pronunciation, except perhaps *corosives* in this line:[1]

With corosives my panting heart to perse
128

Certain compounds are treated as though they were two monosyllables, which by his theory are adjusted as 'occasion requireth.' Gascoigne shifts the stress of 'unto' as it suits him.

And yet my life is *únto* thee resinde
84

The noble face was *únto* thee but newe
275

Then staye a while: give eare *únto* my rime
187

Únto my nature and complexion
310

The phrases, of course, sometimes fit the metrical pattern only at the cost of some distortion:

Yet hauld I in, the mayne *shéate óf* the minde
145

And to my long *hóme, thús* my life it hasteth
248

My swelling heart, *bréakes wíth* delay of paine
345

Even in the first foot, where poets have always felt free to use a trochee, where Gascoigne himself in other poems places words which cannot be said with a weak stress followed by a stronger, in this

---

[1] Helge Kökeritz, *Shakespeare's Pronunciation* (New Haven, 1953), 336. He believes this word was stressed on the first syllable. Here he has evidence of spelling variants, and what seem to be clear cases in Shakespeare, 1H6, III, iii, 3, and 2H6, III, ii, 403. In general, however, I do not trust his judgments based on his assumption of a rigid coincidence of metrical pattern and word-stress—even in the case of Gascoigne. See his circular reasoning on 332–335, all of it dependent on his assumptions about metre.

poem there occur only words which either clearly fit the metrical pattern or can be adjusted to it since they are monosyllables:

> *And to* my long home. . . .
>
> 248
>
> *Thinke on* the Tythe. . . .
>
> 89
>
> *When in* the depth. . . .
>
> 95

With these adjustments of syllable and stress allowed by his system, Gascoigne achieves in 'Dan Bartholomews Dolorous discourses' a regular correspondence of language and metrical pattern. If the words are not always perfectly in 'their mother phrase,' they never go beyond the leeway allowed in *Certayne Notes*: 'And yet I will not altogether forbidde it you, for in some places, it may be borne, but not so hardly as some use it which wryte thus:

> Now let us go to Temple ours,
> I will go visit mother myne, &c.'

In this poem Gascoigne does not go beyond a simple inversion such as this,

> In happy haven, which *saufer was* than Dover
>
> 150

Most of the lines fall out with an easy correspondence of phrase and metrical pattern. The lines tend to be grammatical units, and if they are read with the steady emphasis on the metrical stresses which is made possible by all the devices of Gascoigne's versifying, they do sound 'obvious and harsh.'[1] But when the reader allows the phrases to retain the flavour of speech they rightfully possess, the lines are easy-going, and even have a kind of energy. There is none of the cramped effect too common in Googe or Turberville. Gascoigne is, if anything, long-winded, but he does have change of pace. His metrical principles have a place for the natural phrases of speech, and this permits him to keep a sense of reality in his verse. It may be a rather incongruous sense sometimes, but it absorbs into the conventions both very emotional and very trivial experience. Gascoigne does this literally, without necessity of allegory or elaborate rhetorical figures. For him one of the worst things about being in love is that he cannot enjoy his dinner, as a person like him would normally expect to:

> And when my Fellowes call me downe to dyne,
> No chaunge of meate provokes mine appetite.
>
> 285

[1] Prouty, *Gascoigne*, p. 130.

The lover in 'Dan Bartholomew' suffers the usual Petrarchan freezing and burning:

> I freeze in hope, yet burne in haste of heate
>
> 346

but here Gascoigne's homely literalness is almost comic, for the man is also freezing and burning in the waters of Bath:

> But when I here, the Bell hath passed prime,
> Into the Bath I wallowe by my wyll,
> That there my teares (unsene) might ease my griefe
>
> 325

The range is not great, but as the metrics are always in touch with speech, the experience is in touch with reality.

> Well let this passe, and thinke uppon the joye,
> The mutuall love, the confidence, the trust,
> Whereby we both abandoned annoye,
> And fed our mindes with fruites of lovely lust.
> Thinke on the Tythe, of kysses got by stealth,
> Of sweete embracinges shortened by feare.
> Remember that which did maintaine our helth,
> Alas alas why shoulde I name it here.
> And in the midst of all those happie dayes,
> Do not forget the chaunges of my chaunce,
> When in the depth of many waywarde wayes,
> I onely sought, what might thy state advaunce.
>
> 85–96

That is what Gascoigne does in a poem which is perfectly regular metrically. But as I have said, he is not always regular; and the regularity or irregularity can occur in any of the larger poetic forms. The blank verse of *The Steel Glass*[1] has in all its 1,113 lines only about two dozen which present any discrepancy between language and metrical pattern. There are about a dozen lines whose initial feet cannot be iambic:

> *Only* that king. . . .
>
> 9
>
> *Brethren* by like. . . .
>
> 73
>
> *Cruel?* nay just. . . .
>
> 718

[1] *Works*, II.

82

About half as many lines are feminine, with eleven syllables, and a few lines can be found in which a word seems misplaced.

> When wrong *triumphes* and right is overtrodde.[1]
> 21

Run-on lines are very rare, and a pause occurs relentlessly after the fourth syllable. It is indicated by punctuation in the infrequent cases where the phrase does not require it.

> But holla: here, I see a wondrous sight,
> I see a swarme, of Saints within my glasse:
> Beholde, behold, I see a swarme in deede
> Of holy Saints, which walke in comely wise,
> Not deckt in robes, nor garnished with gold. . . .
> 783–787

The blank verse of *Jocasta*[2] is really irregular. In the acts signed by Gascoigne, there are irregularities in the first feet, in feet within the line, and eleven-syllable lines, all in great profusion. Particularly the nouns of family relation fail to agree with the metrical pattern.

> The traine of Jocasta my deare mother.
> II, 1, 17

In other verse Gascoigne almost never allows himself an extra syllable within the line, as he does here.

> Th' unworth|ie ex|*ile thy broth*|er to |the gave
> II, 1, 58

> My fath|ers pall|*ace the hol*|ie aultars
> II, 1, 110

Although the contrast is never so great as in blank verse, in poulter's measure Gascoigne has the same inconsistency: regularity in one poem, irregularity in another. In a poem of 46 lines, 'When perelesse Princes courtes,'[3] eight lines have one or more words which do not fit the metrical pattern, three lines have extravagant poetical licences
 o   s| o   s | o s|os
(Promot*ion* not devot*ion*), and there is a rhyme of a stressed and an

---

[1] Kökeritz, *op. cit.*, says *triumph* may have the stronger stress on the second syllable, as a verb; but see above, p. 80.
[2] *Works*, I, 244.
[3] *Ibid.*, 69.

unstressed syllable. The metre here tends to become a free-swinging ballad measure:

> The woman wantonnesse, shee commes with ticing traine,
> Pride in hir pocket plaies bo peepe, and bawdry in hir braine.
> Her handmaides be deceipte, daunger and dalliaunce,
> Riot and Revell follow hir, they be of hir alliaunce.
>
> 29–32

Apparently, Gascoigne recognizes the difference:

> And thus this foolishe jest, I put in dogrell rime.
>
> 45

But he can write in the same racy, colloquial, joking vein and keep to the letter of his principles. A very similar poem, 'A gloze upon this text, Dominus iis opus habet,'[1] in 100 lines exhibits no real irregularities except in these two lines:

> They bringe some fowle at Midsommer, a dish of Fish in Lent,
> At Christmasse a capon, at Mighelmasse a goose.
>
> 74–75

Within his principles Gascoigne can manage the same swing in which the sing-song of poulter's resembles the chant of nursery rhyme and yet theoretically retains a regular metre.

> Give Gave is a good man, what need we lashe it out.
>
> 13

The thump of poulter's, so fatal to serious verse, is here as appropriate as in *Taffy is a Welshman, Taffy is a thief*. In fact, Gascoigne must have recognized the absurdity, the effect of something close to nonsense, that the emphatic stresses required by the measure bring to the conventional matter of poulter's. Occasionally he writes it in Surrey's vein, as in 'The lamentation of a lover,'[2]

> Now have I found the waie, to weepe and wayle my fill,
> Now can I ende my dolfull dayes, & so content my will.
>
> 1–2

But as often it becomes burlesque, and the Petrarchan complaints explode into jokes, as in 'The Anatomye of a Lover.'[3]

> The Anvile is my heart, my thoughtes they strike the stroake,
> My lights and lunges like bellowes blow, & sighes ascend
>   for smoake.
> My secreete partes are so with secreete sorrowe soken,
> As for the secreete shame thereof, deserves not to be spoken.
>
> 17–20

---

[1] *Ibid.*, 70.   [2] *Ibid.*, 45.   [3] *Ibid.*, 37.

Poulter's measure at last has come to an end in a fitting absurdity.

In other forms, when the recognition of the measure does not depend upon over-emphasis, Gascoigne's careful fitting of language to metrical pattern has its own kind of success. The effect of the metre is not the kind we usually call musical, nor is it often expressive, serving to add new meaning to the language of the poem. It may be simply a composition on the theme of the iambic foot, like this stanza from 'Gascoignes De profundis.'[1]

> Before the breake or dawning of the daye,
> Before the lyght be seene in loftye Skyes,
> Before the Sunne appeare in pleasaunt wyse,
> Before the watche (before the watche I saye)
> Before the warde that waytes therefore alwaye:
> My soule, my sense, my secreete thought, my sprite,
> My wyll, my wishe, my joye, and my delight:
> Unto the Lord that sittes in heaven on highe,
> With hastye wing,
> From me doeth fling,
> And stryveth styll, unto the Lorde to flye.
>
> 56–66

Here the words often correspond exactly to the foot. The foot is repeated again and again, simply and clearly, in groups that make a unit of five in each of the first three lines, of two and three in line four, of five again, and units of one foot in the sixth and seventh lines; and so on. At every point the language is clearly in correspondence with a pattern. These repetitions centre on the bold repetition of

> Before the watche (before the watche I saye).

This is what Gascoigne can do with the idea of fitting the word to the foot, the phrase to the measure.

In the form that after poulter's was his favourite, rhyme royal, he often achieves a similar success, and sometimes there appears another value of the iambic pattern and the careful observance of the measure. Here the stanza serves as a form to display the syntax of the language. The clauses are balanced against the lines and the sentences knitted up in balance with the form the rhyme-pattern offers. The key line is the fifth. It has to balance in meaning and in syntax the first four lines. The mark of its proper function is its rhyme, the last of the sequence ababa. This line must also prepare for the refrain of the last two lines.

[1] *Ibid.*, 60.

> The vaine excesse of flattering fortunes giftes,
> Envenometh the minde with vanitye,
> And beates the restelesse braine with endlesse driftes,
> To staye the staffe of worldly dignitie:
> The begger stands in like extremitie.
> Wherfore to lacke the moste, and leave the least,
> I coumpt enough as good as any feast.
>
> *Memories*, II, 1–7[1]

One of the great values of the strict iambic pattern is that it can give an exact weight and value to each syllable of a polysyllabic word. The controlled emphasis on *Envenometh, dignitie, extremitie* is consonant with the thought, which is of a balance of two extremes, and with the form, a balance of sentences and rhymes. Alliteration and internal rhyme, in lines where they do not need to serve as primary indicators of the structure, can function as they do here to bring resonance and a certain additional unity to the order of the language. Again, the stanza is a sort of exercise on the theory of the iambic foot. No new meaning emerges with a new intonation pattern. Only the exact significance of the words and phrases is emphasized by their precise manipulation. Every syllable is in place.

Apparently Gascoigne did not realize that syllables could be recognizably out of place. In this poem there are seven stanzas of rhyme royal. Six times comes the refrain,

> I coumpt enough as good as any feast.

The seventh time the line is this:

> It is enough and as good as a feast.

Typically, what Gascoigne means this time is his own verse—it is enough, pretty bad, but it will do, he says. Neither the principle of regularity nor Gascoigne's usual practice can account for this line. After the firm, expected stress on *good* six times,

> o   s | o   s | o   s | o s| o   s
> I coumpt enough as good as any feast,

we read now,

> o s| o   s | o   s| o   s| o   s
> It is enough and as good as a feast.

Gascoigne would not claim credit for shifting the stress suddenly in this way. The metre has created a phrase which after six stresses on *good* we can only read with the extreme emphasis of finality, as góod

1 *Ibid.*, 63.

as a fēast.[1] It is only his monosyllable 'circumflex' at work. But such effects are not what Gascoigne was seeking.

He was stricter at the musters than anyone before him. He writes a verse which almost, but not quite, demands a perpetual double attention to every syllable, to its place in speech and to its place in an abstract pattern. His own principles did not allow him to make the most of that. His vision was single. But Gascoigne, who loved mottoes, provides one here for himself.

> And though the musicke of my verse,
> Be plainsong tune both true and just:
> Content thee yet to here my song,
> For els thou doest me dooble wrong.[2]

[1] The expression was proverbial, lending perhaps extra emphasis and finality. Tilley, 188, E-158, gives 'Enough is as good as a feast' as recorded in 1546, 1553, and c. 1565.

[2] *Works*, I, 458.

IV

The Shepheardes Calender

The Shepheardes Calender is generally said to be the turning point of Elizabethan poetry. Certainly it was something new, and it was immediately recognized as new.[1] The centre of what was new in it was its metres; it had a great variety of measures, great variety in the way the measures were handled in detail, and great freedom. The long way taken by generations of poets in using the new measure of Wyatt was no longer followed. They had tried to learn, largely from Surrey's adaptations of Wyatt's measure, how 'each word in place with such a sleight is couched,' as Turberville put it.[2] Gascoigne had finally said exactly what the places were and how each word was to be put into them. There was only one set of places, and there was only one way to couch the words there. There were plenty of stanzas; not so many as there were to be later, but that was not the main point; there was only the iambic line to make them of. It is immediately apparent in *The Shepheardes Calender* that there are other kinds of lines, and that each word is not in the place Gascoigne had said it must be; often the place itself, the order of a metrical pattern, is not there.

The variety and freedom of metre in *The Shepheardes Calender* consists of three things. There is a variety of stanza forms. There is a variety of measures or metrical patterns. There is a variety of ways the words are placed in relation to these patterns. These new things had to be taken seriously; they occurred all in one book with a general plan; this plan, or framework, might seem superimposed, even an afterthought, but the book was not a miscellany or a

[1] *The Works of Edmund Spenser, A Variorum Edition*, v. I, ed. C. G. Osgood and H. G. Lotspeich (Baltimore, 1943), Appendix IV, 'Early Fame,' 641–645.

[2] Turberville, *Epitaphes, Epigrams, Songs and Sonets* (London, 1567), No. 11, 'Verse in Prayse of Lord Henry Howard Earl of Surrey.'

handful of sundries. And the poet obviously had major intentions. No one had to be reminded that eclogues had been the first production of 'the Romish *Tityrus.*' The apparatus of E. K., whatever else it might be, was expert promotion. So were the *Three proper and wittie familiar Letters* and the *Two other very commendable Letters* published in 1580. All these gave the book weight, and emphasized the way the varieties of metre reflected on each other. None of the radical measures could seem mere 'forgetfulness or carelessness' in the company of all the others. Although they were not in themselves original, the forms were many and varied, and it is easy to see why the book was a startling novelty.[1]

[1] The originality of the stanzas or ways of combining lines is largely that there are so many of them all together. If one includes the verses 'To His Booke,' eight-syllable triplets; the 'Envoy,' twelve-syllable couplets; and the pair of twelve-syllable lines quoted by E. K. in the October Gloss, there are fourteen different ways of grouping the various kinds of lines (see Appendix A, 'Verse forms'). Four of these are quatrains or variations on the quatrain. *January, December,* and the *August* dialogue are in one of the most popular of sixteenth-century forms, the quatrain and couplet, ABAB CC. The *November* dialogue and *April* dialogue are in quatrains linked by the rhyme. The links begin with the third quatrain in *November*; in *April* the linking is intermittent. The eight-line stanza of *June* is composed of two quatrains on two rhymes, ABAB BABA. *October* is a six-line stanza, ABBA BA. These simple variations are similar to many of the stanza forms in Tottel, or parts of them: there we find lines arranged in many combinations, ABAB AB CDCD EDE FF, ABAB BABA BABA BCC, ABAB ABBA BABA, ABAB ABCB, ABAA BB, and so on.

July is in the 'common' metre, or fourteener broken and rhymed in lines of eight syllables and six, ABAB. *March* is in the 'romance' metre of 'Sir Thopas,' AAB CCB; A and C have eight syllables, B usually seems to have seven.

August contains the first poem printed in English closely to resemble the sestina. Some think he got the idea from Sidney. (See Spenser Variorum, *Minor Poems,* I, 349.)

February, May, and *September* are in varieties of four-beat couplets.

The songs of *August, April,* and *November* combine long lines with short. *August's* song, ABAB, usually has the A lines of eight syllables, the first B of five, the second of seven. It resembles popular songs of the day. See Bruce Pattison, *Music and Poetry of the English Renaissance* (London, 1948, 173). The nine-line stanza of *April's* song combines lines of ten, four, and eight syllables, with many lines varying from these quantities. *November's* song has a ten-line stanza of lines of twelve syllables, ten syllables, eight, and four. One stanza has a rhyme-scheme different from the others. Combinations of lines of different lengths were common in the song-books and miscellanies. See *A Handfull of Pleasant Delights,* ed. H. E. Rollins (Cambridge, Mass., 1924), dated about 1566 by Rollins. There are things like this (No. 2):

> You lordings, cast off your weedes of wo
>   me thinks I heare
> A trumpet shril which plain doth show
>   my Lord is neare:
> Tantara tara tantara....   *(cont. next page)*

It is not so easy to see why it was not also bewildering. While *The Shepheardes Calender* is obviously a turning point of some kind, it indicates so many directions that one attempting to follow it would not know which way to go. To predict Spenser's development from it would have been impossible. Only a small portion of its metrical variety resembles the metrics of the great Elizabethan poetry which is said to begin with its appearance. About the *April* song, for instance, Professor Renwick has said, 'of all the *Calender* this "lay" was probably the most striking to contemporaries, and the most influential.'[1] But those who were influenced must have been very critical and selective. Spenser's irregularities in the *April* song are surely as striking as anything else about it, and they were not imitated.

The irregularities are striking not only in that song. They are so severe in many places that they cause a blurring of two of the three features that constituted the new variety and freedom of the metres of *The Shepheardes Calender*. The way the lines are grouped to form stanzas or other units is always easily seen even when it is inconsistent from one part of a poem to another. But the structure of the lines themselves is not always clear: sometimes it is impossible to say what Spenser's metrical pattern was, or even if he had one in mind. Consequently, it is sometimes impossible to say just how he means to place his words in relation to a metrical pattern. Some lines seem to offer no explanation for being what they are.[2]

See also *Paradise of Dainty Devices*, 1576–1606, ed. H. E. Rollins (Cambridge, Mass., 1927), No. 81:

> If euer man had loue to dearly bought,
> Lo I am he that plaies within her maze:
> And finds no waie, to get the same I sought,
> But as the dere are driven vnto the gaze.
> And to augment the grief of my desire,
> My self to burne, I blowe the fire:
> But shall I come by you,
> Of forse I must fly you.

Turberville (No. 79, etc.) and Gascoigne (De Profundis, etc.) had used them to some extent. But Spenser's combinations were new. They were made probably in imitation of Ronsard, or perhaps of the madrigals which must have been sung in England by this time, although they were not printed, translated, or generally imitated, until a few years later. (See Pattison, *op. cit.*, 'A manuscript collection of Italian compositions has been found dating from the sixties,' p. 96.)

[1] W. L. Renwick, ed., *The Shepheard's Calender* (London, 1930), 190–191.

[2] Some of the lines, obviously, could be edited towards regularity; but textual changes made in the interests of improving the metres, like those in most modern editions of Shakespeare, have no real authority. Studies of orthography and Elizabethan printing may well produce more reliable texts not only of Spenser but of all the poets considered in this book. But I work with the printed text as it exists in the editions most generally accepted by scholars.

Those puzzling lines may be due to the truly radical nature of Spenser's metrical experiments. The variety of stanzas is his most obvious innovation, but the least important; he experimented in the basic structure of the line, but again, the most obvious thing is not the most important. He uses two easily recognized kinds of structure: the four-beat line and the iambic line. This in itself was unusual, for the four-beat line, while not quite unknown, was very much out of date and thought to be very crude. The three poems in this crude measure are among those described by E. K. as 'mixed with some satyrical bitternesse,' and satire was supposed to be crude and rough, partly because the word was associated with satyr, the rough creature of the woods. Thomas Drant in 1566 gives the derivation in verse:

> Or Satyra, of Satyrus, the mossye rude,
> Uncivile god: for those that wyll them write
> With taunting gyrds and glikes and gibes must bere the lewde,
> Strayne curtesy: ne reck of mortall spyte.[1]

Also, Spenser may have justified his interest in the measure on the grounds that it was fitting for his simple folk to use not only rude diction, but rude and archaic metres, as the use of this metre was justified in *The Mirror for Magistrates*. It was a special kind of verse, for a special purpose; probably it was never intended to appear as a general possibility for English metre. Certainly, alongside the iambic, it provided variety.

But Spenser was not satisfied with this. Both four-beat measures and iambic measures he uses in a wide variety of ways, so wide, in fact, that the measures sometimes seem to be neither one nor the other. Perhaps he even had a third thing in mind. We know that shortly after he had finished *The Shepheardes Calender*, or possibly before it was quite ready for press, he was deeply interested in writing English verses in classical measures. This was at the time he coveted for English poets the right to scan their lines by a system that had little to do with the actual sound of the words in the lines. 'Accents,' or stress, would be disregarded in such a system, and syllables themselves would be subject at least to the usual poetic licence.[2]

If anything like this or perhaps another strange system crept into *The Shepheardes Calender* we would never know it. Who could tell

---

[1] From Thomas Drant, *A Medicinable Morall, that is, the two Books of Horace Satyres, Englyshed.* . . . London, 1566, as given by M. C. Randolph, 'Thomas Drant's Definition of Satire,' *Notes & Queries*, CLXXX (1941), 415–418.

[2] The classical versifying experiments are considered later in Chapter V.

that these lines were intended to be classical measures, if Spenser
had not said so?[1]

> See yee the blindefoulded pretie god that feathered archer,
> Of louers miseries which maketh his bloodie game?
> Wote ye why his moother with a veale hath coovered his face?
> Trust me, least he my loove happely chaunce to beholde.[2]

In considering the metrical patterns and the ways Spenser uses
them, the large division, of course, is between the four-beat measures
of *February*, *May*, and *September*, and everything else. When the
verse is looked at closely, the division is not quite clear-cut; but it is
useful. Within the category of the poems which seem to be largely or
even partly iambic, a division into three groups is possible. The
'common' measure of *July* and the 'romance' measure of *March*
make the first. The second is made of the songs of *April*, *November*,
and *August*. The third group contains all the lines that seem to be
more or less pentameter. *January*, *April* (1–36), the *November* dialogue, *June*, *October*, and the *August* sestine are the most nearly
regular. *December* has a distinctive way of using the ten-syllable line
in relation to an iambic pattern. The *August* dialogue and the few
lines that close *April* are extremely irregular; they may not be intended to have any relation to an iambic structure.

1. *The Four-Beat Line: February, May, September*
More than a third of all the lines in the *Calender* are in the four-
beat measures. Calling them 'four-beat measures' means that they
are written with a metrical pattern in mind. This metrical pattern is
not exactly the same as that of the old four-beat verse; many of the
requirements of that verse are not met here. There is no way of knowing whether Spenser failed to recognize these requirements or whether
he disregarded them in his experiment, or series of experiments, based
on a simplified version of the four-beat metrical pattern. Of course,
one can also assume that Spenser did not have any consistent metrical
pattern in mind here, but chose to write three long poems which
would never fall into any discernible consistent structure. Following
this assumption, one would have to suppose that Spenser has taken
care to insure that his lack of organization, or freedom, might not

---

1 Alternate dactyllic hexameter and dactyllic pentameter:

A. $-$ u u $\mid$ $-$ u u $\mid$ $-$ u u $\mid$ $-$ u u $\mid$ $-$ u u $\mid$ $-$ u
   $-$ $-$ $\mid$ $-$ $-$ $\mid$ u u $\mid$ $-$ $-$ $\mid$ $-$.
B. $-$ u u $\mid$ $-$ u u $\mid$ $-$ $\mid\mid$ $-$ u u $\mid$ $-$ u u $\mid$ $-$
   $-$ $-$ $\mid$ $-$ $-$ $\mid$

2 *Works*, IX, 16.

appear to become a principle itself. For various structures do appear from time to time, out of repetitions in the organization of the language into lines, even if the reader applies no metrical pattern as he reads.

> s o   o s o   o   s   o   s
> Who will not suffer the stormy time,
> Where will he liue tyll the lusty prime?
> *Feb.*, 15–16

> o   s   o   o s o   o   s   o   s
> Then paye you the price of your surquedrie
> With weeping, and wayling, and misery.
> *Feb.*, 49–50

> o   s   o   s   o   s   o   s   o   s
> There at the dore he cast me downe hys pack,
> And layd him downe, and groned, Alack, Alack.
> Ah deare Lord, and sweete Saint Charitee,
> That some good body woulde once pitie mee.
> Well heard Kiddie al this sore constraint,
> And lengd to know the cause of his complaint:
> Tho creeping close behind the Wickets clinck. . . .
> *May*, 245–251

> o   s   o   s   o   s   o   s
> Ah fon, now by thy losse art taught
> That seeldome chaunge the better brought.
> Content who liues with tryed state,
> Neede feare no chaunge of frowning fate:
> But who will seeke for vnknowne gayne,
> Oft liues by losse, and leaues with payne.
> *Sept.*, 68–73[1]

But these structures suggest themselves only to be withdrawn. Reading the poems as mixtures of various metrical schemes seems to be based on the idea that Spenser is trying here to be 'like Chaucer,' as Chaucer might have appeared without sounding the final *e* and without the benefits of modern editing in producing iambic penta-meters. Spenser's lines, then, would have no real metrical pattern, but only a chaotic mixture of possibilities in which each line was its own law within the limits of eight syllables to eleven. It seems to me rather that Spenser is working with a very powerful metrical pattern which he expects will exert an unusual degree of influence over the

---

[1] These and all subsequent quotations from *The Shepheardes Calender* are from *Works*, ed. E. A. Greenlaw, *et. al.*

language of the line.[1] The metrical pattern of four beats to the line is to be maintained at no matter what expense to the language. When the language has to be distorted in a very arbitrary way to achieve this pattern, the results are crudities in mis-using language, the decorum of shepherds—not new or shifting metrical patterns. The pattern is simply four beats to a line, and they can come anywhere. Within those large possibilities, Spenser uses a number of different relations between the pattern and the language. Some of them, the easiest to describe and classify, have been seen above. Others occur in a scattered way throughout the three poems. No one relation ever becomes completely dominant.

Certain gross differences appear between the poems of *February*, *May*, and *September*, when their elements are added up. Eighty per cent of the lines in *February* have nine syllables, and most of the rest have ten. In *May* the nine-syllable and ten-syllable lines are about equal in number. In *September* about sixty per cent of the lines have nine syllables and about thirty per cent ten syllables. Each of the poems has a few eight-syllable and a few eleven-syllable lines. These figures are not very certain because the syllables are often uncertain. In other verse where Spenser's intention to be regular apparently allows more secure judgment of what is syllabic and what is not, his licences are many, following the customs of the day. *Heaven* may be one syllable or two,[2] and *-ed* endings may or may not be

---

[1] The assumption about the imitation of Chaucer is stated by W. L. Renwick: 'The verse of these three eclogues can be understood at all only as an attempt to reproduce the effect of Chaucer's verse read without the final e's, for though the majority of the lines are of nine syllables, there may be as few as eight and as many as eleven.' (*Edmund Spenser*, p. 100.) A better understanding was shown by Thomas Gray long before the final e confused the issue. 'The "Riding Ryme" I rather take to be that which is confined to one measure, whatever that measure be, but not to one rhythm; having sometimes more, sometimes fewer syllables, and the pause hardly distinguishable, such as the Prologue and History of Beryn, found in some MSS of Chaucer, and the Cook's Tale of Gamelyn, where the verses have twelve, thirteen, or fourteen syllables, and the caesura on the sixth, seventh, or eighth, as it happens. This having an air of rusticity, Spenser has very well adapted it to pastoral poetry, and in his hands it has an admirable effect. . . .' ('Observations in English Metre,' *Works*, ed. Gosse [London, 1884], I, 339.) Gray observes that the variations in syllables do not mean departures from 'one measure.' The models he proposed are more likely than 'Chaucer,' if a source must be provided. See also Lewis, *English Literature in the Sixteenth Century*, 361; he notes as precedents, among others, the four-beat metres of 'The Blacksmith,' 'Thomas of Woodstock,' 'Flodden,' and 'James I' in the *Mirror*, 'not to mention Barclay, Hawes, Skelton's rhyme royal, and the pseudo-Chaucerian *Pilgrim's Tale*.'

[2] So mought| our Cudd|ies name| to Heau|en sownde.
And, whence| thou camst|, flye backe| to *heauen*| apace.
                                        Oct., 54, 84.

syllabic.[1] The number of syllables alone means little, however. It is not consistent enough to be a principle in itself. It does mean that the dips between the four lifts, or beats, tend to be longer in *May*, which has the most ten-syllable lines.

The relation between the metrical pattern and the language is the important and interesting thing in these four-beat poems. The essential distinction is the simple one that some lines are easy to read, some are hard. All must be fitted somehow to the metrical scheme. *February* opens with lines that move with their phrases and stresses in easy compliance with the requirement of four lifts. Minor ambiguities make no difference. What does it matter if the third lift, in the first line, falls on *rancke* or on *Winters*? Or, in the second line, does it matter if it is *neuer* or *ginne* that is most strongly stressed?

> Ah for pittie, wil rancke Winters rage,
> These bitter blasts neuer ginne tasswage?
> The kene cold blowes through my beaten hyde,
> All as I were through the body gryde.
> My ragged rontes all shiver and shake,
> As doen high Towers in an earthquake:
> They wont in the wind wagge their wrigle tailes,
> Perke as Peacock: but nowe it auales.
>
> *Feb.*, 1–8

Here there is something very like the half-lines of earlier four-beat measures, and this phrasing contributes to the ease of the accommodation of language and metrical requirement. Even so, there are adjustments to be made. The third line might sound like this in speech: the kéen cóld|| blówes thróugh my béaten híde||. The first two lines have already created the expectation that there will be only four strong metrical stresses or lifts, and probably the reader will find that the first two override the phrase-pattern, with this result,

ø s | ø   s | ø   s| ø   s
The kene cold blowes through my beaten hyde.

May begins somewhat differently. After the first few lines, there are two places where the longer phrases continue through the line-end, and then at the beginning of the next line, close in such a way

---

[1] And fault|lesse fayth|, is *turned*| to faith| lesse fere.
   That lyues| on earth|, and lou|*ed* her| most dere.
                                   June, 110, 112.
Spelling is sometimes but not always an indication, as in
   Then should| my plaints|, *causd* of| discur|tesee.
                                   June, 97.

as to suggest that they ought there to provide two lifts. The rest of the line shows that this expectation was wrong.

> Is not thilke the mery moneth of May,
> When loue lads masken in fresh aray?
> How falles it then, we no merrier bene,
> *Ylike as others*, girt in gawdy greene?
> Our bloncket liueryes bene all to sadde,
> For thilke same season, when all is ycladd
> With pleasaunce: the grownd with grasse, the Wods
> *With green leaues*, the bushes with bloosming Buds.
>
> 1–8

Lines requiring various kinds of violence to their language occur in all three poems. In many lines the language itself does not present four relatively-strong stresses, as in these lines below.

> I wonne her with a gyrdle of gelt.
> *Feb.*, 65
>
> See howe he venteth into the wynd.
> *Feb.*, 75
>
> Which I cond of *Tityrus* in my youth.
> *Feb.*, 92
>
> The ranckorous rigour of his might.
> *Feb.*, 185
>
> So longe haue I listened to thy speche,
> That graffed to the ground is my breche.
> *Feb.*, 241–242
>
> Enaunter their heritage do impaire.
> *May*, 78
>
> She stoppeth the breath of her youngling.
> *May*, 100
>
> I haue of thy health and thy welfare.
> *May*, 216
>
> Open the dore at his request.
> *May*, 226
>
> Tho opened he the dore, and in came
> *May*, 278
>
> In the basket for the Kidde to fynd.
> *May*, 289
>
> Since when thou hast measured much grownd.
> *Sept.*, 21
>
> Thus chatten the people in theyr steads.
> *Sept.*, 120
>
> How, but with heede and watchfulnesse.
> *Sept.*, 230

There are also many lines which present too many relatively-strong stresses, so that the action of the metrical pattern is to suppress one of them, as in these lines. The choice of the syllable to be suppressed is sometimes arbitrary.

Must not the world wend in his commun course.
Feb., 11
Selfe haue I worne out thrise threttie yeares.
Feb., 17
Some in much ioy, many in many teares.
Feb., 18
Colours meete to clothe a mayden Queene.
Feb., 132
And oft his hoarie locks downe doth cast.
Feb., 181
And often halowed with his holy water dewe.
Feb., 210
Ah *Piers*, bene not thy teeth on edge, to thinke.
May, 35
Passen their time, that should be sparely spent.
May, 41
Butter enough, honye, milke, and whay.
May, 115
Most is, a fooles talke to beare and to heare.
May, 141
Sicke, sicke, alas, and little lack of dead.
May, 264
Of which her sonne had sette to dere a price.
May, 299
Thrise three Moones bene fully spent and past.
Sept., 20
And nowe the Westerne wind bloweth sore.
Sept., 49
That here by there I whilome vsd to keepe.
Sept., 63
And casten to compasse many wrong emprise.
Sept., 83
Marrie that great *Pan* bought with deare borrow.
Sept., 96
For bigge Bulls *of Basan* brace hem about.
Sept., 124

In all three poems the lines often assume a more or less regular movement. They seem to be organized by feet, three iambs and an anapaest.

The iolly shepheard that was of yore,
Is nowe nor iollye, nor shepehearde more.
Sept., 26–27

97

When this pattern is broken, the essential metrical requirement of four lifts to the line continues.

> In forrein costes, men sayd, was plentye:
> And so there is, but all of miserye.
> I dempt there much to haue eeked my store,
> But such eeking hath made my hart sore.
>
> *Sept.*, 28–31

The reader must be willing to forget the expectation of alternate weak and strong stresses, and allow the four lifts to come as they will, according to the old privileges of the measure. A line like the last above has 'clashing' lifts, and the last two lifts may fall where they will.

> ø   s   s ø   s   ø   s
> But such eeking hath made my hart sore.
>
> ø   s   s
> hath made my hart sore.
>
> ø   s   ø   s   ø
> hath made my hart sore.

The kind of four-beat verse Spenser writes is not dependent on a close correspondence of the metrical pattern and the phrases of speech. It does not depend on the phrases to carry the metrical pattern, as does the four-beat measure used by Ferrers in 'Thomas of Woodstock.' There the metrical pattern is never called upon to assert itself. In Spenser's four-beat measures, the metrical pattern has to assert itself if the verse is to retain its structure. The effect is entirely different from that of Ferrers' lines,

> This noble father to maynteyne my state,
> With Buckyngham Erldom dyd me indowe,
> Both Nature and Fortune to me were grate,
> Denyeng nothing which they myght allowe.
>
> *Thomas of Woodstock*, 15–18

Ferrers had to observe the phrasing by half-line with perfect consistency to control the stress-patterns of his phrases. He very rarely used the tertiary stress of a polysyllabic word as a lift; it would create an expectation that would destroy his phrasing. Spenser uses such syllables or does not use them as he pleases. It does not matter to him if the practice is inconsistent.

> s   s   s   s
> That his father left by inheritaunce.
>
> *May*, 89
>
> s   s   s   s
> When shepeheards had none inheritaunce.
>
> *May*, 105

98

6

434723774874563743625324735665678

THE SHEPHEARDES CALENDER

For *Pan* himself was their inheritaunce.
May, 111

In *February*, *May*, and *September*, then, Spenser is using a metrical pattern at its extreme of one kind of power. It is a 'musical' use of the metre, very different, of course, in effect, from other kinds of musical effects Spenser attains. It is remote from speech, and is intended to be. There are no subtleties of relation between metre and intonation patterns, any more than there are any subtleties of thought or imagery or plot in these poems. Whatever one's judgment of them may be, it ought to begin with a proper understanding of their metre. One must not shrink from distorting the phrases to accommodate the four beats. They should pound along come what may, like nursery rhymes. When the metrical intention of these poems is properly understood, their simple nature may be appreciated. The 'rustic' diction may be seen as part of the strategy necessary to allow this remoteness from the realities of speech. The solemn, wooden moralizing assumes its proper weight; it is uncomplicated by reality, not to be pondered, and it is not all like Chaucer. There is about as much reference to real speech as there is to real experience, and this is thoroughly congenial to Spenser. It is often his way with his metre as with his thought.

2. *The 'common' and 'romance' measures: July and March*

There is nothing remarkable about the common measure, or divided fourteener, of July. Here Spenser is not experimenting. He uses the measure with no great freedom; if anything, his verse is more regular than that of many poets of the day. His standard kind of stanza is metrically very like Turberville's in that poet's treatment of the same themes from Mantuan. (Turberville does not rhyme at the break, and he throws in some poulter's measure from time to time.)

> Besyde, as holy fathers sayne,
>   there is a hyllye place,
> Where *Titan* ryseth from the mayne,
>   to renne hys dayly race.
> *July*, 57–60

> They say there is a place where as
>   the Sunne from Sea doth rise,
> Which (if I well remember) seemes
>   unto our mortall eyes. . . .
> Turberville, 8th Ecl., 107–110[1]

[1] *The Eclogues of Mantuan*, translated by George Turberville (facsimile), ed. Douglas Bush (New York, 1937).

Spenser's variations are similar to those of Turberville, but he uses them less often, and he does not use Turberville's run-on lines. In three lines Spenser depends on the metrical pattern to regulate the stresses, or he has a clashing stress:

> Whose balefull barking bringes in hast
>
>   o   s
> *pyne, plagues*, and dreery death.
>
> > *July*, 23–24

> The wastefull hylls vnto his threate
> is a *playne ouerture*.
>
> > *July*, 27–28

> that with *fond termes*, and weetlesse words.
>
> > *July*, 35

Here is Turberville:

> Wher is of frogs, *gnats*, flies & wormes
> and other like *good* store
> Among the Willowes, Alder boughes
> and rotten Reedes, with more
> Than I can name. . . .
>
> > *8th Ecl.*, 29–33

> As rough as hogs, as leane as rakes
> raggd, leaping at a crust.
>
> > *8th Ecl.*, 153–154

> But afterward when greedy Lust
> and licorous lips began
> To tast the fruite that was forbid,
> and that hee ate up all
> The Apples, keeping none for God
> when he for fruite did call. . . .
>
> > *8th Ecl.*, 113–118

But Spenser did not object to placing words out of 'their mother phrase and proper Idiom.' He would have written 'and that the apples all| he ate up. . . .'[1]

> Whilome there vsed shepheards all
> to feede theyr flocks at will. . . .
>
> > *July*, 65–66

The presence of the measure in the book is of some interest, but

---

[1] 'Gascoigne disapproved of placing the adjective after the noun . . .; he himself almost never employed the construction. Sidney, as well, used it rarely. On the other hand, it is so common in the poetry of Warner and Spenser that under their weighty influence it became a general practice again among the poets of the late sixteenth century.' Veré L. Rubel, *Poetic Diction in the English Renaissance* (New York, 1941), p. 231 n.

there is nothing remarkable in the way it is used. The same thing is true of the 'romance' measure of *March*.

> The ioyous time now nigheth fast,
> That shall allege this bitter blast,
> And slake the winters sorowe.
> Sicker Willye, thou warnest well:
> For Winters wrath beginnes to quell,
> And pleasant spring appeareth.
> *Mar.*, 4–9

Of the 117 lines, a few have nine or ten syllables where eight are expected. The shorter lines are all but one of seven syllables, unless we choose to syncopate a syllable.

> But soone it sore encreas*ed*.
> *Mar.*, 99
>
> Ne wote I, how to cease *it*.
> *Mar.*, 102

There are some initial trochees, and a few other feet are trochaic.

> *Sicker Willye*, thou warnest well.
> *Mar.*, 7
>
> That nowe *sleepeth* in Lethe lake.
> *Mar.*, 23
>
> *Mought her necke bene ioynted* attones.
> *Mar.*, 53
>
> That seeing I, *leuelde* againe.
> *Mar.*, 85

It has been claimed that this poem 'illustrates the eagerness with which "the new poet" was experimenting, and it shows the powers which he was bringing to bear upon his experiments.'[1] The poem is something of a novelty in its revival of the measure. Less radical than the experiments of *February*, *May*, and *September*, it seems very close to the verse of *April*, a fairly conventional employment of one kind of iambic measure. It does not seem to be a very powerful experiment, But then, it has also been said that *March*, with its little Cupid story, is a profound myth, 'an inimitable poetic description of puberty.'[2]

[1] George Saintsbury, *Cambridge History of English Literature* (New York, 1910), III, 258.
[2] Leo Spitzer, 'Spenser, Shepheardes Calender, March,' *Studies in Philology*, XLVII (1950), 494–505.

3. *The Songs of August, April, and November*

The *August* song is similar in several ways to *March*, but it is much more interesting. It is a song for two voices. The first carries the theme along, in lines of eight syllables. The second brings in a partial refrain and echo, in a line of five syllables and a line of seven (sometimes eight). The differences between the two voices are interesting, and the organization of each kind of line is interesting in itself.

> *Perigot.*　It fell vpon a holly eve,
> *Willye.*　　　hey ho hollidays,
> *Per.*　　When holly fathers wont to shrieve:
> *Wil.*　　　now gynneth this roundelay.
> *Aug.*, 53–56

There are eighteen stanzas. Of the 36 lines of Perigot, 21 are perfectly regular, like those above in the first stanza. Four of his lines have initial trochees. Eleven lines have some variation from the regular in which the language does not exactly correspond to the metrical pattern. The variations do not exceed certain limits, and the limits are those which were to win acceptance as marking the kind of variations that were acceptable to standard English verse. This poem has the appearance of a deliberate experiment consciously controlled. Of Perigot's lines, for instance, those that are the first lines of the stanzas and those that are the third lines of the stanzas present almost exactly the same proportions of variation. Ten of the first-lines are perfectly regular, and eleven of the third-lines; two lines of each kind have initial trochees; four lines of each kind present some difference between the phrase pattern of stresses and the metrical pattern. Two of the first-lines and one of the third-lines have nine syllables. Each of the variations is worth noticing. As I have said, they occur within the limits of what were to become acceptable deviations of the language from the metrical pattern. Their appearance here is significant, but of course not at all definitive, in the great welter of variations that occur in *The Shepheardes Calender*.

One of these lines is indeterminate; the metrical pattern is not immediately reproduced in the language, and there are two possibilities of attaining four strong metrical stresses. The line can go either one way or the other.

> o　　o　s　o　s　　　s　o　　　s
> As the bon|i lasse| passed| bye,
>
> s　　o　s　o| s　　o| o　　s
> As the boni lasse pass ed bye.
> *Aug.*, 77

It has eight syllables, of course, in either case (unless *passed* is a monosyllable). But it is the only line in the poem which is not readily reconciled to the metrical pattern. For the context of this poem, too many syllables vary from their proper position in the metrical pattern. Two lines present two trochaic feet.

> *Tripping over* the dale alone.
> *Aug.*, 63
> *There it ranckleth* ay more and more.
> *Aug.*, 101

The five other lines vary from the metrical pattern in a way that is particularly interesting. The phrase patterns demand departures from the strict metrical pattern, but the lines can be reconciled to that pattern according to a strict application of Gascoigne's theory of monosyllables. The monosyllable, he said, may be regarded as of an indifferent degree of stress, capable of adjustment to the metrical requirement. This kind of variation becomes a standard practice in metrics. It is an adjustment that is purely theoretical; the metrical pattern is not expected to have much influence on the actual reading of the line. It does account for its structure.

>   o s
> Well deck*ed in* a frock of gray.
> *Aug.*, 65

> o   s   o s o   s
> *and in* a kirtle of greene saye.
> *Aug.*, 67

>   o s
> A chape *let on* her head she wore.
> *Aug.*, 69

>   o   s o   s
> I left the head *in my hart roote.*
> *Aug.*, 99

>   o   s o s
> Ne can I find *salue for* my sore.
> *Aug.*, 103

The nine-syllable lines use the privilege of introducing an extra syllable occasionally, a privilege which also is used by all but the most strict metrists.

>   o o s
> But wheth*er in payne* full love I pyne.
> *Aug.*, 109

>   o o s
> So learnd I loue *on a holly*e eue.
> *Aug.*, 121

I

so o
Of sweete *Violets* therein was store.
Aug., 71

The lines of Willye are completely different. His first lines, the second of each stanza, all have five syllables. Eleven of these have the same stress pattern, although how many strong stresses it is intended to present is not certain. The lines are like these:

> hey ho hollidaye.
> *Aug.*, 54
>
> hey ho Bonibell.
> *Aug.*, 62
>
> hey ho gray is greete.
> *Aug.*, 66
>
> hey ho pinching payne.
> *Aug.*, 110

Four of his lines present a second pattern.

> hey ho the high hill.
> *Aug.*, 58
>
> hey ho the Sunne beame.
> *Aug.*, 82
>
> hey ho the Moonelight.
> *Aug.*, 90
>
> hey ho the fayre flock.
> *Aug.*, 118

Three lines have still another pattern.

> hey ho the thonder.
> *Aug.*, 86
>
> hey ho the glyder.
> *Aug.*, 94
>
> hey ho the arrowe.
> *Aug.*, 102

If the lines are to be consistent in the number of strong metrical stresses, all must have one metrical stress after the *hey ho*. The last kind of line can not have two there, as the others can, if the language is not to be distorted. In any case the stress cannot be in the same position from one line to the next.

Willye's other lines, the last of each stanza, have seven syllables except for three which have eight. Seven of these lines present this pattern:

> now gynneth this roundelay.
> *Aug.*, 55
> the greene is for maydens meete.
> *Aug.*, 68
> as clear as the christall glasse.
> *Aug.*, 80

Three have this pattern:

> so cleaues thy soule a sonder.
> *Aug.*, 98
> such woundes soone waxen wider.
> *Aug.*, 96
>
>   o s|
>   s o
> love is a curelesse sorrowe.
> *Aug.*, 104

The third pattern has three lines. They have the possibility of three or four stresses.

> she can trippe it very well.
> *Aug.*, 4
> woode as he, that did them keepe.
> *Aug.*, 76
> let thy follye be the priese.
> *Aug.*, 116

There is one more pattern for the seven-syllable lines:

> it was a desperate shot.
> *Aug.*, 100
> and mone with many a mocke.
> *Aug.*, 120

The eight-syllable lines, like one group of the seven-syllable lines, are particularly out of order; they seem to present the possibility of four strong stresses.

> the while the shepheard selfe did spill.
> *Aug.*, 60
> she sweeter than the Violet.
> *Aug.*, 72
> so loue into thy heart did streame.
> *Aug.*, 84

These lines of Willye's are based on a metrical system which allows the stresses of speech to occur in any order, and in such a way that there is no consistency from one line to another, even in the number of relatively strong stresses. This may mean that the lines are supposed to have only the patterns of the language that occur in each one, so that these three lines are not expected to have the same metrical form:

> hey ho hollidaye,
> *Aug.*, 54

> hey ho the Sunne beame,
> *Aug.*, 82

> hey ho the Thonder;
> *Aug.*, 95

Nor are these three lines expected to share a common pattern:

> now gynneth this roundelay.
> *Aug.*, 56

> she can trippe it very well.
> *Aug.*, 64

> the while the shepheard selfe did spill.
> *Aug.*, 60

Or it may mean that the lines are expected to have the same metrical requirement, regardless of the language—even if the language is distorted. Any one of these requirements is possible.

> s o s
> hey ho hollidaye.
> *Aug.*, 54

> o s s
> hey ho the fayre flock.
> *Aug.*, 118

> s o o
> hey ho hollidaye.
> *Aug.*, 54

> o o s
> hey ho the fayre flock.
> *Aug.*, 118

> o s o
> hey ho the Thonder.
> *Aug.*, 95

It may even be that both Willye's lines share with Perigot's lines
the basic requirement of four stresses, as John Erskine believed:

<blockquote>

s   s   s   s
It fell vpon a holly eue,

s   s s s
hey ho hollidaye,

s   s   s   s
When holly fathers wont to shrieve:

s   s   s   s
now gynneth this roundelay.[1]
</blockquote>

Aug., 53–56

In any case, the two speakers have different voices. Perigot's lines
are iambic with limited possibilities of variation. The language and
the metrical pattern are closely adjusted to one another. However
Willye's lines are read, they do violence to one element: either the
language refuses to take account of a metrical order, or the metrical
order refuses to consider the pattern of sounds of the language. The
concurrence of the two voices leads some readers to describe the
whole poem as 'rough.' Of course it is not. It must be the result of
calculation. The effect could be called 'musical,' but it is more than
that. Confronting the iambic line of Perigot with Willye's refrain
does produce a rather intricate pattern of sound. These sounds are
language, however. The 'music' is a distortion of the sounds of
language. The intonation is affected and thus the meaning is affected
by these distortions.

There is not very much meaning at stake here. Perigot's lines
organize carefully a few simple statements by balancing the intonations of the voice with an abstract pattern. Willye's lines, in one way
or another, throw that balance off, as his language itself, echoing
Perigot, throws off whatever responsibility to meaning Perigot may
have established.

<blockquote>
Per.   The glaunce into my heart did glide.

Wil.   hey ho the glyder.
</blockquote>

Aug., 93–94

The language and the metre conspire together to produce this nonsense. It is a deliberate conspiracy and it produces very cheerful
nonsense.

The *April* song, like that of *August*, is a mixture of lines modulated
by the demands of both language and metre and lines that must
outrage one if they are to satisfy the other. Unlike *August*'s song,
April's variety seems to assume no order. Nor does the disruption of

---

[1] John Erskine, *The Elizabethan Lyric*, New York, 1903, p. 110. The scansion
is Erskine's.

107

the original order serve the purpose of the song, as *August*'s does. The matter of *April* is as simple as that of *August*. It presents a number of attractive scenes of pretty things with pretty names, and it praises the Queen for her beauty. But the irregularities of the metres, disturbing the presentation of these things, add nothing to them as appropriate as Willye's bumptious foolishness was to *August*'s song.

The first stanza establishes a correspondence of the language to a metrical pattern of iambic lines of ten, four, and eight syllables.

> Ye dayntye Nymphs, that in this blessed Brooke
> doe bathe your brest,
> For sake your watry bowres, and hether looke,
> at my request;
> And eke you Virgins, that on *Parnasse* dwell,
> Whence floweth *Helicon* the learned well,
> Helpe me to blaze
> Her worthy praise,
> Which in her sexe doth all excell.
> *April*, 37–45

In the second stanza there is but one small departure, and that may be reconciled.

> o   s |o   s|o   s | o   s |o   s
> For shee is Syrinx daughter without spotte.
> *April*, 50

In speech, the stress pattern would be something like this: dáughter without spót. The line may be justified as presenting the substitution of an ionic foot |ooss| for two iambic, or the word *without* may be reconciled, theoretically, to the iambic pattern. Compounds such as *without*, *into*, are freely used in this way by Gascoigne, as though they were two monosyllables.

In the third stanza four lines have variations and these also may be reconciled to the metrical pattern as standard, permissible departures or as theoretically regular lines. Two lines have extra syllables,

> With Damaske ros*es and Daff*adillies set.
> *April*, 60

> And Prim*roses greene.*
> *Avril*, 62

One line probably reverses the order of stresses in the first foot, but it is another compound word.

> *Bayleaues* betweene.
> *April*, 61

The last line of the stanza has its quota of eight syllables, but in speech it would present only three noticeably strong stresses. If there are to be four, the metrical pattern must supply one of them. Theoretically it could be supplied so as to present a perfectly regular iambic pattern: no word would have its stress-pattern distorted. The pattern of the phrase would be distorted.

```
     o   s| o    s|  o    s|o s
Embellish the sweete Violet.
```
April, 63

Another reading would be somewhat closer to the normal phrase. It produces clashing stresses, and the purely metrical stress on the last syllable of *violet* remains:

```
     o   s| o    o   s  | s o s
Embellish the sweete Violet.
```

Again, in the fourth stanza occur lines which may be reconciled as more or less standard variations or poetic licences. The first line needs some help from the metrical pattern to get its five stresses. When the extra one is supplied, the most likely solution is a line of three trochaic feet and two iambs. The trochaic feet, it should be noted, are made of monosyllables, and thus are doubly acceptable.

```
  s   o| s   o|  s   o| o   s|o    s
Tell me, haue ye seene her angelick face.
```
April, 64

The fourth line has an extra syllable; like those in the two lines of the third stanza, it causes no important interference with the pattern of the line.

```
  o   o    s |  o    s
can you well compare.
```
April, 67

In the third line of the stanza, if the metrical pattern is to be satisfied there must be some adjustments made in the language. These can be covered by the standard poetic licences. *Heavenly* has its second syllable syncopated.[1] 'Haueour' seems to be subjected to diaeresis so that it has three syllables.

```
  o   s|  o  s|o s|  o   s |  o    s
Her heauenly haueour, her princely grace.
```
April, 66

---

[1] See above, p. 94. Spenser seems to have thought that *heaven* had only one syllable in speech, so that the licence in its use, according to him, was using it as two syllables: '*heaven*, being used shorte as one sillable, when it is in verse stretched out with a *diastole*, is like a lame dogge that holdes up one legge.' Letter, *Works*, IX, 16.

109

In the fifth stanza all the short lines which began as four-syllable lines, in the first stanza, have become five-syllable lines. The first line has a minor variation.

Again, in the sixth stanza all the short lines have five syllables, but they maintain easily the pattern of two relatively strong stresses. None of the other lines is perfectly regular. For the first time, some of the lines can be adapted to a requirement of five strong stresses only at considerable expense to their phrases, and with some uncertainty at best.

> Shewe thy selfe *Cynthia* with thy siluer rayes,
>   and be not abasht:
> When shee the beames of her beauty displayes,
>   O how art thou dasht?
> But I will not match her with *Latonaes* seede,
> Such follie great sorow to *Niobe* did breede.
>   Now she is a stone,
>   And makes dayly mone,
> Warning all other to take heede.
>
> *April*, 82–90

The extra syllable in the first line is no problem, and the metrical pattern easily supplies a strong stress to *with*. The fifth line departs from the pattern in two feet, but not widely. *Match her* may be iambic almost as well as trochaic. The extra syllable in the next foot is by now an expected variation.[1] The last line is irregular, but again it is a familiar set of variations. The fact that they occur together in one line is less familiar. The first foot is trochaic, and the last two feet combine in the way that can theoretically be considered to satisfy the metrical pattern, $\overset{o}{oth}|\overset{s|o}{er\ to\ take}\ \overset{s}{heed}$; or if it is considered that the metrical pattern itself here takes on a variation, it can be said that these two feet together form an ionic. It is the third line that causes trouble. It presents only four stresses that can qualify as representatives of metrical strong stresses.

$$\overset{s}{When}\ shee\ the\ \overset{s}{beames}\ of\ her\ \overset{s}{beauty}\ \overset{s}{displayes}.$$

In this case there is some justification for a strong stress on *her*: the *Queen's* beauty, contrasted to the moon's. Again, in the sixth line there is an excuse for the clashing stresses that must be present if there are to be five strong stresses in the line. The line has twelve syllables,

$$\overset{s}{Such}\ \overset{s}{follie}\ \overset{s}{great}\ sorow\ to\ \overset{s}{Niobe}\ did\ \overset{s}{breede}.$$

[1] Or may be scanned thus: But I will not $\overset{s}{match}$ her $\overset{s}{with}$ La$\overset{s}{to}$naes $\overset{s}{seede}$.

In the seventh stanza the longer lines all present some variation or other. But two of the shorter lines depart from their pattern widely. They have six syllables, and if they are read as the other short lines have been read, with the expectation of a generally iambic pattern, they present three stresses instead of two.

> She is my goddesse plaine,
> And I her shepherds swayne.
>
> *April*, 97–98

The eighth stanza has one line with ten syllables which receives five strong stresses but in a very irregular order, whichever possibility is selected.

> Bene they not Bay braunches, which they doe beare.
>
> *April*, 104

In the ninth stanza the shorter lines are again all of five syllables, and each clearly presents two relatively strong stresses. The long lines are all difficult. The first line has ten syllables, and places can be found for five strong stresses, but the syntax is distorted. The third line has only nine syllables, and there is no place for a fifth strong stress.

> $\quad$ s $\quad$ s $\quad\quad$ s $\quad\quad$ s
> They dauncen deffly, and singen soote.
>
> *April*, 111

The fifth line will receive five stresses, but there is no way to make them anything but extremely irregular.

> s $\quad\quad$ s $\quad$ s $\quad$ s $\quad\quad$ s $\quad$ s
> Wants not a fourth grace, to make the daunce euen?
> s $\quad\quad$ s $\quad\quad$ s $\quad\quad$ s $\quad$ s
> Wants not a fourth grace, to make the daunce euen?
>
> *April*, 113

The theoretical resolution in this line of monosyllables requires the distortion of more stresses than Spenser has allowed heretofore in this poem. The sixth line is also irregular. If it is to have five strong stresses, no location of them can avoid awkwardness.

> Let that rowme to my Lady be yeuen.
>
> *April*, 114

The tenth stanza has only lesser variations. In the remaining three stanzas many lines can be adjusted to their metrical patterns only with difficulty. Several of them present other arrangements of stresses so clearly that it is impossible to be certain that Spenser did not

111

mean to abandon the metrical pattern here, rather than to make extreme variations on it.

Three of the eight-syllable lines (two of them here with nine syllables) offer considerable resistance to an iambic metrical pattern.

Such for a Princesse bene principall.
April, 126
Shall match with the fayre flowre Delice.
April, 144

This line is supposed to rhyme with *Daffadowndillies*.

I will part them all you among.
April, 153

The longer lines, now of nine, ten, or eleven syllables, sound more like four-beat verses than like the kind of thing the poem began with.

Ye shepheards daughters, that dwell on the greene.
April, 127
Let none come there, but that Virgins bene.
April, 129
Strowe me the ground with Daffadowndillies.
April, 140
And Cowslips, and Kingcups, and loued Lillies.
April, 141
Now ryse vp *Elisa*, decked as thou art.
April, 145
I feare, I haue troubled your troupes to longe.
April, 149

Certainly these lines have variety; they are different. But they seem to serve no purpose. If the poem is an experiment, it is an experiment in progressive deterioration. The final state of disorganization casts doubt on the variations that occurred earlier in the poem. The earlier lines can be explained, but in the company of so much that cannot, are the explanations valid?

In *November*'s song the variations from the iambic structure of the lines rarely exceed the limits of later standard practice. The thirteen ten-line stanzas present only a handful of these variations, and they are readily classified. Only one stanza, the seventh, raises serious questions. There are two departures from the rhyme scheme. In the first stanza 'ryme' is supposed to rhyme with 'nyne.' The fifth stanza has an altered scheme: the fifth and ninth lines rhyme with the first and third, instead of with the second and fourth as they do in the

112

other stanzas. There are only five variations in the number of syllables to a line. One of these may be accounted for by elision, *now's* for *now is*:

> Now is time to dye. May time was long ygoe.
> *Nov.*, 81

The other lines with an extra syllable are these,

> The songs that Colin made *in her prayse*.
> *Nov.*, 78

> O Lobb, thy losse no long*er lament*.
> *Nov.*, 168

Only two lines appear to lack a syllable. One of them, as W. L. Renwick suggests, may get the syllable it needs if we consider what Spenser does elsewhere: *chaplets* he usually spells *chapelets*, and uses the *e* as a syllable.[1]

> The colourd chaplets wrought with a chiefe.
> *Nov.*, 115

The other line short by one syllable cannot be explained by this rather speculative interpolation. It simply lacks a syllable. The pattern of strong stresses is not disturbed. The number of strong stresses in the line is immediately apparent, and the line may gain some emphasis from its abruptness. But it is a departure from the metrical pattern maintained for this type of line in the rest of the poem.

> Dead and lyeth wrapt in lead.
> *Nov.*, 59

About one in ten of the lines have some variation in the pattern of stresses. Some of these can scarcely be called real variations; the metrical pattern simply lends a degree of stress to a syllable which would be not at all strongly stressed in speech, but which lies between two weak-stressed syllables; thus it receives the extra stress without really distorting the pattern of speech, and the metrical pattern is very easily satisfied. The lines are these:

> With cakes and cracknells *and* such country chere.
> *Nov.*, 96

> Her soule vnbodies *of* the burdenous corpse.
> *Nov.*, 166

[1] In *August*, 70, it seems to be used as a syllable, and perhaps in 69. Renwick cites also *Astrophel*, 42, and FQ IV, xi, 46, where the word has three syllables if it is intended to fit an iambic pattern (Renwick, *The Shepheard's Calender*, p. 222).

113

There is another of this kind, this one made somewhat more complicated by its position:

> Whence is it, that the flouret *of* the field doth fade.
>
> *Nov.*, 83

This is the first line of a stanza, which according to the metrical pattern should have twelve syllables and six strong stresses. In this particular line the stress is supplied exactly as in the iambic pentameter lines above, but it is easier here than it is in those lines to miss the fact that the pattern requires the addition of a stress. Even in *The Shepheardes Calender* the reader is generally more prepared to find a line with five strong stresses than he is for anything else. And there was that line in the third stanza with its extra syllable (there elided, possibly for formal reasons): *Now is time*. This makes it possible that the line could be mistaken, the reader could fail to note that a degree of stress must be supplied to *of*. But the mistake would be the reader's, in this case; and in this poem Spenser has the right to expect careful reading.

In three lines there is a kind of variation in which the language does not exactly meet the requirements of the metrical pattern, but can be reconciled to it at least theoretically. Variations like these need not distort the language, and need not break the metrical pattern. They are a standard device of English verse. As words, taken one by one, the language fits; as phrase, it does not; and the discrepancy is only in one foot to the line.

> The faded lockes *fall from* the loftie oke.
>
> *Nov.*, 125

> And flouds of teares *flowe in* theyr stead perforse.
>
> *Nov.*, 127

> She hath the bonds *broke of* eternall night.
>
> *Nov.*, 165

The position of these variations is also interesting. They come after the fourth syllable, and Spenser was undoubtedly thinking of that as the place of a pause, the caesura; a reversed foot there is only less common than at the beginning of the line, in the standard practice of verse. Again, Spenser has the right to expect that the careful reader will note these things. Having noted them, there is not much else to do; the technique meets the demands of technique, and those who appreciate techniques will like to see this.

The seventh stanza as a whole demands this kind of observation. Only the two six-syllable lines and two lines of refrain are quite obviously regular. In the other lines, either language or metrical pattern must be distorted. The entire movement of the language is not that of the metrical pattern. The first line is somewhat like that of the first line of the fourth stanza, noted above; it is most easily read as a line with five relatively strong stresses. But the adjustment required to get six strong stresses is much more severe. The syllable which must receive the extra degree of stress does not lie between two weak-stressed syllables, as it does in the line from the fourth stanza. Nor is its adjustment the only one the line requires. The line might sound like this, disregarding the metrical pattern.

O thou greate shepheard Lobbin, how great is thy griefe.

Nov., 113

A complete re-interpretation of the line is necessary, if it is not to remain extremely irregular. Only *how* can receive the extra strong stress if there is to be a semblance of the intonation of speech. *How great is thy griefe* may be an intensification of the more normal way of saying it. It is still a long way from the metrical pattern, farther than the structure of this poem seems to allow. To bring it closer is to destroy any intensified intonation gained by the stress on *how* and to transform the statement. It would no longer sound like something that could be said; at best it might be a sort of incantation, although word for word, quite theoretically, it is possible.

O thou greate shepheard Lobbin, how great is thy griefe.

The pattern is not restored at once. As I said, this is the first line of a stanza that demands a great deal of metrical interpretation. Two of its lines, the fifth and the ninth, are the most extreme departures of the entire poem. The way they depart, out of the necessity of the inherent stresses of some of their words, reinforces the tendency of the language of other lines in its resistance to the metrical pattern.

> O thou greate shepheard *Lobbin*, how great is thy griefe,
> Where bene the nosegayes that she dight for thee:
> The colourd chaplets wrought with a chiefe,
> The knotted rushrings, and gilte Rosemaree?
> For shee deemed nothing too deere for thee.
>   Ah they bene all yclad in clay,
>   One bitter blast blewe all away.
>   O heauie herse,
> Thereof nought remaynes but the memoree.
>   O carefull verse.

Nov., 113–122

I have noted above the suggestion that 'chaplets' might be read 'chapelets,' with the *e* as a syllable. If that suggestion is taken, the lines all have the number of syllables expected of them. This is important, because in this poem the number of syllables in a line tells what its place in the structure is. If the stress pattern is not immediately apparent, the number of syllables tells what it should be. The extra syllables in 78, and in 168, are not disturbing to their own lines, since the stresses are perfectly clear there. But they contribute to the possibility of misunderstanding other lines which might seem to have extra syllables but do not. If anapaestic feet are admitted to the poem, then the first line of this troublesome stanza, with its twelve syllables, could still be read as a five-stress line, in violation of the poem's structure. A line lacking a syllable is even more serious than the doubtful stresses. The structure of the poem depends on differences of two syllables in the length of lines: a line with an odd number of syllables falls between the boundaries. And lines short by a syllable, unlike lines with an extra syllable, necessarily present a different stress pattern. This need not be serious if the syllable that appears to be missing is the first in the line, as in *Dead and lyeth wrapt in lead* from the first stanza. But the ambiguity of 'chaplets' is a bad slip. Throughout the poem Spenser seems to be observing a principle: if the stress pattern is not perfectly regular, the number of syllables allows the structure of the line to be identified, and often allows a theoretical reconciliation of language and metre. 'Chaplets' comes at the worst possible place in the poem, and so do the fifth and ninth lines of this stanza. They are the only lines in the poem which cannot be reconciled to the metrical pattern. By themselves, and in another place, neither might seem too extreme; they would not endanger the structure of the poem. Here they do. They demand a trochaic movement.

| s o| s o |

For shee *deemed nothing* too deere for thee.

Nov., 117

| s o| s o |

Thereof *nought remaynes but* the memoree.

Nov., 121

This might appear to confirm the movement of the language in the other lines of the stanza. But if it does, the structure of the poem is broken. Lines of four stresses appear where they do not belong.

o s | o s | o o o s | o s

Where bene the nose*gayes that she dight* for thee:

Nov., 114

```
o   s   o      s e      s  |  o   o   s |
```
The colourd chaplets wrought *with a chiefe,*
Nov., 115

```
o    s   o   s | o      o    s |   o      s
```
The knotted rush*rings, and gilte* Rosemaree.
Nov., 116

The danger comes not only from the individual line and the echoes which seem to answer it in the stanza and in the poem. It comes from the entire *Shepheardes Calender* itself. There is too much variety. There are so many different ways of handling the different measures that the distinctions between them are not always clear. There is a justification for readers who believe that the four-beat measure intrudes sometimes among Spenser's pentameters, or that the pentameter line intrudes in the four-beat measures.[1] In *April's* song the question becomes not so much one of occasional intrusion as a dispute over ownership: the iambic pattern disappears in a series of four-beat lines. All this must necessarily reflect on the stanza of *November's* song. Its general structure is the most complex of all the poems in the *Calender.* Its looseness in detail at some points reflects again on the entire experiment of the book. The lack of control there raises the question of control in another sense; an experiment cannot have meaning without the presence of a control, a standard of comparison. Is there evidence in *The Shepheardes Calender* that Spenser knew what precise control of metrics can mean, and that his irregularities are departures from control and not attempts to reach it? Perhaps the brilliant play of Perigot's and Willye's song suggests it; but that song seems an isolated tour-de-force, not a base for further operations. Of course we can extend the context from line through stanza and poem and the entire book to the literature of Spenser's time, and say, as it has usually been said, that it is in the poetry of Gascoigne and his contemporaries that the control of the experiment lies. This may be true. I have argued that this metrical tradition was real. *November's* song, with its contrast to the anarchy of *April's,* almost provides the answer, but not quite.

4. *Pentameter Lines: August, April* (154–161); *January, April* (1–36), *June, August* (sestine), *October, November* (dialogue); *December*
    The many ten-syllable lines of the *Calender* give an idea of what Spenser may have regarded as a normal range of metrical variation, and what he used that variation for. In the poems (or the more or less self-contained parts of poems) made entirely of lines based on a ten-syllable metrical pattern, there are 699 lines. Of these, the poems

---

[1] Francis B. Gummere, for instance, classified lines within various poems as four-beat or pentameter. *American Journal of Philology,* VII, 63–70.

of one group are in slightly different degrees close to the metrical pattern. There are 451 lines in this group. The *August* dialogue and the last section of the *April* dialogue, together ninety-two lines, are so irregular that the pattern is in question. The *December* poem, 156 lines, lies between these two extremes. It has irregular lines but not without what seems to be a system.

The lines of dialogue that follow *April*'s song are the most doubtful in *The Shepheardes Calender*. There are only eight lines. Five of them have ten syllables, two have nine, one has eleven. Only one of the lines, the second, can easily be regular iambic pentameter; and one other, the seventh, can be if the phrases are allowed to suffer some distortion. The others will not fit at all. Perhaps the dialogue is really a version of the four-beat measure. Ten-syllable lines do not dominate in Spenser's long four-beat poems, and the first part of the *April* dialogue, before the song, is clearly iambic; but the keynote of the *Calender* is variety, not consistency.

Thenot
And was thilk same song of *Colins* owne making?
Ah foolish boy, that is with loue yblent:
Great pittie is, he be in such taking,
For naught caren, that bene so lewdly bent.

Hobbinol
Sicker I hold him, for a greater fon,
That loues the thing, he cannot purchase.
But let vs homeward: for night draweth on,
And twincling starres the daylight hence chase.
Apr., 154–161

There is no way to describe all these except to say that no two of them are alike. If we insist that the lines must share something besides their rhymes, then they will have to be four-beat, for some of them have no possibility of receiving five strong stresses. If we believe they should have as nearly as possible the same pattern as the rest of the *April* dialogue, they are very irregular indeed. I see no way to decide. We cannot say simply, Spenser meant them to be just what they are and that is all; what they are depends on what metrical pattern we apply. One might hope that Spenser meant us to remember the iambic pentameter of the beginning of *April*, and to read the lines with the iambic pattern in mind. That way they all go flat, so to speak: Hobbinol's second line gives up before it gets to the last syllable, the last strong stress; he is tired, perhaps bored, and it is time to go home. It would be a modern kind of thing in metre, not at all Spenserian. Just this once he may have tried it out; but I doubt if he really meant to.

118

The *August* dialogue is as irregular as these eight lines from *April*. It must have been a deliberate experiment, but we have only the results; from these it is hard to see exactly what the experiment was. At least one element is clear; all but about a half-dozen of the 84 lines have exactly ten syllables, or can easily be accommodated to ten syllables with the usual licences. This cannot be anything but intentional. But about the stresses, there is nothing at all consistent. It may be that Spenser intended only to count the syllables and let the stresses fall as they would. It may be he intended to present the experiment of a number of lines with ten syllables and five metrical stresses written so that the strong stresses would fall in a great variety of orders and would sometimes not fall at all, but would have to be pushed into the line at the expense of distorting the phrases. That is how the lines appear, if one tries to read them with five strong stresses. Or it may be that he intended to write ten-syllable four-beat lines. In that case also the metrical pattern will not apply without violence. The language of many lines does not co-operate at all.

Classification of the lines by either system becomes extremely arbitrary once the lines that fit easily are sorted out. If one seeks to read them all with five strong stresses apiece, there are thirteen lines which appear at once as regular iambic pentameter, lines like these:

> Ah *Willye*, when the hart is ill assayde.
> > *Aug.*, 5
>
> I pyne for payne, and they my payne to see.
> > *Aug.*, 18
>
> With mery thing its good to medle sadde.
> > *Aug.*, 144

Another dozen or so lines become regular with the easy addition of a degree of stress to some syllable lying between two weak-stressed syllables, as in these lines:

> That hath so raft vs *of* our meriment.
> > *Aug.*, 14
>
> How doleful*ly* his doole thou didst rehearse.
> > *Aug.*, 193

After that, classification means little. There are lines which offer five strong stresses, but in an irregular pattern; some of these lines may be reconciled to an iambic pattern theoretically, some may not.

> Ah *Willye* now I haue learnd a newe daunce.
> > *Aug.*, 11

  s   s   s   s s
Sike a song neuer heardest thou, but *Colin* sing.
Aug., 50

   s   s   s   s   s
My old musick mard by a newe mischaunce.
Aug., 12

   s   s   s   s   s
Of Beres and Tygres, that maken fiers warre.
Aug., 28

Still others refuse to accept the five strong stresses in any order.
With pyping and dauncing, didst passe the rest.
Aug., 10

And here with his shepehooke hath him slayne.
Aug., 34

Sicker make like account of his brother.
Aug., 43

Most of the lines present the possibility of five strong stresses, if
they can fall anywhere; at the same time they present the possibility
of four beats.

The loe *Perigot* the Pledge, which I plight:
A mazer ywrought of the Maple warre:
Wherein is enchased many a fayre sight
Of Beres and Tygres, that maken fiers warre:
And over them spred a goodly wild vine,
Entrailed with a wanton Yuie twine.
Aug., 25–30

This kind of verse stands in clear contrast to the ten-syllable verse
that is consistently iambic for hundreds of lines. Both stand in contrast to the slightly disordered lines of *December*.

Definite limits are observed in the verse of the first part of the
April dialogue, the *November* dialogue, the *August* sestina, *January*,
June, and *October*. There may be extra syllables in a line, although
there are none in the *April* or *November* dialogues, and very few in
the other regular poems. Most of these are feminine lines,

If any gods the paine of louers pitie,
Jan., 14

And bowe your eares vnto my dolefull dittie.
Jan., 16

A few have an anapaestic foot,

*To the wat*ers fall their tunes attemper right.
June, 8

Let breake your sounder sleepe and pit*ie augment*.
Aug., 189

120

January ends with one regular twelve-syllable line, and in the *August* sestina there is a twelve-syllable line that also appears to be deliberate. There are no lines lacking in a syllable in any of the poems of this group.

There are initial trochees, both those demanded by a word and those suggested by a phrase.

> *Quenching* the gasping furrowes thirst with rayne.
> > *Apr.*, 6

> *All in* a sunneshine day, as did befall.
> > *Jan.*, 3

The metrical pattern is often called upon to be satisfied with a weak stress falling between two other weak stresses where a strong stress is required.

> So faynt they woxe, and feeble *in* the folde.
> > *Jan.*, 5

> Him Loue hath wounded *with* a deadly darte.
> > *Apr.*, 22

> Accorde not *with* thy Muses meriment.
> > *Nov.*, 34

> Renne after haste*ly* thy siluer sound,
> > *June*, 61

> In rymes, in riddles, *and* in bydding base,
> > *Oct.*, 5

> The hollow Echo *of* my carefull cryes,
> > *Aug.*, 160

Here and there a word is allowed to reverse a foot, or the intonation of a phrase will do it occasionally.

> Should Colin make *iudge of* my fooleree,
> > *Nov.*, 28

> Then should my plaints, *causd of* discurtesee,
> > *June*, 97

Run-on lines are very scarce. There are only a few as clear as this,

> Well couth he wayle hys Woes, and lightly slake
> The flames, which loue within his heart had bredd.
> > *June*, 85–6

The regular line dominates. *January* is typical, and one stanza should serve to present its quality.

121

All so my lustfull leafe is drye and sere,
My timely buds with wayling all are wasted:
The blossome, which my braunch of youth did beare,
With breathed sighes is blowne away, and blasted,
And from mine eyes the drizling teares descend,
As on your boughes the ysicles depend.

Jan., 37–42

Here is a stanza of George Gascoigne's to put beside Spenser's.

The Sunny dayes which gladde the saddest wightes,
Yet never shine to cleare my misty moone:
No quiet sleepe, amidde the mooneshine nightes,
Can close mine eyes, when I am woe begone.
Into such shades my peevishe sorrowe shrowdes,
That Sunne and Moone, are styll to me in clowdes.[1]

The difference between the two stanzas is minute, yet it is larger here than it would be for most of the lines of this kind in *The Shepheardes Calender*. This stanza of Spenser's is not quite the average for *January*; it contains the only reversed foot in that poem. There are reversed feet in Gascoigne, too; plenty of them, as there are plenty of eleven-syllable lines; but he wrote many long poems which had none, and presumably he would have banished them all if it had not been a bother. There are a few in all the basically regular poems of *The Shepheardes Calender*, except the very short part of *April*. There is only one here, but *January* is short. They are all like this; only one such foot to a line, and they never disturb the easy recognition of the stress requirements of the line.

Thy Muse to long *slombreth* in sorrowing.

Nov., 3

Here wander may thy flock *early* or late.

June, 11

Such pleasaunce makes the Gras*hopper* so poore.

Oct., 11

Those are the conditions of Spenser's regularity. If *January*, *June*, *October*, the dialogue of *April* and *November*, can be seen as separate from the other kinds of verse in the *Calender*, and uncontaminated by them, this kind of regularity represents the control of the experiment. The metrical pattern is clear, and its relation to the language is very close to that described by George Gascoigne. Exactly how close it is impossible to say. For Gascoigne, the metrical pattern ruled the intonations of speech, but the intonations of speech were

[1] Gascoigne, *Works*, I, 40.

122

important too. The mother phrase was not to be distorted. The diction of *The Shepheardes Calender* is famous for its artifice, not for its resemblance to speech. Often it departs from speech not by its elegance but by its archaic 'rudeness.' At one extreme this produces the music of the *August* song. The stately sonorities of Spenser's later poetry are also made with a language somewhat removed from that of speech, but in another direction. In that way the two kinds of verse, very different in effect, have a similar basis in theory.

> All as the Sunny beame so bright,
>   hey ho the Sunne beame. . . .
> *Aug.*, 81–82

> Eftsoones the nymphes, which now had flowers their fill,
> Ran all in haste to see that silver brood. . . .[1]

In contrast to these are certain lines of a kind that can occur anywhere in *The Shepheardes Calender*, but seem to occur most often, most deliberately, and with the best results in *December*. In these lines, the reader is aware of the metrical pattern; it has been fully established by the domination of perfectly regular lines. The reader sees also that the metrical pattern is not exactly the same as the intonation of the language, but can be expected to add something to the language now and then, as it can add a strong stress to the phrase *of a bushye brere* in the second line below; or if not to add to the language as the line would be spoken, to be satisfied with the possibility.

> The gentle shepheard satte beside a springe,
> All in the shadowe of a bushye brere,
> That *Colin* hight, which wel could pype and singe,
> For he of *Tityrus* his songs did lere.
>   There as he satte in secreate shade alone,
>   Thus gan he make of loue his piteous mone.
> *Dec.*, 1–6

In the third stanza a new kind of line appears. There have been occasions before this when the phrases were not in themselves exactly iambic, especially at the beginning of lines. *There as he satte* can be read as iambic, if anyone should insist, but the phrase suggests something else. This particular line demands something else.

> Hearken awhile from thy greene cabinet.
> *Dec.*, 17

Hearken is of course a departure, and *from thy green cabinet*

[1] *Prothalamion*, 55–56.

certainly sounds like one. The first might be expected, the other is probably a surprise. Exactly what solution is made depends on the reader, but a solution is possible. If he wishes, he can read *from thy* green cabinet, or something in between the two, and maintain the metrical pattern, at the same time clarifying the rhyme with the next line,

> The rurall song of careful Colinet.
>
> *Dec.*, 18

'Greene cabinet' is Marot's *verd cabinet*,[1] a decorative oddity; it may be worth the attention it receives by its metrical position, as a decoration. The main point it makes is that the metrical pattern need not be always and exactly in correspondence with every phrase. Other lines like this appear:

> Why liuest thou stil, and yet hast thy deathes wound?
>
> *Dec.*, 95

The sixteenth stanza presents a concentration of slight metrical departures. Its last line is remarkable for its variation.

> And thus of all my haruest hope I haue
> Nought reaped but a weedye crop of care:
> Which, when I thought haue thresht in swelling sheaue,
> Cockel for corne, and chaffe for barley bare.
> Soone as the chaffe should in the fan be fynd,
> All was blowne away of the wauering wynd.
>
> *Dec.*, 121–126

The sentiment is familiar enough by this point. It has been repeated many times, in *January* and in this poem, over and over again.

> Thus is my sommer worne away and wasted,
> Thus is my haruest hastened all to rathe:
> The eare that budded faire, is burnt and blasted,
> And all my hoped gaine is turnd to scathe.
> Of all the seede, that in my youth was sowne,
> Was nought but brakes and brambles to be mowne.
>
> *Dec.*, 97–102

> My haruest wast, my hope away dyd wipe.
>
> *Dec.*, 108

> Theyr rootes bene dryed vp for lacke of dewe.
>
> *Dec.*, 111

[1] Clement Marot, *Oeuvres*, ed. Georges Guiffrey (Paris, 1875–1931), 'Eglogue au Roy,' II, 286.

The stanza looks better in isolation than it does in the company of this repetition, which accumulates without progressing, and, according to Spenser's usual practice, suffers from a random kind of generalization which always seems to come at the wrong time.

> Thus is my haruest hastened *all* to rathe.
> *Dec.*, 98
> And *all* my hoped gaine is turnd to scathe.
> *Dec.*, 100

This is Sackville's *all*; it serves to cover anything that may have been left out in the catalogue, or it serves, sometimes, as an intensive modifier, according to the Elizabethan practice.[1] But this last purpose is largely defeated by the frequent use of the word, which is so convenient metrically; it is one of those monosyllables that can easily accept either the stronger or weaker stress, and, meaning so little, it can come in nearly anywhere:

> The gentle shepheard satte beside a springe,
> All in the shadowe of a bushye brere.
> *Dec.*, 1–2
>
> the while the rest
> Vnder the tree fell all for nuts at strife.
> *Dec.*, 34–35

Spenser, however, does not go to the extremes of Sackville:

> In blacke *all* clad, there fell before my face
> A piteous wight, whom woe had *al* forwaste,
> Furth from her iyen the cristall teares outbrast,
> And syghing sore her handes she wrong and folde,
> Tare *al* her heare that ruth was to beholde.
> Induction, 73–77

It may seem for one moment of speculation, as though the other lines in the poem served only as preparation for this one stanza; almost, indeed, as if the entire *Calender* had this purpose. It is true that the sentiment would profit by facing the world alone, but the metrical preparation was necessary. The iambic line has to be recognized as a force to be granted sway wherever possible, as it is in *January, April, June, November, October*; then the possibility of variations is established in *December*, with no great immediate purpose—until we reach this stanza. Here the run-on of the first line, the abrupt initial trochee of the fourth, begin to arouse attention, but not too much. 'When I thought haue thresht' is probably rather

---

[1] E. A. Abbott, *A Shakespearian Grammar* (London, 1871), p. 37.

a crude way of dropping a syllable. There may be some lack of clarity about whether it was the crop or the threshing or both that was so unsatisfactory. The interest is still in the slight metrical departures; but the next-to-last line must not depart. It must be iambic, not

$$\overset{o}{\quad}\overset{o}{\quad}\overset{s}{\quad}$$
Soone as the chaffe should *in the fan* be fynd.

Dec., 125

Except for one line four stanzas later which confirms this line, the last line of the stanza is the most irregular in all the poems of this group:

All was blowne away of the wauering wynd.

All was seems familiar; like *All in the shadowe*, line two. But it cannot be only a simple initial trochee. Probably we shall read it like this: *All was blowne away.* . . . This pattern has not occurred before. The next foot may be anapaestic, for that has a precedent,

$$\overset{\sigma}{\quad}\overset{o\ s}{\quad}$$
For ylike to me was libertee and lyfe.

The line may even have two of these feet, although that would be unprecedented in this entire group of poems. This would give it eleven syllables, and ten is the normal number. Perhaps *wauering* should be *wau'ring*, as *soveraigne* is *sov'raigne* in line seven. The line would then have to come out this way:

$$\overset{s}{\quad}\overset{o}{\quad}\overset{s}{\quad}\overset{o}{\quad}\overset{s}{\quad}\overset{o}{\quad}\overset{s}{\quad}\overset{o}{\quad}\overset{s}{\quad}$$
All was blowne away of the wau(e) ring wynd.

It can be spoken, and the way it must be spoken rescues even Spenser's *all* from its usual emptiness. The line has a quality not possessed by the other lines with the same sentiment,

My timely buds with wayling all are wasted. . . .
My haruest wast, my hope away dyd wipe. . . .

Because it can be spoken, and the demands of speech do not exactly fit the metrical pattern, the reader who is aware of the metrical pattern established by the other lines must grant some attention to this line. When the attention is given, it is rewarded. There is none of that disappointment that Coleridge said could be in these cases 'like that of leaping in the dark from the last step of a staircase, when we had prepared our muscles for a leap of three or four.'

But it would be too fanciful to call this the record of a great deliberate poetic achievement. Finally, Spenser's variety, and his experiments, do not really add up to anything coherent. Nobody can be sure that *December* was the last of the *Calender* poems to be written. And Spenser can be disappointing enough, even in *December*. Most of it sounds exactly like George Gascoigne.

> The carefull cold hath nypt my rugged rynd. . . .

There are even times when all the twisted iambs of the 1550's and 1560's sound again:

> The loser Lasse I cast to please nomore,
> One if I please, enough is me therefore.

If Spenser's experiments were intended to find a viable method of escape from this, they cannot be said to have been successful. He seems to have tried nearly everything in *The Shepheardes Calender*, but the experiments, where they can be understood, seem basically the same. In the ragged four-beat verse with its powerful metrical pattern, in the lyrics with too many variations, in the regularity of *January*, everywhere, I should say, except in the counterpoint of *August*'s song and the variations of *December*, some deep sacrifice is made in one of the two elements of metre. If there is a clear metrical pattern, the language of speech in one way or another is altered so that its controlling patterns of sound are weakened in order to give the metrical pattern the maximum sway; or the metrical pattern gradually fades out of hearing, as in the *April* song. Reducing the tension between the sounds of language and the symbols of sound in the metrical pattern, these poems reduce the possibilities of tension between the reality of experience represented by intonations of speech and the form of artifice. For all the variety of effects that Spenser gains, this is essentially the method of most poetry between Tottel's *Miscellany* and Sidney. Perhaps it freed Spenser for the great fantasy also framed 'to an olde rusticke language';[1] but in itself *The Shepheardes Calender* seems not the beginning of a new way in metre, but a turning round and round at a dead end.

[1] Sidney, *The Defence of Poesie* (1595), *Works*, III, p. 37.

V

Classical Metres

A FEW months before *The Shepheardes Calender* was published, Spenser was writing poems based on the adaptation of classical metres to English. This was an experiment more radical than any of those in the *Calender*. The metres of the *Calender* all appear to be made in one way or another of the familiar elements of stress, syllable, or both, together with rhyme. In the language of the time, they are all 'rimes.' The new experiment was 'versifying,' based on the elusive element of quantity.

For all that has been written about this episode, the exact nature of the experiment is still not completely known. Perhaps it never can be. But when what is known about it is placed in the perspective of the metrical history of the sixteenth century, the effect of the experiment can be seen, if not all its details. It appears to have been successful in ways that could not have been foreseen by the experimenters. Verses did not replace rhymes; but the attempt ended in the recognition of a new way of understanding and using the old metres of English. It accomplished what the experiments of *The Shepheardes Calender* could not do.

The history of the long movement that lay behind the experiment in classical metres is well known, and in general the fate the movement succumbed to is clear. This history does little to explain the importance of the experiment to English poetry; in fact it has probably helped to obscure that by appearing to explain what it does not. At best, it tells why the poets came to classical metres, but not what they found there or what they took away. This external history can be given very briefly. Some renaissance scholars had hoped to re-establish Latin as the language of poetry; but there existed also in the fifteenth century the idea that poetry in the modern tongues could be subjected to the discipline of Latin metres, as Latin had been to Greek. The movement had its followers throughout Europe, and the early Tudor Humanists took it up with enthusiasm in England. Cheke talked of it, and Ascham hoped that the 'rude beggerly ryming' of Chaucer, Wyatt, and Surrey would be supplanted by true verses. Verse might not be as glorious as oratory, but it had been one of the glories of Rome. Therefore it would help make England glorious too. As successor to these men, Gabriel Harvey had the same hope. He was the first to receive any encouragement of it, for no English poets of ability responded to the idea until, as Spenser wrote to Harvey in October, 1579, Philip Sidney and Edward Dyer 'proclaimed in their ἀρείῳ πάγῳ a generall surceasing and silence of balde Rymers, and also of the verie beste to.' They had 'prescribed certaine Lawes and rules of Quantities of English sillables, for English verse,' and Spenser reported that he was drawn to their faction.[1] Of what they may have produced, we have the two poems in Spenser's letters to Harvey,[2] eight poems in Sidney's *Arcadia*, two brief translations by Sidney, and one poem from a manuscript of his *Certaine Sonets*.[3] There were a few other English attempts in the 1580's and 90's: Stanyhurst's translations from the *Aeneid*, Webb's from Vergil's eclogues; Abraham Fraunce, protégé of Sidney, wrote a long poem in quantitative hexameters; Campion's *Observations in the Art of English Poesie* offered examples of quantitative verse and an argument for it. Echoes of the movement may appear in Milton's scorn of rhyme in the preface to *Paradise Lost*, but it is generally understood that the entire project has its epitaph in Samuel Daniel's *A Defence of Ryme* (1603). To him it was all pedantic nonsense: 'our vnderstandings are not to be built by the square of *Greece* and *Italia*. We are the children of nature as well as they.'[4] His verdict is surely right; what he says is only a statement of the course followed by the poets, even by Spenser and Sidney. 'Werre it not farre better to hold vs fast to our old custome, than to stand thus distracted with vncertaine Lawes....'[5] In a way the whole movement was an attempt to impose on the poets a system alien to English tradition and contrary to the very nature of the language. Few have ever been sorry it failed.[6]

[1] *Works*, X, 'The Prose Works,' p. 6.   [2] *Ibid.*, pp. 7, 16.
[3] The translations, Sidney, *Works*, II, 307. The poem was not printed until it appeared in *Works*, IV, 401.
[4] Samuel Daniel, *Poems and A Defence of Ryme*, ed. A. C. Sprague (London, 1959), p. 139.   [5] *Ibid.*, p. 149.
[6] The history of the movement is given in detail in J. E. Spingarn, *A History of Literary Criticism in the Renaissance*, 2nd ed. (New York, 1908), pp. 298 ff., *et passim*, and in J. W. H. Atkins, *English Literary Criticism: The Renascence* (London, 1947).

This is the general history of the Elizabethan interest in classical metres, and the judgment upon it. Why Gabriel Harvey was interested one can understand, and in a general way it is easy to see what was wrong with the programme. But why Spenser and Sidney were so interested is another matter, and it may be that for them the experiment was not really a failure. It seems likely that their work in classical metres contributed to a new understanding of the kind of metre they inherited, and a new employment of it. The 'old custom' Daniel was upholding was not as old or as simple as he seems to be saying. Much of the metrical system he used had existed only in fragments before 1580.

As with many questions of metre, the central difficulties about the classical metres of Spenser and Sidney are due not to any misunderstanding of the metrical patterns involved, but to misunderstandings of the language. The metrical patterns were those of Latin verse; these would have been clear to Sidney and to Spenser.[1] For the hexameter, the pattern consisted of feet in which an abstract unit called a long syllable was joined with another of the same kind or with two abstract units called short syllables. When the Roman poets ordered their language to correspond with this pattern of abstract elements, they found similar elements in the language, syllables generally recognized as long or short. These they could arrange to correspond to the abstract longs and shorts, and to these elements found in the language they could add other elements which for purposes of verse they could use in the same way, the syllables which were long 'by position,' as it has generally been described.[2]

The trouble was that in English there was then, as there is now, a terrible confusion about 'long' and 'short' sounds in the language. The words are used to refer to the very different things of vowel quality and to actual duration of sound. Our dictionaries commonly call the vowels and diphthongs of *bate, beet, bite, boat, Butte* 'long a, long e, long i, long o, long u,' and the vowels of *bat, bet, bit, bought, but,* 'short a, short e, short i, short o, short u.' Of course, this has nothing to do with quantity, with duration. But the confusion exists in all literary studies of English quantitative verse.[3] It creeps into

[1] T. W. Baldwin, *William Shakspere's Small Latine & Lesse Greeke* (Urbana, Ill., 1944), v. II, chapter XLI, 'Upper Grammar School: Shakspere's Exercise of Versifying,' pp. 380–416.

[2] The description of classical metres, one hears, is about to be revised by new linguistic discoveries.

[3] K. B. McKerrow, 'The Use of So-called Classical Metres in Elizabethan Verse,' *The Modern Language Quarterly*, IV (1901), 172–180, and V (1902), 61–63; T. S. Omond, *English Metrists* (Tunbridge Wells, 1903); Enid Hamer, *The Metres of English Poetry* (London, 1930); G. D. Willcock, 'Passing Pitefull Hexameters,

studies useful to the inquiry into the nature of the Elizabethan experiments and makes them less useful than they might be.[1] English vowels and their syllables do vary in duration, in actual quantity, but not in a way that distinguishes them from one another; quantity is phonetic in our language, but not phonemic. *Dies* and *bees* are longer than *died* and *bead*, which are longer than *dike* and *beak*. The actual duration of the vowel or diphthong varies with its phonetic environment; it has nothing to do with the difference between the vowel of *beet* and the vowel of *bet*. (Of course, this does not mean that a poet couldn't use that difference as a principle of his poetry, if he really wanted to, and didn't mind being hard to follow.)

For their exercises in Latin verse, Sidney and Spenser would have had the quantities of syllables explained in their school texts, the authorized grammar book or some similar work.[2]

It is impossible to say what elements in English they found to use in correspondence with the metrical elements of 'long' and 'short.' The 'certaine lawes and rules of quantities of English sillables for English verse' are lost. The clues provided by the letters between Spenser and Harvey are by no means clear, and the clues offered by their surviving verse in these metres seem inconsistent in a rather brief examination. Supposing the verses of Sidney were all written according to the same rules, they might be deciphered—if someone had an exact knowledge of the pronunciation of Sidney's dialect, observed a due consideration for any conventions of pronunciation Sidney might have used in this verse, and kept this in mind as he classified the several thousand syllables Sidney used, according to the place each has in the metrical pattern and in the context of the language. In the meantime, the exact system followed in this verse is unknown. But before considering the verse itself for such conclusions as can be drawn without a complete understanding of it, the comments in the letters of Spenser and Harvey and a few words by Sidney must be examined.

A Study of Quantity and Accent in English Renaissance Verse,' *The Modern Language Review*, XXIX (1934), 1–19; 'Gabriel Harvey,' J. C. Maxwell, *Essays in Criticism*, I (1951), 185–188.

The best study is G. L. Hendrickson, 'Elizabethan Quantitative Hexameters,' *Philological Quarterly*, XXVIII (1949), 237–260.

[1] As for instance, Kökeritz, *loc. cit.* Kökeritz uses 'long' and 'short' to mean both actual duration of sound and difference in quality, and shifts from one meaning to the other without warning. Thus, he apparently believes that duration of sound was distinctive in Elizabethan English, which would be very interesting in connection with the quantitative poems if one could be sure the belief did not arise at least partly from this confusion of terms.

[2] Baldwin, *loc. cit.*, *passim*. Baldwin reproduces as end-papers two pages of such *Prosodia*. See also Harvey's letter, quoted below.

It may be impossible to be absolutely certain what Spenser meant by 'long' and 'short,' but it seems plain that he regards quantity as something that can be used conventionally in verse; a 'long' in verse need not correspond to anything 'long' in the language. The Latin rules of position can make an English syllable 'long.' It seems also that he thinks there are naturally 'long' and 'short' syllables in the language, and he may be saying that strong-stressed syllables in speech are 'long,' weak-stressed 'short,' and that this is the measure of 'Accentes,' applicable to speech—while the measure of 'Quantitie,' reserved for verse, is not strictly dependent upon stress:

> For the onely, or chiefest hardnesse, whych seemeth, is in the Accente; whych sometime gapeth, and as it were yawneth ilfauouredly, comming shorte of that it should, and sometime exceeding the measure of the Number, as in *Carpenter* the middle sillable being vsed shorte in speache, when it shall be read long in Verse, seemeth like *a lame Gosling that draweth one legge after hir*: and *Heauen*, beeing vsed shorte as one sillable, when it is in Verse stretched out with a *Diastole*, is like *a lame Dogge that holdes vp one legge*. But it is to be wonne with Custome, and rough words must be subdued with Vse. For why, a Gods name may not we, as also the Greekes, haue the kingdome of oure owne Language, and measure our Accentes by the sounde, reseruing the Quantitie to the Verse?[1]

It appears that Spenser is using 'long' and 'short' without any particular thought of duration, but rather as Gascoigne used these words interchangeably with other terms for accent or stress: 'remembre to place every worde in his natural *Emphasis* or sound, that is to say in such wise, and with such length or shortnesse, elevation or depression of sillables, as it is comonly pronounced or used.' Spenser is saying that in speech 'long' and 'short' mean degrees of stress, but in verse they need not necessarily mean that. The poet can place his words not according to their 'natural *Emphasis* or sound' but according to a convention made by the poet.

At first Harvey seems to agree with him, and says that this is exactly what the classical poets did; but then he suggests that the 'longs' and 'shorts' of the spoken language itself were influenced by the conventions established in poetry.

> In which respecte, to say troth, *we Beginners* haue the start, and aduauntage of our Followers, who are to frame and conforme both their Examples, and Precepts, according to that President which they haue of vs: as no doubt Homer or some other in *Greeke*, and *Ennius* or I know not who else in *Latine*, did preiudice, and ouerrule those, that followed them, as well for the quantities of syllables, as number of feete, and the like: their onely Examples going for current payment, and standing in

[1] Spenser, *Works*, X, 16.

steade of Lawes, and Rules with the posteritie. In so much that it seemed a sufficient warrant (as still it doth in our Common Grammer Schooles) to make τῑ in τιμή, and *V* in *Vnus* long, because the one hath τίμή δ'ἐκ διός ἐστί, and the other, *Vnus homo nobis*, and so consequently in the rest.[1]

Later, Harvey changes his mind. 'Position neither maketh shorte nor long in oure Tongue.' Here it is plain that Harvey means by short and long the different degrees of stress. 'Say you *suddāinly*, if you list: by my *certainly*, and *certainty* I wil not.'[2]

But in neither place does the essential difference of opinion between Harvey and Spenser come to the surface. Spenser is not proposing to change English speech: he believes we should 'measure our Accentes by the sounds.' He is talking about the adaptation of speech to the metrical pattern, insisting that the two things are different, and that the difference may be preserved in a line of verse by observing certain conventions, 'reseruing the Quantitie to the Verse.' Harvey takes exactly the position of George Gascoigne. Metrical pattern and language must coincide perfectly. When, in the first place, he believes poets have the right to use a sound 'short' in speech as 'long' in verse, he thinks that this will actually make the speech sound 'long,' will transform the language. For the moment, he thinks this is all right. Then he decides that he does not want the normal pronunciation changed. He never sees the possibility of 'reseruing the Quantitie to the Verse,' of using language so that it will fit the metrical pattern by convention but not in actual sound. He does not understand the independence of metre and speech.

Sidney's comments on verse and rhyme in *The Defence of Poesie* do little to make clear his position on this matter of quantity. He seems to be saying that quantity is more a matter of actual sound than of convention, but what quantity consists of is not quite clear. At first it is separated from stress, 'accent,' and is said to involve duration, being like the 'time' of music. But then it is related again to stress, when he says that the 'accent' of French and Spanish makes it difficult for them to use dactyls. And the old confusing idea of 'low' and 'high' syllables comes in too.

Now of versefying, there are two sorts, the one aunciend, the other moderne. The auncient marked the quantitie of each sillable, and according to that, framed his verse: The moderne, observing onely number, with some regard of the accent; the chief life of it, standeth in that like

---

[1] *Ibid.*, 464. The accents in the Greek text follow Harvey's usage as given in this source.
[2] *Ibid.*, 474.

sounding of the words, which we call Rime.[1] Whether of these be the more excellent, wold bear many speeches, the ancient no doubt more fit for Musick, both words and time observing quantitie, and more fit, lively to express divers passions by the low or loftie sound of the well-wayed sillable.... Truly the English, before any Vulgare language, I know is fit for both sorts: for, for the auncient, the *Italian* is so full of Vowels, that it must ever be combred with *Elisions*. The *Duch* so of the other side with Consonants, that they cannot yeeld the sweete slyding, fit for a Verse. The *French* in his whole language, hath not one word that hath his accent in the last sillable, saving two, called *Antepenultima*; and little more hath the *Spanish*, and therefore verie gracelessly may they use *Dactiles*. The English is subject to none of these defects.[2]

The verse of Spenser, Harvey, and Sidney is as obscure as their comments, as far as quantity goes. All three use the Latin laws of position, but without consistency. As for 'natural' quantity, it is impossible to say what they thought they were using there. They certainly do not follow the 'long *a*, short *a*' notion, as modern commentators have assumed they should have. They definitely do not use strong stresses as indicators of 'long' syllables. Harvey seems finally to say this is what should be done, but he does not do it in his verses.

About quantities, a few more words, and that incomprehensible subject can be forgotten. Here I draw on a useful study of these verses in *The Metres of English Poetry* by Enid Hamer.[3] Mrs. Hamer apparently believes that quantity ought to be determined on the principles of 'long *a*, short *a*,' but she does succeed in demonstrating the lack of consistency in what these poets use as 'short' and 'long.' She scans Spenser's elegiacs[4] thus:

$$- \; u \; u \quad - \quad - \quad - \; u \, u \quad - \quad - \quad - \; u \, u \quad - \; u$$
See yee the| blindefould|ed pretie| God that| feathered| Archer
      ⌣   ⌣

$$- \quad - \quad - \; u \, u \quad - \quad - \quad u \; u \quad - \; u \; u \quad -$$
Of Lou| ers Miser| ies|| which maketh| his bloodie| Game

---

[1] A few sentences farther on, he is less diffident about 'accent'; 'Now for Rime, though we doo not observe quantitie, yet wee observe the Accent verie precisely.'

[2] Sidney, *Works*, ed. Feuillerat, III, p. 44. One MS of *Arcadia* contains a dialogue on verses and rhymes which echoes this passage. It has nothing more illuminating about quantity. It is printed in Sidney's *Arcadia*, R. W. Zandvoort (Amsterdam, 1929), pp. 11–12.

[3] Enid Hamer, *The Metres of English Poetry*, London, 1930, 294 ff.

[4] Alternate dactyllic hexameter and dactyllic pentameter:

(1) – uu | – uu | – uu | – uu | – uu | u
    – – | – – | – – | – – | | – –

(2) – uu | – uu | – | – uu || – uu| –
    – – | – – | | || |

```
—   u  u   —    —    —  u  u   —    —    —  u  u  —  —
Wote ye why| his Mooth| er with a| Veale hath| coouered|his face
                        ⌣                         ⌣
```

```
—    —    —   u  u   —     — u u    —    u  u  —
Trust me| least he my| Looue|| happely| chaunce to be|holde.
```

She notes what Harvey noted in a letter to Spenser, and asks 'why "he" and "ye," "why" and "my" are short, while "me" is long, and why the first syllables of "feathered" and "Mother" are long when "with" is short, and why "love" and the first syllable of "covered" are long.' She finds similar inconsistencies in Sidney, who uses 'Oh' and 'nye' as long, 'so' and 'I' short, and so on, and in the verses of Harvey. Thus, if quantity did mean anything consistent to these men, we do not know what it was.

The important thing is that whatever they may have been using for 'longs' and 'shorts,' it was not stress; but having formed their feet of these other mysterious elements, they then had to take account of stress. Here a study by G. L. Hendrickson is of great value.[1] Fortunately Mr. Hendrickson is not much concerned with quantity. He simply scans the verse without worrying about true or false quantities, and then considers the metrical stress or *ictus* that falls on the first syllable of each foot in the hexameter, seeing whether or not this coincides with the speech-stress. He finds it often does not, in the verse of Harvey and of Sidney. He concludes that they constructed and scanned their verse in quantitative feet, and were quite aware of the metrical stress on the first syllable of each foot; but they *read* the verse with the normal pronunciation of words. This followed the practice of the time in reading Latin verse, and the verse Sidney constructed on these principles is actually a very close reproduction of the verse of Vergil. Sidney observes the principles of the caesura carefully, and usually avoids the coincidence of metrical stress and speech stress patterns in the first four feet of his hexameters, while regularly causing it to coincide in the last two feet, after the Latin practice. Mr. Henrickson cites the following lines. He has marked the metrical *ictus* beneath the line, and the strong stress of the language above the line. The dotted bars mark caesura. 'It will be noticed,' he says, 'that whether the lines are scanned (.) or are pronounced by Latin or English normal accents ('), the correspondence is essentially complete between each group.'[2]

---

[1] G. L. Hendrickson, 'Elizabethan Quantitative Hexameters,' *Philological Quarterly*, XXVIII (1949), pp. 237–260.
[2] *Ibid.*, 246.

                         better it is to be private
in sórrowes:tórment: than tíed to the pómpes of a pállace
  .   .   .   .   .

inténdunt   :scándit : fatális máchine múros
  .   .   .   .   .

nurse ínward: máladies: which have not scope to be breath'd out
  .   .   .   .   .

in cáelum   : scópuli : qúorum sub vértice láte
  .   .   .   .   .   .

thát to my adváncement: their wísdomes háve me abásed
 .   .   .   .   .   .

párs stupet innúptae   : domum éxitíale minérvae
 .   .   .   .   .   .

dréad not a whít: O góodly crúell: that pítie may enter
  .   .   .   .   .   .

quíd tibi núnc   : miseránde púer: pro láudibus ístis.
  .   .   .   .

If Mr. Hendrickson is correct, as he seems to be, he has shown that
one principle employed in the classical metres was the opposition of
the metrical pattern used to construct the verses and the corresponding elements of sound in the language. Furthermore, the opposition
was not simply negative, the result of ignoring the stress pattern of
the language, but it was a carefully planned opposition. The element
of sound, speech-stress, was deliberately put in position relative to
its abstract simulacrum, the metrical strong-stress or *ictus*. The two
were recognized as different and independent of one another, and
yet necessarily the location of the abstract element influenced the
location of the element of sound in the actual line of verse. The verse
was scanned one way and read another. Even if Mr. Hendrickson's
conclusions about the prominence of the metrical *ictus* in classical
verse are doubted, or its recognition by the Elizabethan is doubted,
the conclusion about the relation of the metrical pattern and the
sound-patterns of the language in the structure of the line of verse
must remain the same. For the structure by quantity, whatever
quantity may have been, was not based on a complete correspondence
of metrical pattern and language. Here the testimonies of the prose
comments of Spenser and of the verse itself are at one, so far as they
can be deciphered. The system is really new to English. It is not
simply the introduction of a few new kinds of feet, the novelty that
Gascoigne had coveted. With this in mind, it is easy to understand
why Spenser was so excited when he saw what Sidney was doing. He
had done enough experimenting in *The Shepheardes Calender* to
recognize that this experiment was of fundamental importance. Here

neither metrical pattern nor language had to give up their own order to be joined in a line of verse; the actual structure of the language could be controlled by the symbolic structure of the metre, yet a difference between the two could still be apparent.[1] When he encountered the versifying of Sidney, Spenser had already begun *The Faerie Queene*; perhaps its metre and style were already clear to him. In *The Shepheardes Calender* he had written a few lines which took full advantage of the attention demanded by wide departures from an established metrical pattern:

> All was blowne away of the wauering wynd.

Beyond this there is only conjecture. But consider one line, somewhat after the method of Mr. Hendrickson in marking the classical hexameters. Of course this is Spenser, and I cannot mark with any confidence how the entire sentence might be said in the normal course of speech. The phrasing is deliberately out of that normal course; Spenser did not say 'The woods shall answer to you'; he says, 'The woods shall to you answer,' and makes us listen to the sound of the line and not simply respond to what it says. But also troubling the sounds of speech, changing them from only what is said to another kind of sound, is the metrical pattern. If they did not still have something of the order of speech, the sounds could fit that pattern perfectly. As it is, they fit closely enough to assure us that every sound is exactly where it should be, according to an order which is yet not

---

[1] As I read Spenser's 'Iambicum Trimetrum' or Sidney's classical verses like 'Fayre Rockes, goodly Rivers,' they are very successful English poems, but this is not my point in this chapter. I cannot manage a scansion by quantities of the iambic trimeters; perhaps it increases the pleasure one finds in the lines to know that there was behind them some system, however inscrutable it may be. But they appear on their own terms as free lines with about five relatively strong stresses each, in a peculiarly easy and relaxed phrasing, full of repetition and charming detail. This direct and fluent language seems to me far superior to anything in *April* or *November*.

> Vnhappie Verse, the witnesse of my vnhappie state,
> Make thy selfe fluttring wings of thy fast flying
> Thought, and fly forth vnto my Loue, whersoeuer she be:
> Whether lying reastlesse in heauy bedde, or else
> Sitting so cheerelesse at the cheerfull boorde or else
> Playing alone carelesse on hir heauenlie Virginals.
> If in Bed, tell hir, that my eyes can take no reste;
> If at Boorde, tell hir, that my mouth can eate no meate:
> If at hir Virginals, tel hir, I can heare no mirth.
> *Works*, X, p. 7.

Sidney's classical verses seem more in his usual style, one of the styles, at least, of the *Arcadia*; a nervous, ingenious, yet strangely languorous monotony. Quotation cannot represent it fairly, for its effect is cumulative.

quite the same as only the order of the sounds themselves. Two
kinds of sounds join here; one of them accommodates itself to the
other, yet each retains some part of its separate identity. These things
together are the famous music.

> The woods shall to you answer and your Eccho ring.
>
> 'Epithalamion,' *Works*, VIII, 242

VI

Sir Philip Sidney

In Sidney's poetry the metrical system of modern English reaches perfection for the first time. Everything that has been fragmentary before is fully realized. The technical details of the relation of language to the metrical pattern are settled in the form they were for centuries to keep (or consciously to depart from), in poem after poem so fluent that the achievement seems effortless.

The English metrical pattern formed of the simulacra of strong-stressed and weak-stressed syllables was long inherent in the language, but only since the time of Gascoigne had it been clearly recognized as something that could also be thought of apart from the language. This pattern was recognized by Sidney and used by him in two ways. Both were triumphs, but the first was only partial and he abandoned it. The second is what everyone after him has always grown up knowing.

In the poems of the *Arcadia*,[1] Sidney brings to perfection the exact, regular correspondence of features of the language to the same features in the metrical pattern. He does this with a thoroughness of organization unknown before in modern English. His measures are far more varied, more intricate, and more precisely observed in detail than those of any poet before him. This organization alone brought new possibilities of significance to the language of poetry. Sidney's rhetorical genius, his psychological insight, and his virtuoso powers of sustaining and augmenting what he had begun, gave this kind of metrical organization a dimension it had never had before.

[1] Sir Philip Sidney, *Complete Works*, ed. A. Feuillerat (Cambridge, 1922–1926). This edition is unsatisfactory, since it is based on first editions rather than on the most authoritative and complete editions. The variations are collated, but the poems are scattered throughout the four volumes, some appearing in whole or in part only among the textual notes. An edition of Sidney's poems is badly needed.

In the sonnets of *Astrophel and Stella*,[1] he moved into another way of using the English metrical system. Here he uses the language in relation to the metrical pattern no less exactly than he did in the *Arcadia* poems; every syllable matters just as much as it did there; but the relation of the syllable of language to its simulacrum in the metre is more formal, more a matter of technical agreement. A convention has been completely established, and within its limits, the language can count for more than ever before. The metrical control allows the full sense of the difference between the metrical pattern and the language to become plain. The art of poetry achieves the degree of sophistication that allows it to recognize its own limitations; for it is seen that speech is one thing and metre another, although the two must meet. With this recognition, the basic resources of the language can be exploited, not as the order of rhetoric but as the order of speech, and consciously so. In Sidney's poetry, this recognition leads to wit. His wit produces frequently in his verse the effect of irony, a light, perhaps only wry irony, but it is enough to make him the master of more than one tone. With the ability to control and change the tone of his speech, he produces the effect of voices speaking, of drama. Through drama comes that effect as of the richness of experience—'Full, material, circumstantiated' as Lamb said—the effect that has misled most discussions of *Astrophel and Stella* into biography. Greater poets than Sidney, although perhaps not greater in sheer literary talent, soon used these resources to go far beyond any depth he ever reached. But he made the medium, and it began with metre.

Sidney's earliest poems may be the lines in *The Lady of May*, a masque performed in 1578. Next he wrote the *Arcadia* poems, probably between 1577 or 1578 and 1580, and probably also, the twenty-five poems printed in 1598 as 'Certaine Sonets.' In 1580 and 1581, it seems, he wrote *Astrophel and Stella*. His translations of the *Psalms* cannot be dated.[2]

[1] Sidney, *Astrophel and Stella*, ed. Alfred Pollard (London, 1888). This is based on the authoritative text of 1598.

[2] Dates are uncertain for particular poems. The *Psalms* are thought by Wallace, Sidney's biographer, to be late, but in some ways they resemble the earliest work in *The Lady of May*. There, as in the *Psalms*, Sidney indulges in that inversion Gascoigne abhorred, *That goddess mine* (*Works*, 2, 338); *He rests me in greene pasture his* (3, 214). He rarely does it elsewhere. Even the extravagant variety of form in the *Psalms* seems an early characteristic; no two of the forty-three Sidney translated have the same stanza. But see Hallett Smith, 'English Metrical Psalms,' *Huntington Library Quarterly*, XIX (1946), 269, for another opinion.

A note prepared for *Holinshed's Chronicles* by Edmund Molyneux, Sir Henry Sidney's secretary, before Sidney's death in 1586, states that Sidney began the *Arcadia* in the summer of 1577. (*Holinshed's Chronicles* [London, 1808], iv, 870.)

The verse in *The Lady of May* is pure Gascoigne in metre, with its
quatrain and couplet, and in language.[1]

> When wanton *Pan* deciv'd with Lions skin,
> Came to the bed, where wound for kisse he got,
> To wo and shame the wretch did enter in,
> Till this he tooke for comfort of his lot,
>   Poor *Pan* (he says) although thou beaten be,
>   It is no shame, since *Hercules* was he.[2]

To list all the forms of the *Arcadia* would be to describe nearly
every one of the eighty-three poems.[3] This is not the variety of *The*

If the poems in classical metres were all written at the same time, Spenser's
letter fixes the date for these as late as 1579.

A letter from Sidney to his brother Robert, October 1580, is generally taken
as referring to the *Arcadia*. 'My toyfull books I will send, with Gods helpe by
February . . .' (*Works*, iii, 132). Most of the poems may have been written before
the prose romance through which they are scattered.

The 'Certaine Sonets' appear in the Clifford MSS of the old *Arcadia*. (Feuillerat, *Works*, 4, vii.)

At the same time, Sidney may have been writing the sonnets of *Astrophel and
Stella*. Sonnet XXX, *Whether the Turkish new-moone*, echoes Sidney's letter to
Langust of October, 1580 (Pollard, *Astrophel and Stella*, 190). Sonnet XLI,
Having this day my horse, my hand, my launce, perhaps refers to a journey
arranged for the visit of the French ambassadors between April 15 and August,
1581. Sidney's Stella, Penelope Devereux, was married in September or October
of 1581; the marriage had been arranged in the spring of 1581. Most of the sonnets and songs of the sequence seem to refer to a time after the marriage. (The
material is assembled by Michel Poirier, *Sir Philip Sidney*, Lille, 1948.) Of course,
it is possible that Sidney did not think it dishonourable to write 'this day' at a
time other than the very evening of the tourney he was writing about. Perhaps
there was no tourney; poems are not diaries. But there was a Penelope, she did
have blonde hair and black eyes, she was once to marry Sidney, and she married
Lord Rich, in 1581.

[1] Poirier notes other resemblances to Gascoigne, p. 164.

[2] *The Complete Works of Philip Sidney*, ed. Albert Feuillerat (Cambridge,
1922), ii, 338.

[3] With a coarse sieve the poems may be sorted into these groups (I give the
number of poems in each group):
Sonnets, 21; Couplets, 11; Quatrain and couplet, 9; Sonnet-like, 8; Classical
measures, 8; Varied line-length stanzas, 6; Triple rhyme, 4; Triple rhyme and
internal rhyme, 3; Triple rhyme and couplets, 1; Sestina, 3; Two quatrains and
couplet, 2; Ottava rima, 2; Rhyme royal, 1; 'Crown,' 1; Poulters, 1; Miscel-
laneous, 2. The impossibility of a real classification can be seen when one realizes
that there are fourteen different types of sonnets among the twenty-one, and that
some of these differ again by having attached to them another short poem, or by
being linked in rhyme to another sonnet. There are twelve-syllable, ten-syllable,
and eight-syllable couplets; several different kinds of varied line-length stanzas;
three kinds of sestina; six kinds of classical measures.
Also, see Hallett Smith, 'English Metrical Psalms,' 269–270, for the variety of
forms in Sidney's translations of the *Psalms*.

Shepheardes Calender; it is not an experiment with the elements that form the measure (except for the classical metres). The most remarkable thing is not the variety, even the variety presented by the shifts of form within a poem, but the minute precision of the elements of metre. A difference of one syllable in the length of a line is not, as in Gascoigne, an indulgence; nor as in Spenser, a minor variation of obscure intent. There are no lines in the *Arcadia* poems with extra syllables except the feminine lines. These may be used in alternation with regular lines,[1] the entire poem may be made of them,[2] they may appear in pairs in the longer poems.[3] In some of the poems, the difference of a syllable marks a definite change in the measure.

One syllable can mark a change in the fantastically complex measures of some of the eclogues. *Come Dorus come,*[4] a singing match, begins in triple rhyme with lines of twelve syllables, for seventy-two lines. The last three syllables rhyme. It is a sort of double feminine line; the last two syllables are weak-stressed.

> Come *Dorus* come, Let Songes thy sorrowes signify,
> And, yf for want of use thy mynde ashamed ys,
> That very shame, with Loves hye tytle Dignify.
> No style ys helde for base, where Love well named ys.
> Eche eare suckes up the wordes a true Love scattereth,
> And playne speeche ofte, then quaynte phrase better framed ys.

The measure changes, for twenty-four lines, to eleven syllables.

> Once, a sweete once, I saw with Drede oppressed,
> Her whome I Drede, so that, with prostrate lying,
> Her Lengthe the earthe in Loves cheef Clothing dressed,
> I sawe the Richess falle, and fell a Cryinge,
> Lett not deade Earthe enjoy so deare a Cover,
> But Deck there with my sowle, for youre sake dyinge.

At line ninety-seven the measure becomes ten-syllables, and continues so for thirty-three lines.

> And yf enchauntement can a hard harte moove,
> Teache mee what Circle can acquaynte her spirite
> Affections charmes in my behalf to proove.
> The Circle ys my (Rounde aboute her) sighte
> The power I will Invoke dwelles in her eyes
> My Charme shoulde bee, shee haunte mee day and nighte.

---

[1] *Works*, II, 42.

[2] *Ibid.*, II, 91.

[3] *Ibid.*, I, 218, 294.

[4] *Ibid.*, IV, 54 ff. As is the case with nearly all the *Arcadia* poems, Feuillerat's text has to be corrected on the basis of his collations with manuscripts and the edition of 1596. I have made these corrections where necessary, and use them here without further notice.

At the 115th line the scheme changes to internal rhyme.

> Suche as yow see, suche still yow shall mee fynde,
> Constant, and kynde, my sheepe youre foode shall breede,
> Theyre woolle youre weede, I will yow musick yeelde,
> In flowery fielde, and as the day beginnes,
> With Twenty ginnes, wee will the smalle Byrdes take,
> And pastymes make. . . .

Again, at the 146th line the measure changes and the stanza is made of lines of ten syllables and lines of six, or eleven and seven. The last line of each stanza becomes the first of the next stanza.

> Thus dothe my Lyfe within yt self Dissolve,
>   That I growe like the Beaste,
> Which beares the Bit a weaker force doth guyde.
>   Yet pacyence must abyde.
> Suche weight yt hathe, whiche once ys full possest.
>
> Suche weighte yt hathe, whiche once ys full possest,
>   That I became a Vision,
> Whiche hathe in others hed his onely beeyng,
>   And lives in fancyes seeyng.
> O wretched state of man, in self Division.

The last twelve lines return to the twelve-syllable measure in a rhyme scheme resembling the original triple rhyme complicated with repetitions.

> Of singing take to thee the reputation
>   Good Lalus myne, I yeeld to thy habilitie;
> My harte doth seeke an other estimation.
>   But ah my Muse I would thou hadst agilitie,
> To worke my Goddesse so by thy invention,
>   On me to cast those eyes, where shine mobilitie.
> Seen, and unknowne; heard, but without attention.

In that virtuoso performance, the last line is something of an anomaly. There are other lines whose simplicity makes them stand out from all this contrivance, although they share exactly its pattern:

> That I growe like the Beaste,
> Which beares the Bit a weaker force doth guyde.

This line is of another order. Two of its feet depart from the metrical pattern, if one reads it, as it demands to be read, for the way it would sound in speech. It has the ring of speech. Word for word, however, it does fit the metrical pattern, even the exact iambic pattern. Furthermore, even if it is considered to have metrical departures, the departures are a kind that Sidney establishes so carefully as the only permissible ones that they are a part of his ordered system for the correspondence of language and metrical pattern. Its real departure from the kind of line Sidney writes in the *Arcadia* is the break in the smooth flow of the line caused by the reversal of stress in the third foot together with the pause after *heard* demanded by the powerful likeness to speech.

Sidney's carefully observed departures from the strict iambic do not, in the *Arcadia* poems, ordinarily cause any such break in the line, and do not suggest any such urgency of speech. Of the 3,500-odd basically iambic lines in the *Arcadia* poems, 184 reverse the pattern of stresses in the first foot by the necessity of the stress-pattern of a word:

> *Reason*, in vaine now you have lost my hart
> I, 147[1]

There are about 3,000 lines of ten syllables, or variations like the twelve-syllable double-feminine line of *Come Dorus come*. In forty-two of these lines the pattern of the third foot is reversed by the word-stress.

> Live long, and long *witnesse* my chosen smarte.
> II, 24

In only ten lines is there a reversal in the second foot.

> Our sports *murdering* our selves, our musiques wailing.
> II, 139

In three lines of ten syllables the fourth foot is reversed. Two of these occur together:

> The Ermion, whitest skinne, *spotted* with nought;
> The sheep, mild-seeming face; *climing*, the Beare;
> The Stagge did give the harme eschewing feare.
> I, 135

> But Man which helpeth them, *helplesse* must perish.
> I, 501

In each of these three cases, the reversal occurs after a pause, and on the analogy of the reversal in the first foot of a line. The most frequent reversal, that in the third foot, need not occur after a pause suggested by the language. Four lines of twelve syllables have the fourth foot reversed. Thus, this departure from the strict metrical pattern can occur in any foot but the last. But it occurs at all (except

---

[1] These references are to volume and page in *Works*.

for the first foot) in only about one line of seventy, and two-thirds of the occurrences are in the third foot. It is obviously systematic.

Sometimes the reversal lends some strength to the line, suggesting a particular intensity of speech, as in the line from a sestina,

> Our sports *murdering* our selves, our musiques wailing.
>
> II, 139

But usually the slight variation does not serve any such purpose. Like the reversal of the first foot, it is in these poems simply a part of the order to be observed in the relation of language and metre. For the typical line of the *Arcadia* is cut exactly to the measure. These lines can be used for more than one purpose. The subjects of the poems are various, the rhetoric varies with the subject; there is more variety in the *Arcadia* than one might expect. But the line remains essentially the same.

> Gett hence fowle greeffe, the Cancker of the mynde,
> Farewell Complaynte, the Misers onely pleasure,
> Away vayne Cares, by whiche fewe men do fynde,
>> theyre sought for Treasure.
>
> IV, 214

> Hee sayde the Musick best thilke Powers pleasde,
> Was Jumpp Concorde betweene oure witt and will,
> Where Highest notes to godlynes are Raysde,
> And Lowest sinck not downe to Jott of yll.
>
> IV, 238

> And thus she did. One day to him she came,
> And (though against his will) on him she leand,
> And out gan cry, ah well away for shame,
> If you helpe not our wedlocke will be staind,
>> The goodman starting, askt what did her move?
>> She sigh'd and sayd, the bad guest sought her love.
>
> II, 67

> Shall I that saw Eronaes shining haire
>> Torne with her hands, and those same hands of snow
>> With losse of purest blood themselves to teare?
> Shall I that saw those brests, where beauties flow. . . .
>
> I, 228

> So divers be the Elements disposed
>> In this weake worke, that it can never be
>> Made uniforme to any state reposed.
> Griefe onely makes his wretched state to see
> (Even like a toppe which nought but whipping moves)
> This man, this talking beast, this walking tree.
> Griefe is the stone which finest judgement proves.
>
> I, 227

145

His being was in her alone:
And he not being, she was none.
They joi'd one joy, one griefe they griev'd,
One love they lov'd, one life they liv'd.
The hand was one, one was the sword
That did his death, hir death afford.
As all the rest, so now the stone
That tombes the two, is justly one.

I, 557

In all these the relation of the language to the metrical pattern is essentially the same. The tension between them is slight, easily resolved in the favour of the metrical pattern—as in the first example, a lyrical passage on a familiar theme: the metrical pattern here is expected to be obvious, to be indeed the main interest. The line is smoothed out by the degree of stress lent here and there by the metre—*the Cancker of the mynde*, so that the last line gets the full advantage of its small metrical surprise, its shortness. It is the note of all those 'singing birds' that soon filled England's nest. The second example, a work-a-day expository verse of uncomplicated ideas, observes the same properties of language and metre, producing the same steady progression of sound and thought.

The third example is good Chaucerian narrative. Neither the exclamation nor the indirect speech of the characters presents much counter to the metrical pattern. This is one way the speeches attain, as they do in Chaucer, their special notes of foolishness or insincerity.

The fourth example with its more emotional subject is like the balanced lines of Marlowe's *Tamburlaine*: declamatory, rhetorical, musical, not really dramatic; the emotion expressed does not interfere with the metrical structure of the line.[1]

The fifth example strains more than the others at the measure, running over its line-end, and, in the obscurity of the fourth line, straining a little at the iambic structure. There is something more of Greville here than merely the echo of his figure of the top; but Sidney cannot give power to generalizations as Greville can, raising them above the level of the sententious.

Then Man, endure thy selfe, those clouds will vanish;
Life is a Top which whipping Sorrow driueth;
Wisdome must beare what our flesh cannot banish,
The humble leade, the stubborne bootlesse striueth.[2]

[1] On the balanced line as it appears in blank verse, see Baker, 58 *et passim*.
[2] *Poems and Dramas of Fulke Greville*, ed. Geoffrey Bullough (New York, 1945), I, 136.

146

Greville's metaphor is at once more extravagant and more condensed than Sidney's simile, but the real strength of the passage lies in the emphasis necessary to reconcile the metrical pattern and the phrases in that third line. Still, Sidney's lines,

This man, this talking beast, this walking tree,

has some power in its expression of disgust. In a small way it illustrates how the echoing phrases of these poems, perfectly ordered within their measures, can mount and accumulate the kind of energy which was described by William Empson, in speaking of *You Goteheard Gods*, as both peculiarly static and yet able to reach a 'sustained magnificence' of crescendo.[1]

The last example is an entire poem, a little epitaph. Its effect is not altogether unique; somewhat similar passages occur in some of the longer eclogues. Here the repetitions take on the tight, bare, intricate and deceptive simplicity of *The Phoenix and the Turtle*. It is perhaps the first of those great metaphysical epitaphs of which Browne's on Sidney's sister is the best. Again, both the measure and the pattern of stresses within the measure find a correspondence in the language which is constantly insisted on, so that it is a feature of the style that unites all the lines of the *Arcadia*, whatever their subject or mood. The prodigious exactness in Sidney's contrivance of these poems brings to all of them the artificiality, in the Elizabethan sense of artfulness as well as in our own sense, that goes with their pastoral setting. And through that, with their themes of art and feeling, 'inward' and 'outward,' 'reason' and 'passion,' chastity and sexuality, this exactness of metre allows Sidney to bring into the language of art the great themes of Elizabethan poetry.

I have said that it was the exercise in classical metres that brought in a new idea of the relation of metrical pattern and language, and consequently a new kind of poetry. In those experiments, Sidney and Spenser must have learned to recognize the possibility that these two elements of verse could be joined without losing their separate identities. They could even exist sometimes in opposition to one another, and yet the metrical pattern could retain its power as the organizing principle of the language in the line.[2]

But whatever its source, there is a new kind of poetry in *Astrophel and Stella*, and it depends on a new kind of metrical practice. The metrical pattern, of course, is the same: simulacra of strong- and weak-stressed syllables in alternation. (Some of the songs change

[1] William Empson, *Seven Types of Ambiguity* (New York, 1947), p. 38.
[2] See above, Chapter V.

147

this slightly: they have a trochaic foot, and a truncated trochaic line.)[1]

Word-stresses maintain about the same relation to the metrical pattern that they have in the *Arcadia* group. Of the 1,512 iambic lines in *Astrophel and Stella*, about one in twelve began with a word that reverses the pattern of stress:

<pre>
          s o
</pre>
Loving in truth, and faine in verse my love to show[2]
I, 1

In the *Arcadia* poems, about one line in twenty began that way. In the third foot of the iambic pentameter lines of *Astrophel and Stella*, there is one reversal of stress for approximately every sixty lines, compared with about one in seventy in the *Arcadia*. I count only those due to word-stress, like that in the third foot (but not in the fourth) of this line:

With sword of wit *giving* wounds of dispraise.
X, 10

Reversals in the other feet are about as rare as they are in the *Arcadia*. There are eight such variations in the fourth foot, or about one in 180; there are about one in a thousand in the *Arcadia*. There is only one in the second foot; there are ten, or one for about every 300 lines, in the *Arcadia*. In the six-foot twelve-syllable lines the only reversals that occur in either group of poems are in the fourth foot, and these are very rare. There are no lines in either work lacking a syllable; there are no lines with extra syllables.[3]

<pre>
      s o| s   o | s o| s
</pre>
[1] Astrophel with Stella sweet
<pre>
      s   o| s   o| s   o| s
</pre>
Did for mutual comfort meete
<pre>
      s   o|s   o | s   o| s o
</pre>
Both within themselves oppressed
<pre>
      s   o' s o| s o| s   o
</pre>
But each in the other blessed.
(Eighth Song).

[2] The reference is to the sonnet number and line, in the text of Pollard as cited above. I take the liberty of removing some of Pollard's punctuation.

[3] The elision is systematic, but at least once, in the first example below, it is phonetically odd.

That Plat*o I* read for nought but if he tame.
XXI, 5.
And yet she heares, and yet no pit*ie I* find.
XLIV, 5.
Most rude dispaire my dail*y un*bidden guest
CVIII, 7.
And in my joyes for thee my onl*y a*noy.
CVIII, 14.
For the last line, 1st Quarto has *onel'anoy*.

While Sidney observes the same system of relation between the word-stresses and the metrical pattern, the relation of the patterns of the phrases to the metrical pattern is quite different. From the earliest sixteenth-century attempts at the regular iambic line, in Surrey and in Sackville, there had been, of course, a reliance on the metrical pattern to carry through a phrase, supplying a degree of stress where the spoken phrase would lack it, or suppressing a stress where need be:

> o s| o s|
> His foode for most, was wylde *fruytes of the tree.*
> > *Induction,* 260
>
> *Earth, ayer,* and all resounding playnt and moane.
> > *Induction,* 511

And there had been in Wyatt, and in John Dolman's 'Hastings' in *The Mirror for Magistrates,* a frequent disregard of the metrical pattern in the interest of the phrases of speech. Sidney manages to combine a formal satisfaction of the metrical pattern with phrases whose stresses frequently violate that pattern. First, of course, he observes his syllables meticulously, and his word-stresses. After that, the stresses of the language may depart from the pattern in any way.

> Not at the first sight, nor with a dribbed shot.
> > II, 1
>
> And strange things cost too deare for my poore sprites.
> > III, 11
>
> Crie Victorie this faire day all is ours.
> > XII, 11
>
> And staid pleasd with the prospect of the place.
> > XX, 10
>
> To shew her skin, lips, teeth, and head so well.
> > XXXII, 11
>
> And then would not or could not see my blisse.
> > XXXIII, 2

This conventional relation to the metrical pattern solves some minor problems of versification that had plagued poets in the days when the pattern was being established. The frequency of the monosyllabic epithet in English had troubled Surrey and Sackville, for phrases like *false fayth* could be used by Chaucer, with the sounded *e,* in a way that these poets could not manage without, it seemed, endangering the iambic pattern: hence the double epithets, *the colde*

149

pale dread, the fowle blacke swelth, the fayre bright day; and *hugie*.[1] It is no problem to Sidney. The speech stresses are this:

> Not at the first sight nor with a dribbed shot,

but the metrical pattern remains absolutely the same. The correspondence is a convention.

> o s| o s| o s | o s| o s|
> Not at the first sight nor with a dribbed shot.

II, 1

With this convention, the metrical pattern is sometimes used as a way of controlling the intonation of the language. The words have their own pattern, usually obvious enough; if the metre is to work in this way, the sentence must first of all appear to be something that might really be said. It had better be colloquial, that is, the full resources of our speech in indicating meaning ought to be in it. It cannot be a statement like this:

> These mountaines witnesse shall, so shall these vallies,
> These forrests eke, made wretched by our musique,
> Our morning hymne is this, and song at evening.
> *You Gote-heard Gods*, X, 143

The language itself makes it clear that this is no ordinary speech, but something more like incantation. It requires the special effects that are the metrical pattern here, or something very close to them, if it is to be spoken. The voice would have to say with its intonation, *This is a very special way of talking.* When the language is this far removed from the more ordinary uses, the intonation suggested by the metrical pattern is probably as good as any. At least it has slight competition.

Sometimes, when the phrases are clear enough, and when there is some urgency in their matter, the metrical pattern may be thought of as making a contribution of the intonation, and so to the meaning. It is an effect much used by Shakespeare, by Donne, and the other metaphysical poets, whose meanings are likely to amount to more than Sidney's. Donne is often concerned with making his lines sound like words spoken:

> Rebell and Atheist too, why murmure I,
> As though I felt the worst that love could doe?
> Love might make me leave loving, or might trie
> A deeper plague, to make her love me too.[2]

[1] See Chapter I, pp. 30 ff.; J. Swart, p. 99 ff.; and Baker, *loc. cit.*
[2] Grierson, I, 54.

The tone as of argument against the self is enforced by the counter-movements of the phrases and the measure, with the sentence running over the line-end to produce an effect of hesitation and surprising resolution like the change of a mood. The metrical pattern is used to gain an unusual degree of emphasis and crowding in the line, as in

> Love might make me leave loving, or might trie

where the pattern of the stresses of speech and the metrical stresses combine to bring emphasis to nearly every syllable;

$$\text{Love might make me leave loving, or might trie. ...}$$

Sidney is not so very different sometimes. In the lines below there is certainly not Donne's degree of cynicism and complexity, but metre is used in the same way. And the argument is conducted in a way that can only be called 'metaphysical,' through contradictions united in an image and in a line whose construction demonstrates the tension of the opposition.

> It is most true that eyes are formd to serve
> The inward light, and that the heavenly part
> Ought to be King, from whose rules who do swerve,
> Rebels to nature, strive for their owne smart.
> It is most true, what we call Cupid's dart
> An image is, which for ourselves we carve,
> And, fooles, adore in temple of our hart,
> Till that good god make church and churchmen starve.
>
> V, 1–8

Here the metre may be said to contribute to the meaning. *The heavenly part ought to be King; ought to be, but is not.* The emphasis does not necessarily exist when the words are not written in Sidney's measure.

Somewhat similar to this employment of metre is the sheer surprise caused by the appearance of abrupt phrases which are yet ordered by the metrical pattern behind them.

> Come, let me write. And to what end? To ease
> A burthened hart.
>
> XXXIV, 1–2

> Let her go! Soft but here she comes! Go to,
> Unkind, I love you not.
>
> XLVII, 12–13

> Flie, fly, my friends; I have my death wound, fly;
> See there that boy that murthring boy, I say.
>
> II, 1–2

Still, this does not really say what this kind of metre is for. Even in the greatest poets, the metre is not always working to provide new intonations, or to help surprise the reader; these things are done mostly by the phrases themselves, by the language. They would not in themselves be sufficient reasons for writing in metre. It may be that this is the best kind of metre for the short and intense poem where there are not many words and the precise intonation of each one makes a great difference. Also, as we say today, the counterpoint of metrical pattern and normal intonation draws our concentrated attention to the way we will understand the language. We have to decide how to say things when we are presented with two choices, and probably our second thoughts will be best; at any rate, we will have thought.

But even bad metre makes us think twice, unless, like poulter's, it may tend to prevent our thinking at all, by insisting on itself. For as I have said, most poulter's is either insistent or nothing. What is the merit, then, of Sidney's metre? Surely it cannot be merely its supreme degree of contrivance. What he gave English poetry was available after him to lesser as well as to greater writers.

His achievement was to recognize the symbolic nature of the elements he worked with. In contriving effects of language, he came to realize that his true theme, matter, and form were all of them language. At the beginning of this chapter I made the claim that it was this recognition of Sidney's about metre that allowed him to practise his art with a new degree of sophistication. This sophistication is first the virtuoso technique: it is sophisticated because it involves the recognition that the poem is made of two things, pattern and language. Gascoigne had known that, but he had not known that the two could remain separate. He thought the language, with its intonations, its integral organizing features, had to become one with the pattern when the two met in a line of verse. 'The fault of the latter verse is that this worde *understand* is therein so placed as the grave accent falleth upon *der*, and thereby maketh *der*, in this worde *understand* to be elevated. . . .' Sidney's sophistication was to see that the two things could remain separate. This is so much a part of our understanding—or it was until recently, for now it seems that the idea of a separate metrical pattern is thought of as rather old-fashioned—so much a part of our understanding, at any rate, of how these things were once regarded, in our textbooks, that it is hard to imagine that it was not always so. But the recognition of an irreducible difference of form and substance in art must have been a profound experience, once. It seems to me that this difference must have led Sidney to the recognition of similar and equally profound

152

differences. It is a recognition of the limitations of poetry. This of course is one of Sidney's themes:

> Loving in truth, and faine in verse my love to show.

He is the first English poet to make poetry a major subject of his poems.[1] From that, the dichotomies march out two by two. The language of poetry and the language of feeling:

> You that do search for everie purling spring
> Which from the ribs of old Parnassus flowes. . . .
> > XV, 1–2

Any language, and feeling:

> Because I oft in darke abstracted guise
> Seeme most alone in greatest companie,
> With dearth of words . . .
> > . . . while thought to highest place
> Bends all his powers, even unto Stella's grace.
> > XXVII, 1–3, 13–14

> Dumbe swannes, not chatring pies, do lovers prove.
> They love indeed who quake to say they love.
> > LIV, 13–14

Thought, and experience:

> You that with Allegorie's curious frame
> Of others' children changelings use to make,
> With me those paines for Gods sake do not take.
> > XXVIII, 1–3

> How can words ease, which are
> The glasses of thy dayly-vexing care?
> > XXXIV, 2–3

> I am not I; pitie the tale of me.
> > XLV, 14

> Stella, the fulnesse of my thoughts of thee
> Cannot be staid within my panting breast,
> But they do swell and struggle forth of me,
> Till that in words thy figure be exprest:
> And yet, as soone as they so formed be,
> According to my lord Loves owne behest,
> With sad eyes I their weake proportion see
> To portrait that which in this world is best.
> > L, 1–8

But this is a theme that runs throughout the sequence, without

---

[1] But see Hallett Smith, *Elizabethan Poetry* (Cambridge, Mass., 1952), on Spenser's themes in *The Shepheardes Calender*, p. 38, *et passim.*

getting anywhere as an idea. To trace it is not very interesting on that level. Sidney's recognition of the profound difference between art and experience often only encouraged in him his decorative fancies, and a silly kind of prettiness. But this weakness is closely related to two kinds of strength, with which it should not be confused. There is trivial decoration in all the business about Cupid,

> In her cheekes pit thou didst thy pitfould set,
> And in her breast bo-peepe or couching lyes,
> XI, 11–12.

Sidney has also the ability to work in miniature with very small actions that very accurately dramatize the reality of a theme. In the eighth song there is one of these occasions. This is the best-known of the songs from the sequence; the lovers are meeting, both of them downcast by Stella's marriage; there is much more between them than at any other time:

> Him great harmes had taught much care,
> Her faire necke a foule yoke bare;
> But her sight his cares did banish,
> In his sight her yoke did vanish.

In such direct approach and with considerably less diffidence than he has usually suffered from, Astrophel tries to make love to her. She refuses him; it is 'Tyran honour' again. But this time honour is more than a word or an idea. It is shown in a tiny but real action.

> Therefore deere this no more move,
> Least though I leave not thy love,
> Which too deep in me is framed,
> I should blush when thou art named.

It is not only an action, however small; it is an appeal beyond convention to the primitive but perhaps unanswerable sense of the personal and social reality of the convention. Here the ability to deal in miniature is genuinely delicate.

The other use of the miniature proceeds directly from the recognition of the difference between the language of poetry and experience, which began with the recognition of what metre is. This is also from a song, one of the *Certaine Sonets* first published in 1598.[1] It is about the nightingale. The poet compares his own unhappiness

[1] *Works*, II, 303.

to the unhappiness of Philomela, and tells her that she can take comfort from the fact that he is even more unhappy than she is.

> Thine earth now springs, mine fadeth,
> Thy thorne without, my thorne my heart invadeth.

Why is he more unhappy than she is? In a line which according to the larger metrical plan has to be the centre of a rather long lyric stanza, he explains why.

> Since wanting is more woe than too much having.

Too much having is almost a callous joke, very nearly an obscenity. But the joke is not really at the expense of Philomela, who suffers 'for Thereus force on her chaste will prevailing.' The brutal reminder is a joke on the poet. As he does perhaps not often enough, Sidney has caused the reality to interrupt the convention, in the form of wit.[1] *Too much having* reflects on the other member of the antithesis, *wanting*, and makes it clear enough what it is the poet is wanting. But the final effect is not grotesque, it is a deepening of the rather conventional complaint with which the poem begins. Through the wit of the antithesis we are reminded of the reality lying behind the whole love convention. When we again come to the refrain,

> 'Thy thorne without, my thorne my heart invadeth,'

it may be with some sense of the psychological complexities of the situation; not explicitly, for we have been reminded of them by wit rather than by direct statement. The manner is only playful, the wit rather trifling; but the end is surprise and dramatic recognition. Through an artifice of pretence the poet has brought us to reality.

[1] Hallett Smith comments on a somewhat similar effect in the ninth Song of *Astrophel and Stella*: 'Sidney is pushing homely pathos to the point at which it is felt as humor also. . . .' *Elizabethan Poetry*, p. 22.

Conclusion

ART comes to reality through artifice, through imitation; for poetry, the artifice begins with language. Sidney discovered how to maintain a maximum tension between the language of the poem and the abstract pattern of the metre; the language is colloquial, with the full resources of speech, and the pattern is strict; the two are bound together in a state of mutual strain according to a set of conventions. The development that began with Wyatt's interest in the sounds of speech and continued through the poets who subjected these sounds of speech to the metrical pattern, distorting them in the process, came to a conclusion in the poetry of *Astrophel and Stella*. There the basic system of using metre and language was established for the English poetry of the three centuries that followed.

Of course, poetry need not be in the metre of Sidney. There is a difference but no basic quarrel between his strict iambic line and the old four-beat line or any other metrical pattern, so long as there is something that can be recognized as a pattern, independent of the particular language of each line of the poem. Even the line division itself, any kind of line, may do; any essential feature of the language, including junctures, may be imitated. Stress need not be the chief feature of English metre. But I should think that there must be a pattern or at least the sense of one even when we cannot quite find it out.

Metre is the sign that the language of the poem is an imitation. When the elements of language chosen to make the metre and the elements of language inherent in the speech the poet must use are brought together in the poem, they exist there in such a way that they imply one another, and yet retain their separate identities. It is thus that the language of speech is made into art, if art is imitation. For what poetry imitates is the structure of the language itself, this great system of sounds we use so cleverly, transmitting our signals to one another about everything in the universe. We have always read the code so easily that we can have had but little idea what its elements really were, as we voiced and hissed, and stressed, and paused. The poets have always known, and they know today. It is what they have been talking about all the time, even when, as in the sixteenth century in England, it took a while for them to get it all straight.

Stanza Forms

This table simply lists the measures or stanza forms occurring in the works discussed by my study, with the addition of *The Paradise of Dainty Devices*, the most popular of the miscellanies after Tottel. For each form, the column below the title of the book gives the number of times that form was used in that book. The total gives the number of poems in the book.

	Tottel	Mirror, 1559–1563	Paradise	Googe	Turberville Epitaphes	Gascoigne Posies	Sidney Arcadia	Shepheardes Calender
Sonnet	56		1			32	21	
16 syll. broken	1				1			
Poulter's	43		13		1	30	1	
Poulter's broken	3			4	55	2		
14er	19		22			1		
14er broken	6			21	22			1
Quatrain and couplet:								
14 syll. broken					1			
12 syll.	1		1			1		
10 syll.	7		17		22	16	7	3
8 syll.	19		11	2	4	6	2	
Quatrain ABAB 10 syll.	6		3		9	9		1
Quatrain ABAB 10 syll. broken				5				
Quatrain ABAB 10 syll. broken concl. coupl.				15				
Quatrain ABBA 10 syll.	1				2			
Quatrain ABAB 8 syll.	23		2	1	3			

	Tottel	Mirror 1559–1563	Paradise	Googe	Turberville Epitaphes	Gascoigne Posies	Sidney Arcadia	Shepheardes Calender
Quatrain broken 8 syll.				1				
Quatrain 6 syll.	10				1			
Triple rhyme 10 syll.	6						8	
Four-beat	2	1						3
Classical							8	
Couplets:								
12 syll.	1		4		1		4	
12 syll. broken					2			
10 syll.	18	1	3		7		5	
10 syll. broken					1			
8 syll.	2		1		4	1	3	
6 syll.					1			
Blank verse	2							
Rhyme royal:								
12 syll.	1	2						
10 syll.	12	22	1		4	12	1	
8 syll.	6							
Ottava rima	26				1		3	
Sestine							3	1
Other stanzas:								
Varied line length	9	1	7		9	3	6	4
10-syll. stanzas	21	1	1		10	7	12	3
8-, 6-, 4-syll. stanzas	6		2		1			
Int. Rhyme			22				3	
Total	307	28	111	49	162	120	87	16

APPENDIX B

-eth and -es

There were two forms of the indicative third person singular inflection of the verb available to Wyatt and to the editor of Tottel. They could write *laugheth* or they could write *laughs* (*laughes*). As far as I can determine neither Wyatt nor the editor had a truly consistent system for making the choice. There is of course a metrical problem here. Does -*eth* represent a syllable, does -*es* represent a syllable, does -*s* represent no syllable?

The Wyatt manuscripts of the Satires, in Muir's version, contain 27 uses of the -*eth* form and 9 uses of the -(*e*)*s* (omitting *hath* and *doth*). Tottel's version contains 15 uses of the -*eth* form and 22 uses of the -(*e*)*s*.[1]

To investigate these uses I will assume for a while that -*eth* is syllabic and -(*e*)*s* is not. (There is in these poems no case where -(*e*)*s* as a syllable would effect any 'improvement' in metrical regularity in either version.) On this assumption, it appears that in both Tottel and Wyatt -*eth* and -*s* are sometimes manipulated for metrical convenience. Wyatt writes,

II, 26. Her Cater *sekes* and *spareth* for no perell.

Tottel repeats this, and adds a similar case by changing one verb in a line and not another, giving this line:

I, 53. Grinne when he *laughes*, that *beareth* all the sway.

Whenever Tottel changes -*eth* to -*s* in the Satires, the change is metrically convenient. He never changes -*s* to -*eth*. All 12 of his changes reduce an 11-syllable line of Wyatt's to a regular 10-syllable line (in one case, II, 37, with a variation in one foot).

[1] Tottel increases the count by a change made for political reasons: lines 22 and 23 of Satire III read in Wyatt:
So sackes of durt be filled vp in the cloyster
That servis for lesse then do thes fatted swyne.
The plural *servis* becomes the singular inflection in question by this change:
So sackes of durt be filde. The neate courtier
So serues for lesse, then do these fatted swine.

159

I, 53.   Grynne when he *laugheth* that *bereth* all the swaye.   W.
         Grinne when he *laughes*, that *beareth* all the sway.   T.
I, 54.   Frowne when he *frowneth* and grone when he is pale.   W.
         Frowne, when he *frownes*: and grone when he is pale.   T.
I, 94.   Nor Fflaunders chiere *letteth* not my sight to deme.   W.
         Nor Flaunders chere *lettes* not my syght to deme.   T.
I, 95.   Of black and white, nor *taketh* my wit awaye.   W.
         Of blacke and white, nor *takes* my wittes awaye.   T.
II, 23. Richely she *fedeth* and at the richemans cost.   W.
         Richely she *fedes*, and at the richemans cost.   T.
II, 27. She *fedeth* on boyled, bacon meat, and roost.   W.
         She *fedes* on boyle meat, bake meat, and on rost.   T.
II, 31. And at this jorney she *maketh* but a jape.   W.
         And at this iourney *makes* she but a iape.   T.
II, 32. So fourth she *goeth* trusting of all this welth.   W.
         So forth she *goes*, trusting of all this wealth.   T.
II, 37. And with her foote anon she *scrapeth* full fast.   W.
         And with her fote anone she *scrapes* full fast.   T.
III, 49. Hath lept into the shopp; who *knoweth* by rote.   W.
         Hath lept into the shoppe; who *knowes* by rote.   T.
III, 51. Sumtyme also riche age *begynneth* to dote.   W.
         Sometime also riche age *beginnes* to dote.   T.
II, 22. Her tender fote. She *laboureth* not as I.   W.
         Her tender fote, she *labours* not as I.   T.

Here the first line may have been regular in Wyatt by syncopation:
lab'reth.

Tottel passes by 15 opportunities to change *-eth* to *-s*. Five of these 15
lines were perfectly regular in the first place, and remain so in Tottel.

II, 19. And hens from me she *dwelleth* not a myle.
II, 20. In colde and storme she *lieth* warme and dry.
II, 83. It *irketh* straite and by it self doth fade.
III, 1. A spending hand that alway *powreth* owte.
III, 37. Vse vertu as it *goeth* now a dayes.

Three of these lines in which no change of *-eth* occurs were irregular in
Wyatt and became regular in Tottel by means other than a change in the
verb inflection (or, in one case, by a change in the inflection of another
verb in the same line).

I, 53.   Grynne when he laugheth that *bereth* all the swaye.   W.
         Grinne when he laughes, that *beareth* all the sway.   T.
I, 72.   That *raileth* rekles to every means shame.   W.
         That *rayleth* rechlesse vnto ech mans shame.   T.
I, 80.   This *maketh* me at home to hounte and to hawke.   W.
         This *maketh* me at home to hunt and hauke.   T.

Six of the lines have 11 syllables in Wyatt and retain 11 syllables in Tottel if we assume that -*eth* is always a syllable. All but one of the lines could have been reduced to 10 syllables, if not all of them to perfect regularity in stresses, by a change of -*eth* to -*s*.

I, 47.	And he that *dithe* for hungar of the golld.	W.
	And he that *dieth* for honger of the golde.	T.
I, 49.	*Passithe* Apollo in musike manyfolld.	W.[1]
	Passeth Appollo in musike manifold.	T.
II, 26.	Her Cater sekes and *spareth* for no perell.	W.
	Her cater sekes, and *spareth* for no perill.	T.
II, 74.	*Goeth* gyde and all in seking quyete liff.	W.
	Goeth guide and all in seking quiet life.	T.
III, 4.	There *groweth* no mosse; these proverbes yet do last.	W.
	There *groweth* no mosse. These prouerbes yet do last.	T.
III, 36.	Full nere that wynd *goeth* trouth in great misese.	W.
	Full neare that winde *goeth* trouth in great misease.	T.

One line has 10 syllables in Wyatt apparently by syncopation of the *e* in the -*eth* ending of *sufferth*. But Tottel prints this as *suffreth*, syncopating the *e* of *suffer*. Metrically it is the same, and it is not necessary to consider this an exception to the assumption about the syllabicity of -*eth*, for my purposes:

I, 70.	And he that *sufferth* offence withoute blame.	W.
	And he that *suffreth* offence withoutt blame.	T.

However, the spelling of this last line in Wyatt, and Tottel's failure to make the change from -*eth* to -*s*, when it would produce regularity (if -*eth* is always syllabic and -*s* is not), suggest that -*eth* was not always considered a syllable. Both men may have considered a line like

Goeth guide and all in seking quiet life

a perfectly regular 10-syllable line, reading *goeth* as one syllable. But in another line,

So forth she *goeth*, trusting of all this wealth,

where *goeth* as one syllable gives the line a total of 10, Tottel has changed to *goes* from Wyatt's *goeth*. In still another line, *goeth* must be two syllables to produce a regular 10-syllable line. The four occasions of *to go* in this inflection are these.

II, 74.	*Goeth* gyde and all in seking quyete liff.	W.
	Goeth guide and all in seking quiet life.	T.
III, 36.	Full nere that wynd *goeth* trouth in great misese.	W.
	Full neare that winde *goeth* trouth in great misease.	T.
III, 37.	Vse vertu as it *goeth* now a dayes.	W.
	Vse vertue, as it *goeth* now a dayes.	T.
II, 32.	So fourth she *goeth* trusting of all this welth.	W.
	So forth she *goes*, trusting of all this wealth.	T.

[1] In this line, -*eth* follows a sibilant, and it is necessarily syllabic there; also -*s* was generally avoided after a sibilant.

161

Tottel's practice, then, seems to have had very little consistency. He appears to have had no objection to the form in *-eth*, as such. Both forms can occur in the same line. He changes to *-s* 12 times, and does not change 15 times. Each time he does change, the change makes the line more regular. When the line containing *-eth* is already regular, he makes no change; but in five cases, he makes no change when the change *would* have produced regularity. It is not possible to tell whether or not *-eth* is always syllabic. If we could assume that sometimes it was and sometimes it was not, we could attain the maximum number of regular lines. However, that assumption about *-eth* would have to be based on an assumption that Tottel had a very determined intention to regularize. While that is obviously his general intention, there are many lines which remain irregular despite that general intention, even when it would seem to be no great trick to regularize them. When there are lines which cannot be regularized by *any* alteration of pronunciation, it is not consistent to claim that we must alter the pronunciation where an alteration will produce a metrically regular line.

There is another possibility (outside that of perfectly arbitrary syncopation) which would allow reading lines like these as regular lines:

> And he that *dieth* for honger of the golde.
> There *groweth* no mosse. These prouerbes yet do last.
> Full neare that winde *goeth* trouth in great misease.

There may have been in speech rival forms of *-eth* and *-s*, allowing, as in the postulated case of Romance accent, a free choice between the two. Again, like the Romance accent, this is difficult to determine since most of the evidence comes from verse, and depends upon an assumption of the poet's metrical intention. The problem is worth reviewing, however. The history of this inflection is linked from beginning to end with the metrical practices of poets. There is an order, obscure in detail but discernible, in the way the practice of the poets in the use of these two forms is gradually regularized. To calculate Tottel's place in that order is to establish one point of his position in the movement to regularity and to indicate how one small item in a changing language found its place in the consistent system of metrics.

The change of the ending of the present indicative third person singular verb began in the English of London at almost the time this variety of English itself became established as a sort of standard. By 1450 or 1500 what is now called Modern English came into general use for writing, replacing for this purpose the Middle English local dialects. Varieties of these continued to exist in speech, and the Standard itself compared to our own Standard was still a mixed dialect in which 'very often the old and the new co-existed for well over a century.'[1]

---

[1] William Matthews, 'The Vulgar Speech of London in XV–XVII Centuries,' *Notes & Queries*, 172 (1937), p. 242.
The rest of this account is drawn from Otto Jespersen, *Growth and Structure*

The beginnings of the substitution of -(e)s for -eth are obscure, and the process has never really been completed although -eth survives today only in very special uses—which seem to reflect, oddly enough, the way its rival, -(e)s, first made its appearance in the records of the Southern dialect—it is scattered here and there in verse in rare examples far out-numbered by the dominant form.[1]

Histories of our language agree that the early -s forms 'were evidently borrowed from Northern poetry and were used for the sake of the rime.'[2] It had formerly been believed that the practice of the poets 'for purposes of metre or rhyme' was the means by which the new forms were intro-duced, that they moved from poetry to prose to speech, but this view is no longer held.[3] At any rate, signs of the change first appear on record in poetry. Lydgate frequently has the -s form. So does Hawes. In general, its use gradually increases in poetry throughout the sixteenth century, as we shall observe in more detail later. By the middle of the seventeenth century, the use of -eth in poetry can be said to have ended as a continuous tradition.

of the English Language (ninth edition), New York, 1955; H. C. Wyld, A History of Modern Colloquial English (London, 1920); Samuel Moore, Historical Outline of English Phonology and Morphology (Ann Arbor, 1925); and from Erik Holmqvist, On the History of the English Present Inflections Particularly -th and -s (Heidelberg, 1922). Holmqvist is particularly interesting because in his detailed study he includes much of the material upon which his judgments are based, and because he is particularly concerned to attempt an explanation of several apparent anomalies in the history of the use of these forms.

[1] 'At the present day the -eth forms are unknown in colloquial English any-where, but are often used in poetry, chiefly because they provide an additional syllable for purposes of metre, and they are familiar to all through the Bible and the Prayer Book.' Wyld, 12. (Jespersen says that 'old people in the hilly parts of Somersetshire and Devonshire' still say [iwɔ.kþ] for 'he walks,' 211.) The first line of Ezra Pound's translation of The Classic Anthology Defined by Confucius, (Cambridge, 1954), is 'Hid! Hid! Hid!' the fish-hawk saith. I would guess, though, that the form is much less used in competent poetry today than it was even 30 or 40 years ago.

[2] Holmqvist, p. 159. Wyld, p. 333. Wyld also suggests the influence of is, ibid., 336.

[3] Jespersen's rather ambiguous statement in the early editions of Growth and Structure of the English Language was that use of the -th ending 'remained the usual practice till late in the 16th century, when s was first introduced by the poets.' (2nd edition revised [Leipzig, 1912], p. 192.) In later editions, the use in writing and the use in speech is clearly separated: 'This remained the usual form in writing till the 16th century, when s began to be used in poetry.' (9th edition [Garden City, 1955], pp. 211–212.) The question is discussed by Holmqvist, 159–160, and by Wyld, 335. Moore believed the change occurred owing to the spread of Northern influence. Wyld believed it occurred by analogy to the 'extremely common auxiliary is' (p. 333). Holmqvist suggests that Northern in-fluence worked through Leicestershire, perhaps in connection with the propa-ganda of Lollardy (144–145). Jespersen says: 'If the s of the third person singular comes from the North, this is true of the outer form only: the "inner" form . . . is the Midland one.' That is, s substitutes for another sound within the Midland pattern of inflection; the pattern itself is not taken from the North (216).

Milton never used it either in prose or poetry except for *doth* and *hath*, 'where the frequency of occurrence protected the old forms from being modified analogically.'[1] After that, the use was a revival, an archaism, no matter how it might be used in poetry, just as any use of it today must be.

Literary prose was more conservative. It took up -*s* later and in certain ways held on to -*eth* longer as an alternate. Caxton always used the -*eth* ending, so did the Authorized Version of 1611. In the sixteenth century, -*eth* is 'practically universal in literary prose, official documents, and in private letters until well into the third quarter of the century,' according to Wyld.[2] Holmqvist disagrees with the statement only as far as private letters go. But for most literary prose, the change is nearly complete by the beginning of the seventeenth century. 'In the 50-year period 1590–1640 . . . prose writers freely employed both -s and -th forms without feeling conscious of the former as colloquial or the latter as archaic,' R. C. Bambas has written,[3] disagreeing with Wyld, who considered that -*eth* was used rarely in the seventeenth century in prose 'except in the stateliest and most lofty.'[4]

In the written language, then, the change was accomplished during the sixteenth century and the first half of the seventeenth. In poetry, we have seen so far only that the choice seems to have been useful for rhyme and metre, and that the chief poet of the mid-seventeenth century rejects the opportunity. Of the spoken language we have nothing yet. It is hard to say what the poets do besides satisfying their metres. These rival forms seem to carry surprisingly little connotation. 'Where a speaker knows rival forms, they differ in connotation, since he has heard them from different persons and under different circumstances.'[5] But in the mixed dialect of sixteenth-century London, anything like a connotation for these forms appears only at the very end of the century, and then rather doubtfully. Just as Wyatt and Tottel can use both forms in one line, apparently Shakespeare did not mind using them together. 'Shakespeare's practice is not easy to ascertain,' Jespersen says. 'In a great many passages the folio of 1623 has *th* where the earlier quartos have *s* . . . the rule may be laid down that *th* belongs more to the solemn or dignified speeches than to everyday talk, although this is by no means carried through everywhere.'[6] Certainly -*eth* seems to be used for metrical convenience here and there among the far usual -*s* endings.

> Some say that euer gainst that season *comes*
> Wherein our Sauiors birth is celebrated
> This bird of dawning *singeth* all night long,
> And then they say no spirit dare sturre abraode
> The nights are wholsome, then no plannets strike,
> No fairy *takes*, nor witch *hath* power to charme.[7]

[1] Jespersen, p. 213.   [2] Wyld, p. 333.
[3] R. C. Bambas, 'Verb Forms in -s and -th in Early Modern English Prose,' *Journal of English and Germanic Philology*, XLVI (1947), 187.
[4] Wyld, p. 334. Cf. Holmqvist, p. 183.
[5] Bloomfield, p. 394.   [6] Jespersen, p. 212.   [7] Q2.

In addition to the possible tendency to associate -*eth* with elevated tone there appears to be only one more correlation between its use and anything except metrical convenience. After a sibilant, -*s* is often avoided.[1] However, this makes no difference metrically, since -*s* is syllabic after sibilants. There is only one occasion in the Satires of the third person present indicative singular verb ending in a sibilant, I, 49. It has in both versions -*eth*.

Erik Holmqvist presents an interesting conjecture about the use of these forms. He finds that 'syncopation of the inflectional *e* in -*es* appears to have been carried through to a large extent by about 1500.'[2] The gradual syncopation of the -*e* in -*eth* does not proceed in this manner, but seems to be checked in the early sixteenth century, where there are both syncopated and unsyncopated uses, as there appear to be in Tottel. 'Sounding of the vowel [seems] to have been the rule again about the middle of the century.'

'In my opinion,' Holmqvist says, 'this development can only be accounted for on the assumption that, as early as 1500, the inflectional -*eth* had passed out of use, or was in a fair way to do so, in the spoken language, and that the ending, therefore, when still adhered to in literary language, was standardized in its old unsyncopated form.'[3] Holmqvist cites evidence, such as familiar letters, the writings of unlearned, nearly illiterate men like Edmund de la Pole, Duke of Suffolk. These writings were more likely, he believes, to represent the uses of speech than the spelling in literary or official works.

It is not necessary here to postulate such a radical theory. The use of -*eth* or -*s* by Tottel would be explained either by Holmqvist's theory, or by Jespersen's that it was the use of -*s* and not -*eth* which was a licence.[4] In either case, Tottel is inconsistent. Metre does not always explain his choice, nor does his choice always explain his metre, either.[5] That would be what we might wish for, but do not get. It would be a great convenience if metre provided a positive record of the history of the language, but it does not. No poet is that consistent in maintaining a relation between his speech and his metrical pattern. We are on shaky ground when we look to poetry for more than an 'imitation' of the forms of speech.

[1] Holmqvist, p. 184.
[2] *Ibid.*, p. 165.
[3] *Ibid.*, p. 166.
[4] *Jespersen*, 213.
[5] Cf. Bambas, p. 186, on the use in prose: 'In none of the works examined in which both -*s* and -*th* forms occur was there any apparent reason for the writer's choice of forms.'

BIBLIOGRAPHY

Primary Sources

Beowulf. Edited by C. L. Wrenn. London: George G. Harrap and Co., 1953.

BLENERHASSET, THOMAS. *A Revelation of the True Minerva.* Edited by Josephine Waters Bennett. New York: Scholars' Facsimiles and Reprints, 1941.

BRIDGES, ROBERT. *Poetical Works.* London: Oxford University Press, 1936.

CAMPION, THOMAS. *Songs and Masques with Observations in the Art of English Poesy.* Edited by A. H. Bullen. London: A. H. Bullen, 1903.

CHAUCER, GEOFFREY. *The Complete Works.* Edited by F. N. Robinson. Boston: Houghton Mifflin Company, 1933.

COLERIDGE, SAMUEL TAYLOR. *Complete Poetical Works.* Edited by E. H. Coleridge. Oxford: Oxford University Press, 1912.

DANIEL, SAMUEL. *Poems, and A Defence of Ryme.* Edited by Arthur Colby Sprague. London: Routledge and Kegan Paul, Ltd., 1950.

DONNE, JOHN. *Poems.* Edited by Herbert J. C. Grierson. Oxford: Oxford University Press, 1912, reprinted 1938.

DUNBAR, WILLIAM. *The Poems of William Dunbar.* Edited by W. Mackay Mackenzie. Edinburgh: The Porpoise Press, 1932.

GASCOIGNE, GEORGE. *A Hundreth Sundrie Flowres.* Edited by C. T. Prouty. Columbia: University of Missouri Press. Studies XVII, 2, 1942.

— *The Complete Works.* Edited by John W. Cunliffe. Cambridge: Cambridge University Press, 1907.

GOOGE, BARNABE. *Eglogs, Epytaphes, & Sonettes* (1563). Edited by Edward Arber. London: English Reprints, 1871.

A Gorgeous Gallery of Gallant Inventions. Edited by H. S. Rollins. Cambridge, Mass.: Harvard University Press, 1926.

GREVILLE, FULKE. *Poems and Dramas.* Edited by Geoffrey Bullough. New York: Oxford University Press, 1945.

A Handfull of Pleasant Delights (1585). Edited by H. E. Rollins. Cambridge, Mass.: Harvard University Press, 1924.

HOWELL, THOMAS. *Howell's Devises* (1581). Oxford: Clarendon Press, 1906.

— *The Poems of Thomas Howell.* Edited by Alexander B. Grosart. Occasional Issues, VIII (1879).

LANGLAND, WILLIAM. *The Vision of William Concerning Piers the Plowman.* Edited by Walter W. Skeat. Oxford University Press, 1886, reprinted 1954.

MAROT, CLÉMENT. *Oeuvres.* Edited by Georges Guiffrey. Paris: Jean Schemit, 1875–1931.

N   167

MILTON, JOHN. *Works*. Volume II. Edited by Frank Allen Patterson. New York: Columbia University Press, 1931–1938.

The Mirror for Magistrates. Edited by Lily B. Campbell. Cambridge: Cambridge University Press, 1938.

MOORE, MARIANNE. *Collected Poems*. New York: The Macmillan Company, 1951.

MORE, SIR THOMAS. *The English Works*. Edited by W. C. Campbell. London: Eyre and Spottiswoode, 1931.

NASHE, THOMAS. *Works*. Edited by R. B. McKerrow. London: A. H. Bullen, 1904–1910.

Old English Ballads, 1553–1625. Edited by H. E. Rollins. Cambridge: University Press, 1920.

The Paradise of Dainty Devices, 1576–1606. Edited by H. E. Rollins. Cambridge, Mass.: Harvard University Press, 1927.

Pearl. Edited by E. V. Gordon. Oxford: Clarendon Press, 1953.

The Phoenix Nest, 1593. Edited by H. E. Rollins. Cambridge, Mass.: Harvard University Press, 1931.

POUND, EZRA. *The Classic Anthology Defined by Confucius*. Cambridge, Mass.: Harvard University Press, 1954.

SACKVILLE, THOMAS. *The Complaint of Henry, Duke of Buckingham, Including the Introduction, or, Thomas Sackville's Contribution to The Mirror for Magistrates*. Edited, from the Author's Manuscript, with Introduction, Notes, and Collation, with the printed edition, by Marguarite Hearsey. New Haven: Yale University Press, 1936.

SHAKESPEARE, WILLIAM. *Comedies, Histories and Tragedies*. London, 1623 (facsimile, edited by C. T. Prouty). New Haven: Yale University Press, 1954.

— *Hamlet*. London, 1604. (Facsimile, San Marino, 1938.)

— A New Variorum Edition. Volume 24–25. *The Sonnets*. Edited by J. Q. Adams. Philadelphia: J. C. Lippincott.

SIDNEY, PHILIP. *Astrophel and Stella*. Edited by Alfred Pollard. London: David Stott, 1888.

— *The Countess of Pembroke's Arcadia*. Eleventh edition. London: Printed by Henry Lloyd for William DuGard, 1662.

— *Works*. Edited by Albert Feuillerat. Cambridge: University Press, 1912–1926.

Sir Gawain and the Green Knight. Edited by J. R. R. Tolkien and E. V. Gordon. Oxford: Clarendon Press, 1930.

SKELTON, JOHN. *Poems*. Edited by Alexander Dyce. Boston: Little, Brown and Company, 1856.

SPENSER, EDMUND. *Works, A Variorum edition*. Edited by E. A. Greenlaw, et al. Baltimore: Johns Hopkins University Press, 1933–1949.

STERNHOLD, THOMAS. *Psalms of David in Metre*. London: Edward Whitechurche, 1551.

SURREY, EARL OF. *The Poems of Henry Howard, Earl of Surrey*. Edited by F. M. Padelford. Seattle: University of Washington Press, 1928.

The Tale of Beryn. Edited by F. J. Furnivall and W. G. Stone. London: Chaucer Society, 1887.

The Tale of Gamelyn. In As You Like It by William Shakespeare. New York: The Mershon Company, 188[?].

Tottel's Miscellany. Edited by H. E. Rollins. Cambridge, Mass.: Harvard University Press, 1927.

TURBERVILLE, GEORGE. *The Eclogues of Mantuan.* Translated by George Turberville. Edited by Douglas Bush. New York: Scholars' Facsimiles and Reprints, 1937.

— *Epitaphes, Epigrams, Songs and Sonets.* London: Henry Denham, 1567.

— *The Heroycall epistles of the learned poet Publius Ovidius Naro.* Translated into English verse by George Turberville. Edited by Frederic Boas. London: Cresset Press, 1928.

— *The Poems of George Turberville*, in The Works of the English Poets. Edited by Alexander Chalmers. Volume II. London, 1810.

— *Turberville's Books of Hunting, 1576.* Oxford: Clarendon Press, 1908.

VERGIL. *Aeneid.* Edited by Charles Knapp. New York: Scott, Foresman, 1900.

WHITMAN, WALT. *Leaves of Grass.* New York: E. P. Dutton, 1912.

WYATT, THOMAS. *Collected Poems of Sir Thomas Wyatt.* Edited by Kenneth Muir. London: Routledge and Kegan Paul, Ltd., 1949.

YEATS, WILLIAM BUTLER. *Collected Poems.* New York: The Macmillan Company, 1951.

Secondary Sources

ABBOTT, E. A. *A Shakespearian Grammar.* London: Macmillan and Company, 1871.

ALDEN, R. M. *English Verse: Specimens Illustrating Its Principles and History.* New York: Henry Holt and Company, 1903.

ALLEN, GAY WILSON. *American Prosody.* New York and Cincinnati: American Book Company, 1935.

ANDREW, S. O. *Postscript on Beowulf.* Cambridge: University Press, 1948.

ASCHAM, ROGER. *The Scholemaster.* Edited by W. A. Wright. Cambridge: Cambridge University Press, 1904.

ATKINS, J. W. H. *English Literary Criticism: The Renascence.* London: Methuen and Company, 1947.

BAKER, HOWARD. *Induction to Tragedy.* Baton Rouge: Louisiana State University Press, 1939.

BALDWIN, T. W. *William Shakspere's Small Latin & Lesse Greeke.* Urbana: University of Illinois Press, 1944.

BARKAS, PALLISTER, *A Critique of Modern English Prosody (1880–1930).* Halle (Saale): Max Niemeyer, 1934.

BAUGH, ALBERT C. (ed.). *A Literary History of England.* New York: Appleton-Century-Crofts, 1948.

BAYFIELD, M. A. *The Measures of the Poets.* A New System of English Prosody. Cambridge: University Press, 1919.

Beowulf. Translated by John R. Clark Hall. Edited by C. L. Wrenn, with prefatory remarks by J. R. R. Tolkien. London: George Allen and Unwin, 1950.

BERDEN, J. M. *Early Tudor Poetry.* New York: The Macmillan Company, 1931.

BLOOMFIELD, LEONARD. *Language.* New York: Henry Holt and Company, 1933.

BOAS, FREDERICK S. *Sir Philip Sidney, Representative Elizabethan, His Life and Writings.* London: Staples Press, Ltd., 1955.

BRADNER, LEICESTER. *Musae Anglicanae.* London: Oxford University Press, 1940.

BRIDGES, ROBERT. *Milton's Prosody.* Oxford: University Press, 1921.

BROOKS, CLEANTH and WARREN, R. P. *Understanding Poetry.* New York: Henry Holt and Company, 1938.

BUSH, DOUGLAS. *The Renaissance and English Humanism.* Toronto: University of Toronto Press, 1939.

Cambridge History of English Literature. Edited by A. W. Ward and A. R. Waller. Cambridge: University Press, 1919–1931.

CASADY, EDWIN. *Henry Howard, Earl of Surrey.* New York: The Modern Language Association of America, 1938.

CLARK, D. L. *Rhetoric and Poetry in the English Renaissance.* New York: Columbia University Press, 1922.

COLERIDGE, SAMUEL TAYLOR. *Biographia Literaria.* London: J. M. Dent and and Sons, 1947.

COLLINS, ARTHUR. *Letters and Memorials of State* (Sidney Papers). 2 vols. London, 1746.

COURTHOPE, W. J. *A History of English Poetry.* London: The Macmillan Company, 1895–1910.

CROLL, MATTHEW. *The Works of Fulke Greville.* University of Pennsylvania, dissertation, 1901.

DANIELSON, BROR. *Studies on the Accentuation of Polysyllabic Latin, Greek, and Romance Loan-Words in English.* Stockholm: Almqvist and Wiksells, 1948.

EMPSON, WILLIAM. *Seven Types of Ambiguity.* 2nd ed. New York: New Directions, 1947.

ERSKINE, JOHN. *The Elizabethan Lyric.* New York: Columbia University Press, 1903.

FOX BOURNE, H. R. *Sir Philip Sidney.* New York: G. P. Putnam's Sons, 1899.

FOXWELL, A. K. *The Poems of Sir Thomas Wiat.* London: University of London Press, 1914.

— *A Study of Sir Thomas Wyatt's Poems.* London: University of London Press, 1911.

FRIEDRICH, WALTER GEORGE. *The Stella of Astrophel.* A Portion of the Astrophel Elegies, A Collection of Poems on the Death of Sir Philip Sidney (1595). A Critical Edition. Baltimore: Johns Hopkins University, dissertation, 1936.

GRAY, THOMAS. *Works.* Edited by Edmund Gosse. London: Macmillan and Company, 1884.

BIBLIOGRAPHY

GREVILLE, FULKE. *The Life of the Renowned Sir Philip Sidney*. Edited by Howell Smith. Oxford: University Press, 1907.

GUEST, EDWIN. *A History of English Rhythms*. Vol. I. London: William Pickering, 1838.

HAASE, GLADYS D. 'Spenser's Orthography, An Examination of a Poet's Use of the Variant Pronunciation of Elizabethan English.' Unpublished Ph.D. dissertation, Columbia University, 1952.

HALL, VERNON, JR. *Renaissance Literary Criticism, A Study of Its Social Content*. New York: Columbia University Press, 1945.

HAMER, ENID. *The Metres of English Poetry*. London: Methuen and Company, Ltd., 1930.

HAMMOND, ELEANOR. *English Verse Between Chaucer and Surrey*. Durham: Duke University Press, 1927.

HANKINS, JOHN ERSKINE. *The Life and Works of George Turberville*. University of Kansas Publications, Humanistic Studies, No. 25. Lawrence, Kansas: University of Kansas Press, 1940.

HARRIER, RICHARD CHARLES. 'The Poetry of Sir Thomas Wyatt.' Unpublished Ph.D. dissertation, Harvard University, 1952.

HARRIS, ZELLIG S. *Methods in Structural Linguistics*. Chicago: University of Chicago Press, 1951.

HARVEY, GABRIEL. *Ciceronianus*. Edited by Harold L. Wilson. Lincoln: University of Nebraska Press, 1945.

— *Fovre Letters and certaine Sonnets, especially touching Robert Greene and other parties by him abused (1592)*. London: 1922.

— *Gratulationes Valdinenses*. Edited by T. H. Jameson. Yale University dissertation, 1938.

— *Marginalia*. Edited by G. C. Moore Smith. Stratford upon Avon, 1913.

— *Works*. Edited by Alexander Grosart. London: The Huth Library, 1884.

HEFFNER, R-M, S. *General Phonetics*. Madison: University of Wisconsin Press, 1949.

HOLINSHED, RAPHAEL. *Holinshed's Chronicles of England, Scotland and Ireland*. 6 vols. London, 1808.

HOLMQVIST, ERIK. *On the History of the English Present Inflections Particularly -th and -s*. Heidelberg, 1922.

ING, CATHERINE. *Elizabethan Lyrics*. London: Chatto and Windus, 1951.

JAKOBSON, ROMAN and HALLE, MORRIS. *Fundamentals of Language*. Janua Linguarum, Nr. 1, 's-Gravenhage: Mouton and Company, 1956.

JESPERSEN, OTTO. *Growth and Structure of the English Language*. 9th ed. New York: Doubleday and Company, 1955.

JOHNSON, SAMUEL F. *Early Elizabethan Tragedies of the Inns of Court*. 2 vols. Harvard University, dissertation, 1951.

KÖKERITZ, HELGE. *Shakespeare's Pronunciation*. New Haven: Yale University Press, 1953.

LEVER, J. W. *The Elizabethan Love Sonnet*. London: Methuen and Company, 1956.

LEWIS, C. S. *English Literature of the Sixteenth Century.* Oxford: University Press, 1934.

MAYNARD, THEODORE. *The Connection Between the Ballads, Chaucer's Modification of It, Rime Royal, and the Spenserian Stanza.* Washington, D.C.: Catholic University of America, dissertation, 1934.

MIRIAM JOSEPH, SISTER. *Shakespeare's Use of the Arts of Language.* New York: Columbia University Press, 1947.

MOFFET, THOMAS. *Nobilis, or A View of the Life and Death of a Sidney, and Lessus Lugubris.* Edited by Virgil B. Heltzel and Hoyt H. Hudson. San Marino, Calif.: Huntington Library, 1940.

MOORE, SAMUEL. *Historical Outline of English Phonology and Morphology.* Ann Arbor: George Wahr, 1925.

NEWCOMB, E. A. *The Countess of Pembroke's Circle.* University of Wisconsin, dissertation, 1937.

OMOND, T. S. *English Metrists.* Tunbridge Wells: R. Felton, 1903.

ONIONS, C. T. 'Prosody,' in Cassell's *Encyclopaedia of World Literature,* edited by S. H. Steinberg. New York: Funk and Wagnalls, 1954.

The Oxford Dictionary of Nursery Rhymes. Edited by Iona and Peter Opie. Oxford: Clarendon Press, 1952.

The Oxford History of English Literature. Volumes II, parts 1 and 2, III. Oxford: Clarendon Press, 1954.

PATTISON, BRUCE. *Music and Poetry of the English Renaissance.* London: Methuen and Company, 1948.

PIKE, KENNETH L. *The Intonation of American English.* Ann Arbor: University of Michigan Press, 1945.

POIRRER, MICHEL. *Sir Philip Sidney, Le Chevalier Poète Élizabethain.* Lille: Bibliothèque Universitaire de Lille, 1948.

POPE, JOHN C. *The Rhythm of Beowulf.* New Haven: Yale University Press, 1942.

POUND, EZRA. *ABC of Reading.* Norfolk, Conn.: New Directions, n.d.

PRINCE, F. T. *The Italian Element in Milton's Verse.* Oxford: Clarendon Press, 1954.

PROUTY, C. T. *George Gascoigne.* New York: Columbia University Press, 1942.

PURCELL, JAMES H. *Sidney's Stella.* New York and London: Oxford University Press, 1934.

PUTTENHAM, GEORGE. *The Arte of English Poesie.* Edited by Gladys Doidge Willock and Alice Walker. Cambridge: University Press, 1936.

RANSOM, JOHN CROWE. *Poems and Essays.* New York: Vintage Books, 1955.

— *The World's Body.* New York: Charles Scribner's Sons, 1938.

REESE, GUSTAVE. *Music in the Renaissance.* New York: W. W. Norton, 1954.

RENWICK, W. L. *Edmund Spenser, An Essay on Renaissance Poetry.* London: Edward Arnold, 1925, reprinted 1949.

RUBEL, VERÉ L. *Poetic Diction in the English Renaissance.* New York: The Modern Language Association of America, 1941.

SAINTSBURY, GEORGE. *A History of Elizabethan Literature.* New York: The Macmillan Company, 1910.

— *A History of English Prosody.* New York: The Macmillan Company, 1906–1910.

SARGEAUNT, W. D. *The English Syllable or Metrical Unit.* Oxford: Basil Blackwell, 1924.

SARGENT, RALPH M. *At the Court of Queen Elizabeth, The Life and Lyrics of Sir Edward Dyer.* London: Oxford University Press, 1935.

SCHELLING, FELIX. *English Literature During the Lifetime of Shakespeare.* New York: Henry Holt, 1927.

— *The Life and Writings of George Gascoigne.* Philadelphia: University of Pennsylvania Press, 1892.

SCHIPPER, JAKOB, *A History of English Versification.* Oxford: Clarendon Press, 1910.

SCHRAMM, WILBUR L. *Approaches to a Science of English Verse.* University of Iowa Studies, Series on the Aims and Progress of Research, No. 46. Iowa City: University of Iowa Press, 1935.

SHANNON, CLAUDE E. and WEAVER, WARREN. *The Mathematical Theory of Communication.* Urbana: University of Illinois Press, 1949.

SHAPIRO, KARL J. *A Bibliography of Modern Prosody.* Baltimore: Johns Hopkins University Press, 1948.

SIDNEY, PHILIP. *The Correspondence of Sir Philip Sidney and Hubert Languet.* Edited and translated by Steuart A. Pears. London: William Pickering, 1845.

SMITH, G. GREGORY (ed.). *Elizabethan Critical Essays.* 2 vols. Oxford University Press, 1904.

SMITH, HALLETT. *Elizabethan Poetry.* Cambridge, Mass.: Harvard University Press, 1952.

SMITH, SIR THOMAS. *De Republica Anglorum.* Edited by L. Alston. Cambridge: University Press, 1906.

SPINGARN, JOEL E. *A History of Literary Criticism in the Renaissance.* 2nd ed. New York: Columbia University Press, 1906.

STEWART, GEORGE R. *Techniques of English Verse.* New York: Henry Holt and Company, 1930.

STONE, WILLIAM JOHNSON. *On the Use of Classical Metres in English.* London: Henry Frowde, 1899.

STOW, JOHN. *Annales, or Generall Chronicle of England.* London: Thomas Adams, 1615.

— *The Survey of London* (1603). Oxford: Clarendon Press, 1908.

STRYPE, JOHN. *The Life of the Learned Sir Thomas Smith, Kt., D.C.L.* Oxford: Clarendon Press, 1820.

SWART, J. *Thomas Sackville, A Study in Sixteenth Century Poetry.* Groningen: J. B. Wolters, 1949.

TATE, ALLEN. *On the Limits of Poetry.* New York: The Swallow Press and William Morrow and Company, 1948.

TILLEY, MORRIS PALMER. *A Dictionary of the Proverbs in England in the Sixteenth and Seventeenth Centuries.* Ann Arbor: University of Michigan Press, 1950.

TILLYARD, E. M. W. *The Poetry of Sir Thomas Wyatt.* 2nd ed. London: Chatto and Windus, 1949.

TRAGER, GEORGE L. and SMITH, HENRY LEE, JR. *An Outline of English Structure.* Norman, Okla.: Brattenberg Press, 1951.

VERRIER, PAUL. *Essai sur les principes de la métrique anglaise.* Paris: Librairie Universitaire, 1909.

WALLACE, MALCOLM W. *The Life of Sir Philip Sidney.* Cambridge: University Press, 1915.

WATKINS, W. B. C. *Shakespeare and Spenser.* Princeton: Princeton University Press, 1950.

WELLEK, RENÉ and WARREN, AUSTIN. *Theory of Literature.* New York: Harcourt, Brace and Company, 1949.

WHETSTONE, GEORGE. *Metrical Life of George Gascoigne, the Poet.* Briston: Printed by John Evans and Company, 1815.

WHITEHALL, HAROLD. *Structural Essentials of English.* New York: Harcourt, Brace and Company, 1956.

WILSON, F. P. *Elizabethan and Jacobean.* Oxford: Clarendon Press, 1945.

WILSON, MONA. *Sir Philip Sidney.* London: Rupert Hart-Davis, 1950.

WIMSATT, W. K., JR. and BROOKS, CLEANTH. *Literary Criticism, A Short History.* New York: Alfred A. Knopf, 1957.

WINTERS, YVOR. *In Defence of Reason.* New York: Swallow Press, 1947.

WYLD, H. C. *A History of Modern Colloquial English.* 3rd ed. New York: E. P. Dutton and Company, 1937.

YATES, FRANCES A. *A Study of 'Love's Labour's Lost'.* Cambridge: University Press, 1936.

YOUNG, FRANCES BERKLEY. *Mary Sidney, Countess of Pembroke.* London: David Mutt, 1912.

YOUNG, SIR GEORGE. *An English Prosody on Inductive Lines.* Cambridge: University Press, 1928.

ZANDVOORT, R. W. *Sidney's Arcadia.* Amsterdam: N. V. Swete and Zeitlinger, 1929.

ZIPF, G. K. *Psychobiology of Language.* Boston: Houghton Mifflin Company, 1935.

ZOUCH, THOMAS. *Memoirs of the Life and Writings of Sir Philip Sidney.* York: Thomas Wilson and Sons, 1808.

Periodicals

BANKS, T. H. 'Sidney's *Astrophel and Stella* Reconsidered.' *PMLA,* L, No. 2 (1935), 403–412.

BARNETT, GEORGE L. 'Gabriel Harvey's *Castilio, Sire Aulicus* and *De Aulica.*' *Studies in Philology,* XLII, No. 1 (January, 1945), 146–163.

BENNETT, JOSEPHINE WATERS. 'Spenser and Harvey's Letter Book.' *Modern Philology,* XXIX (1931), 163–186.

BERGER, MARSHALL D. 'Vowel Distribution and Accentual Prominence in Modern English.' *Word*, XI, No. 3 (December, 1955), 361–376.

BAMBAS, RUDOLPH C. 'Verb Forms in -*s* and -*th* in Early Modern English Prose.' *Journal of English and Germanic Philology*, XLVI (1947), 183–187.

CROLL, MORRIS W. 'Report of the Committee on Metrical Notation appointed at Philadelphia, 1922' (with R. M. Alden, P. F. Baum, F. E. Schelling, F. N. Scott). *PMLA*, XXXIX, No. 4 (1924), lxxxvii.

FLETCHER, J. B. 'The Areopagus.' *Journal of Germanic Philology*, II (1898–1899), 429–453.

FLÜGEL, EWALD. 'Wyatt.' *Anglia*, XVIII (1896), 263 ff. and 454 ff.; XIX (1897), 175 ff. and 413 ff.

FRIES, CHARLES C. 'Meaning and Linguistic Analysis.' *Language*, XXX (1954), 57–68.

FULTON, EDWARD. 'Spenser and Sidney.' *Modern Language Notes*, XXXI (1916), 373–374.

GUMMERE, FRANCIS. 'The Translation of Beowulf, and the Relations of Ancient and Modern English Verse.' *American Journal of Philology*, VII (1886), 46–78.

HARDING, D. W. 'The Rhythmical Intention in Wyatt's Poetry.' *Scrutiny*, XIV, No. 2 (December, 1946), 90–102.

HARRIER, RICHARD C. 'Notes on the Text and Interpretation of Sir Thomas Wyatt's Poetry.' *Notes and Queries*, 198, No. 6 (June, 1953), 234–236.

HARRISON, T. P., JR. 'Relations of Spenser and Sidney.' *PMLA*, XLV (1930), 712–731.

HEMPHILL, GEORGE. 'Accent, Stress, and Emphasis.' *College English*, XVII No. 6 (March, 1956), 337–341.

HENDRICKSON, G. L. 'Elizabethan Quantitative Hexameters.' *Philological Quarterly*, XXVIII (1949), 227–260.

HILL, ARCHIBALD A. 'An Analysis of the Windhover.' *PMLA*, LXXX (1955), 968–978.

HUBBARD, FRANK G. 'A Type of Blank Verse Line Found in the Earlier Elizabethan Drama.' *PMLA*, XXXII, No. 1 (1917), 68–80.

HUDSON, H. H. 'Sonnets by Barnabe Googe.' *PMLA*, XLVIII (1933), 293–294.

HUGHEY, RUTH. 'The Harington Manuscript at Arundel Castle and Related Documents.' *The Library*, XV (1935), 4th series, 388–444.

JAKOBSON, ROMAN. 'Über den Versbau der Serbokroatischen Volksepen.' Proceedings of the International Congress of Phonetic Sciences. Amsterdam: 1932.

LEWIS, C. S. 'The Fifteenth-Century Heroic Line.' *Essays and Studies by Members of the English Association*, XXIV (1938), 28–41.

LONG, P. W. 'Spenser and Sidney.' *Anglia*, XXXVIII (1914), 173–192.

LOWELL, ROBERT. 'The Muses Won't Help Twice.' *Kenyon Review*, XVII (1955), 317–324.

MCKERROW, K. B. 'The Use of So-called Classical Metres in Elizabethan Verse.' *Modern Language Quarterly*, IV (1901), 172–180; and V (1902), 5–13.

MATTHEWS, WILLIAM. 'The Vulgar Speech of London in XV–XVII Centuries.' *Notes and Queries*, 172 (1937), 2–5 ff.

MAXWELL, J. C. 'Gabriel Harvey.' *Essays in Criticism*, I (1951), 185–188.

MAYNADIER, H. 'Areopagus.' *Modern Language Review*, IV (1909), 289–301

PHILLIPS, JAMES E. 'George Buchanan and the Sidney Circle.' *Huntington Library Quarterly* (November, 1948).

PURCELL, JAMES M. 'Sidney's *Astrophel and Stella* and Greville's *Caelica*.' *PMLA*, L, No. 2 (1935), 413–422.

PYLE, FITZROY. 'The Barbarous Metres of Barclay.' *Modern Language Review*, XXXII (1937), 353–373.

RANDOLPH, M. C. 'Thomas Drant's Definition of Satire.' *Notes and Queries*, CLXXX (1941), 416–418.

RANSOM, JOHN CROWE. 'The Strange Music of English Verse.' *Kenyon Review*, XVIII, No. 3 (Summer, 1956), 460–477.

SAUNDERS, J. W. 'The Stigma of Print, A Note on the Social Bases of Tudor Poetry.' *Essays in Criticism*, I (1931), 139–164.

SCHOLL, EVELYN H. 'English Metre Once More.' *PMLA*, LXIII, No. 1 (1948), 293–326.

SHAFER, ROBERT. 'Spenser's *Astrophel*.' *Modern Language Notes*, XXVIII (1913), 224–226.

SMITH, HALLETT. 'The Art of Sir Thomas Wyatt.' *Huntington Library Quarterly*, XIX (1946), 337.

— 'English Metrical Psalms.' *Huntington Library Quarterly*, XIX (1946), 249–271.

SPENCER, THEODORE. 'The Poetry of Sir Philip Sidney.' *English Literary History* (December, 1945), 267.

SPITZER, LEO. 'Language—the Basis of Science, Philosophy, and Poetry.' *Studies in Intellectual History*. Edited by George Boas. Baltimore: Johns Hopkins University Press, 1954.

— 'Spenser, Shepheardes Calender, March.' *Studies in Philology*, XLVII (1950), 494–505.

SWALLOW, ALAN. 'The Pentameter Line in Skelton and Wyatt.' *Modern Philology*, XLVIII (1950), 1–11.

TRAGER, G. L. and BLOCH, B. 'The Syllabic Phonemes of English.' *Language*, XVII (1941), 223–246.

TWADDELL, W. F. 'Stetson's Model and the "Supra-Segmental Phonemes".' *Language*, XXIX (1953), 415–453.

WHITEHALL, HAROLD. 'The Sounds in Their Courses.' *Kenyon Review*, XVI (1954), 322–328.

WILLCOCK, GLADYS. 'Passing Pitefull Hexameters.' *Modern Language Review*, XXIX (1934), 1–19.

WILSON, H. S. 'Gabriel Harvey's Annotating Bibliography.' *Harvard Library Bulletin*, II (Autumn, 1948), 344–361.

WILSON, H. S. 'Gabriel Harvey's "Lost" Ode on Ramus.' *English Literary History* (September, 1945), 167–182.

— 'The Humanism of Gabriel Harvey.' *Joseph Quincy Adams Memorial Studies*. Washington, D.C.: 1948, 720–721.

WINTERS, YVOR. 'The 16th Century Lyric in England.' *Poetry*, LIII (1939), 258 ff.

YOUNG, G. M. 'A Word for Gabriel Harvey.' *English Critical Essays*. Edited By Phyllis M. Jones. 20th-century ed. London: Oxford University Press, 1935.

Index